D1000547

Winter Park
PUBLIC LIBRARY

Book-A-Year
Endowment

In memory of

Nelson Glass

Presented by

Friends of the
Winter Park Public Library

THE VANISHING OF FLIGHT MH370

Most Berkley Books are available at special quantity discounts for bulk purchases for sales promotions, premiums, fund-raising, or educational use. Special books, or book excerpts, can also be created to fit specific needs. For details, write: SpecialMarkets@penguinrandomhouse.com.

THE
VANISHING
OF
FLIGHT MH370

The True Story of the Hunt
for the Missing Malaysian Plane

RICHARD QUEST

BERKLEY BOOKS, NEW YORK

BERKLEY

An imprint of Penguin Random House LLC
375 Hudson Street, New York, New York 10014

This book is an original publication of Penguin Random House LLC.

Copyright © 2016 by Richard Quest.
Penguin supports copyright. Copyright fuels creativity, encourages diverse voices, promotes free speech, and creates a vibrant culture. Thank you for buying an authorized edition of this book and for complying with copyright laws by not reproducing, scanning, or distributing any part of it in any form without permission. You are supporting writers and allowing Penguin to continue to publish books for every reader.

BERKLEY® and the "B" design are registered trademarks of Penguin Random House LLC.
For more information, visit penguin.com.

Library of Congress Cataloging-in-Publication Data

Names: Quest, Richard, 1962– author.
Title: The vanishing of Flight MH370 : the true story of the hunt for the missing
Malaysian plane / Richard Quest.
Description: New York : Berkley, 2016.
Identifiers: LCCN 2015045541 | ISBN 9780425283011 (hardback) | ISBN 9780698407770 (ebook)
Subjects: LCSH: Malaysia Airlines Flight 370 Incident, 2014. | BISAC: TRANSPORTATION / Aviation /
Commercial. | TRANSPORTATION / Aviation / General.
Classification: LCC TL553.53.M4 Q47 2016 | DDC 363.12/42—dc23
LC record available at http://lccn.loc.gov/2015045541

International edition ISBN: 978-1-101-98918-0

FIRST EDITION: March 2016

PRINTED IN THE UNITED STATES OF AMERICA

10 9 8 7 6 5 4 3 2 1

Cover photograph of plane by Thomas Luethi.
Cover design by Daniel Rembert.

While the author has made every effort to provide accurate telephone numbers, Internet addresses, and other contact information at the time of publication, neither the publisher nor the author assumes any responsibility for errors, or for changes that occur after publication. Further, the publisher does not have any control over and does not assume any responsibility for author or third-party websites or their content.

Penguin
Random
House

*To my colleagues at CNN both in front of and
behind the cameras. Without your collective efforts, this book
would not have been possible. We truly did go "all in" to
cover this story. And we will continue to do so, wherever it goes.*

CONTENTS

INTRODUCTION

"Where's that plane?" If there is one question I get asked most by CNN viewers these days, this is it. From politicians and CEOs to doormen and cabdrivers, time and again they want to know, "What happened to that plane? Where is it?" Malaysia Airlines flight MH370—with 239 people aboard—departed from Kuala Lumpur shortly after midnight on March 8, 2014, bound for Beijing, China, and has never been seen since. Despite the largest aviation search in history, virtually nothing was found of the aircraft in the wake of its disappearance. Sixteen months later, thousands of miles from the flight's path, a piece of an airplane's wing washed ashore on Reunion Island. Still, this bit of evidence and a flimsy trail of electronic satellite data are all we have to go on—plus a huge amount of speculation and confusion.

"The most difficult search ever undertaken in human history."[1]

When Australia's prime minister Tony Abbott uttered those words in April 2014, it was not just the usual hyperbole of a politician. What happened to MH370 has been described as a unique, unprecedented, and extraordinary mystery. Planes may crash, but they are not supposed to disappear without a trace. Earlier ocean crashes, such as Air France 447 or Air India 182, have demonstrated that wreckages can typically be located within hours. Airlines today own the most modern aircraft, featuring up-to-date navigation technology, while regulations govern everything from the number of hours a pilot can fly to the fire-resistant fabric used in the passenger seats. Despite the precautions, no one has been able to pinpoint the final resting place of MH370 and those on board. All the while we know that if you lose your iPhone, it can be traced within minutes.

At the heart of this mystery remains the question of the cause of the plane's disappearance. Was it mechanical, or was it criminal: Did someone deliberately take over the aircraft and set it on a course to the south Indian Ocean, intending to kill all on board? Would that someone turn out to be an unknown hijacker or terrorist, or could it have been one of the pilots?

I have spent hours debating the possibilities of what *might* have happened to MH370 with those who declare what *must* have happened. Frequently, whenever I suggest that they keep an open mind because, unsatisfying though it is, we don't know, there is the inevitable "ah, but surely . . ." followed by a series of half-truths, myths, and rumors that have been allowed to enter the debate and fester.

Do I have a view of what might have happened? I do, and I will share it. In doing so, I am not blind to the obvious options, but prefer to keep an open mind on the eventual outcome. As will become clear in the chapters that follow, as a television journalist, I became frustrated, and even angry, with some of the pundits with whom I had to work who were quite prepared to convict the pilots long before any evidence had been found. Instead, this book will stick to the facts as we know them. In the end, you will be left to make up your own mind about where you think the evidence leads.

The disappearance of MH370 has been a serious failure for the multibillion-dollar aviation industry, revealing disturbing facts and behaviors. That one of the most advanced aircraft in the world should vanish, while an airline left hundreds of desperate families waiting for news of their loved ones, is unpardonable. In response, airlines have rewritten their rules from top to bottom. An alphabet soup of international organizations responsible for air travel safety held high-level meetings and set up a task force to look at ways to ensure that planes are always being tracked in real time. Even CEOs I spoke to were as astounded as the general public that planes were not always being tracked to a fine point of precision. Some of the changes did not come soon enough: as suspicion about MH370's pilots increased, discussions were held about a "two-person in the cockpit" rule, stipulating that if one pilot temporarily leaves the cockpit, he or she should be replaced by a flight attendant. Yet the considerable amount of talk led to very little action. If such a change had been made, the crashing of Germanwings 9525, in which a rogue pilot deliberately flew his airliner into a mountain, possibly would not have happened.

When all is said and done, MH370 boils down to one simple fact. For the first time since the Wright brothers first flew, this industry, which prided itself on a policy of "safety first," is having to cope with the unthinkable: a plane disappeared. It is no wonder the head of the airline organization IATA, Tony Tyler, decried, "A large commercial airliner going missing without a trace for so long is unprecedented in modern aviation. And it must not happen again."[2]

The fascination with MH370 goes deeper than an aviation story. International diplomatic and political issues have been raised too. More than 60 percent of the passengers on board the plane were Chinese citizens, and the Chinese government wasted little time in flexing its muscles on their behalf. The relatives of Chinese victims were put up in a Beijing hotel where regular briefings were given by low-level Malaysian government and airline officials. These were acrimonious events, interrupted frequently by hysterical outbursts from distraught family members frustrated at the lack of information they were being given. The way the relatives were treated was shabby at best.

Then there was the role of the Malaysian government itself. Were they a bunch of incompetents who had no idea what they were doing, doomed to make mistake after mistake? Or perhaps the truth was something more sinister: a cover-up for an erroneous military strike? Few people will deny that the first weeks of this crisis were not something of which the Malaysians can be proud. As the tensions rose across the South China Sea, the fate of MH370 rapidly became entwined in a diplomatic game of realpolitik, mystery, intrigue, and failure.

So why did I decide to write this book?

To begin, there is my own personal relationship to this story. Sixteen days before MH370's disappearance, I met and flew with the plane's first officer, Fariq Hamid, filming him for a segment on CNN. Immediately after the story of the plane's vanishing broke, I found that a three-hour flight with someone I had met only once, more than two weeks prior, had now taken on a new importance, and everything about that trip was suddenly the focus of great attention. Conspiracy theorists had a field day. My Twitter account was inundated with comments suggesting that somehow CNN and I had known "something was going to happen" or that we perhaps knew where the plane was. (We didn't, and we don't.)

During that trip to Malaysia in February 2014, I had also spent time with the CEO of Malaysia Airlines, or MH, as it's known by its IATA airline code. The airline was in deep financial trouble well before MH370. Its business model was failing and the carrier was being squeezed. On one side are the Gulf Three carriers—Emirates, Etihad, and Qatar Airways—siphoning off the long-haul customers; on the other side is the low-cost airline AirAsia, also based in Kuala Lumpur. Nutcrackered in the middle, Malaysia Airlines found it impossible to be financially viable. In short, this proud airline, flying for more than half a century, had to find its role in the new world of air travel. Having just traveled to Malaysia to do a story on MH, I was familiar with the difficulties the company was facing and the actions being proposed by the CEO Ahmad Jauhari Yahya (AJ) to put things right. I spent several hours with AJ discussing his strategy for turning MH around. As I will tell you later, I also learned what sort of a leader he would be in the event of an emergency.

From the very first reports of a plane being reported missing to the long weeks and months of searching, I covered almost every aspect of this story: from interviewing grief-stricken relatives; to interpreting and analyzing the sometimes illogical actions of the Malaysian authorities; to explaining then discounting the outlandish and outrageous theories being put forward about what had happened . . . too often being the only voice willing to stand up to the disparaging, unfair comments about the crew on board.

I was very fortunate to be part of a team at CNN that covered this story like nothing we had seen before. Our reportage of MH370 was the first full-scale example of the policies put in place by CNN's new CEO, Jeff Zucker. Jeff had said we should do fewer stories and hit them hard—"own them," as he put it. MH370 took over our airwaves for weeks. Everyone knew this was an experiment for CNN, trying a different way of covering major stories. Would it work? Senior staff would sometimes question the policy while expressing full fealty with it in public. Perhaps this wouldn't matter at another network. But CNN is the most-watched news network in the world. Everyone had a view on how we covered the plane.

I have reported on aviation for the best part of three decades. The first crash I covered was the bombing of Pan Am Flight 103 over Lockerbie, Scotland, in 1988. From Lockerbie to Concorde to Swissair to Air France to Malaysia (370 and 17) and so many incidents in between, I have been involved in the instant analysis required once we get reports that a plane is missing. Months and even years later, I am the correspondent who plows through the accident inquiry reports, trying to make pages of aviation-speak understandable for a general audience. I have sat in numerous cockpits in the air and on the ground. I have "flown" in many simulators and tried my hand "at the wheel." I am not a pilot, and I have never pretended to be. My job is to understand this fascinatingly complicated world, and help the viewer realize what happened and why.

This book is told from the perspective of one who covered this incident and who continues to report on the developments, whether the search and recovery or the steps being taken to make sure it never happens again. It is not an academic textbook, bristling with footnotes. It will not go into every moment of those first days to prove all the inconsistencies that took place. Malaysia's deficiency in handling the communications is well documented; I don't need to go chapter and verse into every misstatement and error. This book will not satisfy the reader who has already made up his mind about what has happened and is prepared to convict either pilot of mass murder. Nor will it satisfy the reader who is determined to believe that the Malaysians made a terrible job of every aspect of the investigation rather than just a lousy job on the information front. It certainly won't satisfy the #avgeek who will be seeking a more in-depth treatise on ACARS, ECAM, Satellite Doppler, and Burst Offset Frequency. Instead I hope to give you a feel for those first frantic days when the search was at its height, followed by the weeks of bewilderment and puzzlement that nothing was found of the jetliner until the flaperon washed ashore.

I have dedicated this book to CNN and my colleagues at the network who worked with me on this story. The sheer dedication everyone brought to the story was extraordinary. This book has been written by drawing on their countless hours of journalism, the thousands of emails that were sent among us, reporting developments, arguing different avenues of inquiry, constantly challenging and debating outcomes. It was a tremendous experience to be a part of such first-class coverage.

I have loved aviation since the first time I flew in the late 1960s, on a holiday flight from Liverpool Speke Airport to Sitges, Spain. The plane was a Cambrian Airways BAC 1-11, a small, noisy craft that would fail all environmental rules today. I remember getting off the plane, walking down the steps, and looking back at this machine glistening in the rain, and thinking, How did that metal get in the air . . . and stay there? I can still spend hours at airports watching planes on takeoff, guessing that moment when one of the pilots will call "rotate" and the plane will bite into the air. As planes get bigger, and the ultra-long-haul flight becomes more common, the fact that MH370 happened is worrying, for it should never have happened. The fact it did is the reason I wrote this book.

THE FACTS

PLANE AND PASSENGERS

Aircraft Reg: 9M-MRO
Aircraft Type: Boeing 777-200ER
Built & Delivered: May 29, 2002 (11 years 9 months 9 days)
Flight Hrs: 53,465
Comms: 3 VHF radios, 2 HF radios, 1 SATCOM, 2 ATC transponders

Souls on Board: 239
Crew: 12
Pax: 227

NATIONALITY OF PASSENGERS
China: 152 (67%)
Malaysia: 50 (16% of passengers; with crew, 20% of souls on board)
Indonesia: 7 (3%)
Australia: 6 (3%)
India: 5 (2%)
France: 4
United States: 3
Canada, Iran, New Zealand, Ukraine: 2 (from each country)
Hong Kong, Netherlands, Russia, Taiwan: 1 (from each country)

THE PILOTS

The Captain: Zaharie Ahmad Shah. Malaysian, age 53. Total flying hours: 18,365 hours. Experience on 777: 8,659 hours. Joined Malaysia Airlines in 1981.

First Officer: Fariq Abdul Hamid. Malaysian, age 27. Total flying hours: 2,763. Experience on 777: 39 hours. Joined Malaysia Airlines in 2007.

WHO'S WHO

Najib Razak—Prime Minister of Malaysia since April 2009

Datuk Seri Hishammuddin Hussein—Defense Minister of Malaysia and, during MH370, Acting Transport Minister

Dato' Sri Azharuddin Abdul Rahman—Director General, Department of Civil Aviation Malaysia

Ahmad Jauhari Yahya (AJ)—CEO of Malaysia Airlines (retired 2015)

Tony Abbott—Prime Minister of Australia, September 2, 2013–September 2, 2015

Warren Truss—Deputy Prime Minister of Australia

Angus Houston—Chief Coordinator, Joint Agency Coordination Centre (JACC)

Jeff Zucker—CEO of CNN Worldwide

THE FLIGHT

MARCH 8 (MALAYSIA STANDARD TIME)

00:27	Push-back
00:41	Takeoff
00:42	Directed to Igari (waypoint)
00:50	Directed to climb FL350
00:50	Read-back FL350
01:01	Advises reached FL350
01:07	ACARS last transmission (provided total fuel remaining)
01:07	Repeats FL350
01:19	Handoff to Vietnam "Contact HCM 120.9 good night"

01:19	Read-back "Good night Malaysian 370" LAST WORDS
01:21	Transponder switched off
01:22	Last ATC radar—probably BITOD
01:25	MH370 deviates from flight plan
02:22	Last primary radar fix (Malaysian radar)
02:25	First handshake FROM the aircraft (of unknown cause)
02:39	Unanswered phone call ground TO plane
03:41	Second handshake FROM the ground
04:41	Third handshake FROM the ground
05:41	Fourth handshake FROM the ground
06:30	Scheduled landing time in Beijing
06:41	Fifth handshake FROM the ground
07:13	Unanswered phone call ground TO plane
07:24	Malaysia Airlines announces plane missing
08:11	Sixth handshake FROM the ground
08:19	Seventh handshake FROM THE PLANE (probably from power loss through fuel exhaustion)
09:15	Failed handshake FROM the ground: plane didn't answer

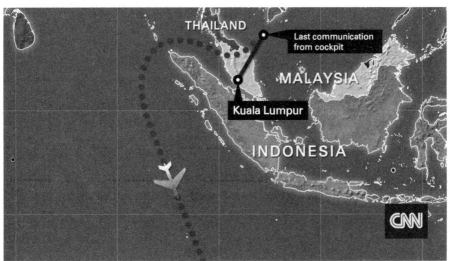

© CABLE NEWS NETWORK, INC. A TIME WARNER COMPANY. ALL RIGHTS RESERVED.

TIMELINE OF SEARCH EVENTS

2014

March 8:	MH370 takes off and goes missing.
March 10:	First mentions of turn-back in press conferences.
March 15:	Malaysia PM admits plane turned back. Sets up corridors.
March 24:	Malaysia PM confirms plane kept flying and went down in south Indian Ocean. Searching begins off Australia coast.
March 28:	Search zone shifts dramatically.
April 7:	*Ocean Shield* hears pings from black boxes—turns out to be false.
April 14:	Bluefin-21 underwater vehicle is deployed to search most likely areas.
May 28:	Bluefin-21 completes underwater search with nothing found.
May 29:	Bathymetric survey of search zone begins.
October 6:	*Go Phoenix* begins underwater search of 26,000 square miles.

2015

January 29:	Malaysia officially declares MH370 an accident; all the passengers and crew are presumed to have lost their lives.
April 16:	Malaysia, China, Australia announce extension of search to 46,000 square miles.
June 3:	Malaysia, China, Australia announce if nothing found, there will be no further extension of search. Effectively, it will be over.
July 20:	Debris believed to be the flaperon from MH370's wing washes ashore on Reunion Island.
September 3:	French officials affirm "with certainty" the debris found on Reunion Island is the flaperon from MH370.

ABBREVIATIONS

AAIB—Air Accidents Investigation Branch; the UK air accident investigating agency.

ACARS—Aircraft Communication and Reporting System; sophisticated data communication system from the plane.

AMSA—Australian Maritime Safety Authority; Australia's maritime regulator.

Annex 13—Agreed international rules on how aircraft accident investigations are to be carried out.

ATC—Air traffic control.

ATSB—Australian Transport Safety Bureau; the Australian air accident investigating agency.

BEA—Bureau d'Enquêtes et d'Analyses; the French air accident investigating agency.

CAAC—Civil Aviation Administration of China; China's regulator.

CVR—Cockpit voice recorder. Records conversations in the cockpit; one of the two black boxes carried by commercial aircraft.

DCA—Department of Civil Aviation; Malaysia's regulator and air accident investigating department.

FAA—Federal Aviation Administration; the US aviation regulator.

FDR—Flight data recorder. Records parameters of the flight; one of the two black boxes carried by commercial aircraft.

FO—First officer; the junior pilot who sits in the right-hand seat.

IATA—International Air Transport Association; organization representing the world's airlines.

ICAO—International Civil Aviation Organization; UN body responsible for international regulation of air transport.

JACC—Joint Agency Coordination Centre; agency created by Australia to coordinate the government's support for the search for MH370.

KLIA—Kuala Lumpur International Airport; also known as KUL.

NTSB—National Transportation Safety Board; the US air accidents investigating agency.

CHAPTER ONE

FIRST HOURS

Richard, a plane has gone missing.

—CNN DIRECTOR OF COVERAGE

I n the world of CNN, I always know when big news has happened—my BlackBerry goes into meltdown. Friday, March 7, 2014, was one of those times. I had been out for a quick drink with friends to celebrate my upcoming birthday, and figuring that if the news desk needed me they could call, I had left my device on the kitchen table. When I got back home, a quick look told me something had happened.

Short, terse, urgent: "Richard, where are you?" "Are you near the office?" "Call in now." They were the usual emails from determined producers who, covering a major story, are anxious to get whatever content they can to "keep the beast fed." According to the time stamps, the emails had started arriving in my in-box faster, the subject lines blaring with more urgent wording. It was 7:25 p.m.

I quickly read the gist of what had happened. A Malaysia Airlines plane had gone missing. The flight number was MH370, and it was flying from Kuala Lumpur to Beijing. No one knew much more. Having covered aviation for decades, I had learned by harsh experience that the first thing to do, even before returning my producer's call, is to find out the basics about what make and type of plane was involved. A fast check of several websites told me one important fact: MH370 was a Boeing 777. That's all I needed to know. This was a large wide-bodied passenger plane with several hundred people on board, and as I remembered, there had never before been a fatal crash of a 777.

Within seconds, an email arrived from the CNN International Desk enclosing the statement from Malaysia Airlines. Released at 7:24 a.m. Malaysia time (7:24 p.m. the previous evening in New York), it confirmed what I had discovered:

> Malaysia Airlines confirms that flight MH370 has lost contact with Subang Air Traffic Control at 2.40am on 8th March. MH370 was expected to land in Beijing at 6.30am the same day. The flight was carrying a total number of 227 passengers (including 2 infants) 12 crew members. Malaysia Airlines is currently working with the authorities who have activated their Search and Rescue team to locate the aircraft.

Immediately, I called the news desk in Atlanta. I wanted to check in and let them know I had received the messages and was now getting ready to come back to work. I could tell by the background noise and the brief, to-the-point replies that everyone was gearing up for what we all knew would be very long hours ahead. With a large, wide-bodied plane officially missing, and hundreds of people of many nationalities likely to be involved, this story was big, and it was going to get even bigger in the coming hours. The word from Atlanta was simple: "Get back to the bureau as fast as you can, we are going to need anything and everything you can offer."

Before heading to the studio, I needed to know more—the aircraft's routing, the weather that lay in its path, the airports involved, the aircraft's date of manufacture, even previous incidents for both the airline and that particular type of airplane. In the immediate hours of television news coverage, knowing these facts is crucial just to keep broadcasting. Spending ten minutes online, reading a variety of websites, and seeing what Twitter's #avgeeks are saying is often the fastest way to get some basic information. After all, there are thousands of people in the aviation business, and when a crash occurs many of them are discussing online what they have seen, heard, or know.

Of course, one can always contact the airline and government agencies directly responsible to get whatever information they will offer, but CNN has many staffers making those calls. Later, I will contact my own inside sources to get off-the-record briefings that will give me far more information than an airline press officer who just happens to be the person who answers the phone. Rather than making calls, in the first hours following a plane crash, I do the basic research and get going. The programs need me on-air, not sitting on hold.

Preparing to head to the studio, I quickly put on a fresh shirt and suit and chose an appropriately dark tie. During the Asian financial crisis in 1997, I'd worn a red tie on the air and received a whole slew of complaints from viewers in Asia saying this was inappropriate because red is the color of prosperity and luck. Making sure I was properly dressed was important. Since I would be talking about plane crashes and missing passengers for hours to come, I wanted to look suitably somber without being funereal.

Arriving at the Time Warner Center, I was told to go straightaway to Studio 73 on the seventh floor. My first broadcast would be on

Anderson Cooper 360°, talking to Anderson. The first report is always the trickiest. I needed to make sure I didn't say anything I would have to backtrack on within a few hours. Anderson asked me the basics, and I was able to give him information about the aircraft and some background on Malaysia Airlines, and then I reported how the plane had been in the cruise, the safest phase of the flight, when it disappeared. With few details, I didn't want to go any further.

After speaking to Anderson, I moved from the large, glamorous studio of *AC360°* to a "flash studio," a small space with a desk, lights, and a single camera. Designed to connect an interviewee to the other parts of the network, it's a quick and easy way of doing many live reports. As the correspondent, I basically sit in the same seat and do multiple reports into lots of different programs. Over the next few weeks I was to spend hours sitting in flash studios at all times of the day and night.

From the flash studio, it was back to the seventh floor to *Piers Morgan Live*. The program was prerecorded on that Friday night, but now, with the breaking news on MH370, the plans drastically changed. The producers abandoned the taped show and prepared for a live program instead. Since Piers was in Los Angeles, I sat in the studio alone. As I waited for the show to begin, the producer said in my ear that Piers was caught in traffic and hadn't arrived at the CNN Los Angeles bureau. If he didn't make it to his studio in time, I might have to anchor the start of the show. I marshaled the few facts and got ready to lead the program. At the last moment Piers arrived, ready to go. I felt both disappointment and relief: disappointment that I would not have a "big moment" and relief that I wouldn't have a chance to "mess it up." Actually, you can't win in this situation; no matter how good you are, the management always resent the fact that they haven't got the person they want, and the best I could have hoped for was a begrudging "he did very well, all things considered." All in all, we were better with Piers!

The interview went long; Piers was filling time and using me to do it. There was an unfortunate moment. Having been on-air now for more than ten minutes, we came back after the break and Piers started up again, introducing me as "the aviation correspondent," which is one of my titles at CNN. He then said something to the effect of "Hang on, Quest isn't an aviation correspondent!" What? I grimaced and battled on through the report. It is never pleasant when a colleague undermines you on-air, even by accident! I made my views clear to Jonathan Wald, his executive producer, who got the point. This wasn't just a petty spat over titles (I have never really cared about them one way or the other). It had to do with credibility. How on earth do we expect the viewer to accept what we are saying when our own colleagues are dismissing what we are claiming to be? Piers had the very good grace to email me, apologizing and explaining that he didn't know that was one of my roles, and when he saw the title in the prompter, he'd assumed it was a mistake. It was a minor moment as I faced the rest of the night's broadcasting.

CNN was now in full "Breaking News" mode. It's a formidable thing to witness. The network with its huge resources was moving into high gear. Like the proverbial oil tanker, it may be slow to start, but once it gets going, it takes on a speed and momentum of its own. At the very minimum, producers were being brought into the newsrooms to help put together and broadcast longer news bulletins dedicated to the story. The international news desk in Atlanta was starting to consider where to dispatch correspondents, producers, and camera crews. Obviously we needed to send staff to Kuala Lumpur, Malaysia, as fast as possible. We also needed to consider sending more staff to Beijing, and possibly Vietnam. Local staff were being brought into the bureau in

Hong Kong, while others were being woken up in London to be ready to cover the extra programming that would be required the next day. Anyone who had any contacts in the aviation industry, or within the governments involved in the search, or who might know anyone who had information, was now being roused to hit the phones. The problem for all twenty-four-hour news broadcasters was, of course, that in those first hours we just simply did not have the facts, and yet we had to keep broadcasting about the story. Essentially, we were relying on the one statement from Malaysia Airlines, admitting the plane was missing, the route it had taken, and the number of people on board.

Armed with these few facts and a lot of background, we got under way. When there's a breaking story of this size, you just have to keep going. So I filled time. I gave lots of background details on the airline, the aircraft, the cities the plane was flying to, the sorts of passengers who were on board. As a journalist, I have two areas of distinct specialization: business and aviation. Networks have correspondents for a reason, not just to give them a pretty title. We have studied the subjects we cover and are able to draw on a deep well of background knowledge. In my case, this goes back more than twenty-five years.

Newbies to twenty-four-hour news find "keeping going" the hardest part of the job. Reporters who are used to tight, structured, network-news live shots of just a couple of minutes suddenly find themselves having to fill hours of airtime. They are overwhelmed by the effort to keep up the momentum without straying too far from the facts.

After the first few hours, I had confirmed the serial number and registration of the aircraft involved, 9M-MRO, as well as its age: it was just under twelve years old. I knew that one of the first questions asked would be about the safety history of the Boeing 777. Thinking of those viewers watching around the world, perhaps in airports, about to board a 777, I usually answer that sort of question with, "So far as we know, very safe." The last thing they want to hear is CNN's aviation correspondent starting to hem and haw about the 777's safety record, raising issues when, at the moment, none existed. I am not being dishonest or disingenuous; there is plenty of time for nuanced answers later on.

In the case of the safety history of the 777, I had nothing to worry about. The 777, which first came into service in 1995, has an exemplary safety record. In almost twenty years, there had never been an accident where passengers had died in a plane crash. In 2013, Asiana 214 crash-landed in San Francisco. Two passengers died after they escaped from the aircraft and were run over by a fire truck responding to the accident. A third passenger died later in the hospital. The only other major 777 incident at the time of MH370 was the crash landing of the British Airways Flight 38 at London Heathrow. That came about because ice had formed in the fuel lines during a frigid flight from Beijing. When the ice jolted free, it blocked the line and starved the engines of fuel. The plane lost power and glided the last few miles to crash just short of the runway. Fortunately, everyone survived.

Having seen the state of the crashed aircraft with both Asiana and British Airways, I find it a miracle that no one was killed when the planes hit the ground—a testament, I have no doubt, to Boeing's ability to build superb airplanes (and the same is true for Airbus!). The 777 was, and still is, among the safest aircraft, and I had no hesitation in saying so on-air, then or now.

The hours went by, and I did report after report. Then something bizarre transpired that would change my relationship to the story of MH370. I received an odd email from Brian Walker, a senior colleague on the international news desk in Atlanta.[1] Brian wrote about a blogger who had been posting pictures on a website. "Richard, this is really weird. This poster says it is a photo of the co-pilot of the Malaysia flight . . . were you ever on one? Could you have met these guys?" In the photograph attached, I was standing in the cockpit behind the pilot who was now being named as the first officer on MH370. I was shocked—indeed, there I was, sixteen days earlier, in the cockpit of a 777 with Fariq Hamid.

This picture, which had been posted on Hamid's Instagram page, was rapidly being circulated now that the names of the flight crew of MH370 were becoming more widely known. The captain was Zaharie Ahmad Shah, and his first officer was Fariq Abdul Hamid. A flurry of emails about this picture went back and forth between me and senior editors in Atlanta, along with our staff in Asia. Obviously, before we could broadcast that I had met and flown with Hamid, we needed to be absolutely certain he was the first officer on that plane. We showed the picture to a senior vice president at Malaysia Airlines, who verbally confirmed that Hamid was indeed the first officer on MH370. I knew then that my relationship to MH370 was about to become a bit more personal.

The photo had been taken during an assignment I had been given in Malaysia, a couple of weeks previously, for CNN *Business Traveller*, the travel show I have presented for twelve years. Ironically, in my live reports over the last few hours, I had been drawing on what I had seen and learned about the airline during my trip to Malaysia without realizing that one of the people I had met was involved with the missing plane. Now it became known that I had a direct connection to a key player.

With this picture circulating, the questions were starting to come thick and fast about the assignment, and what I had seen and learned. The reason we had gone to Malaysia in the first place was because of the rich travel and tourism stories the country had on offer. The country is a wonderful tourist destination in its own right, and it's also a major transfer airport from Europe to Asia and Australia. The airline and the local authorities had promised us excellent access. The core of our program was to be a feature on Malaysia Airlines, which was restructuring to face competition from the newer, nimbler airlines.

The fact that Malaysia Airlines (MH) was in a dreadful financial state was well known. MH had lost money for the past three years. Its load factor—the measure of how full each plane was with paying passengers—was around 4 to 5 percent lower than its competitors. The airline's business was being squeezed between rival airline models. On the one side was Tony Fernandes's phenomenally successful AirAsia, which is headquartered in Bangkok and regularly fills its planes with more passengers than MH. On the other side were the Gulf Three: Emirates, Etihad, and Qatar Airways, which daily send giant wide-bodied planes into Bangkok, and take Malaysia's high-spending business passengers to Europe and the United States.

At all levels of passenger demand, MH was in an impossible position, caught in the middle. Both AirAsia and the Gulf Three were bigger, better resourced, had a considerably lower cost base, and, frankly, were much better run. Their business models had been designed and refined for the new, harsh world of aviation, while poor old Malaysia Airlines was left flying like a traditional flag carrier, with a fleet of aging long-haul planes, out-of-date working practices, and huge losses on the balance sheet.

The problem facing MH was the classic one faced by many national carriers. These dinosaurs have long enjoyed privileged status in their home airports, yet are now facing brutal competition from two different aviation models. Some, like the Hungarian airline Malev, don't survive. Others, like Swissair, get gobbled up by larger neighbors, such as Lufthansa. And there remains an entire cadre of airlines, of which MH is one, that struggle to find a profitable role, constantly trying to reinvent themselves to little effect.

Malaysia Airlines is a proud airline, having carried the national flag from 1947, or 1972, depending on your political definition of when it started flying in different national guises. Whether long haul or regional, MH had decades of know-how, but now needed dramatically to restructure itself if it was to remain viable. Obviously, MH was never going to go out of business; national pride would never have allowed that, and anyway, its major shareholder was Khazanah Nasional, the national sovereign wealth fund that before this crisis owned more than 60 percent of MAS, the holding company. After the twin tragedies of MH370 and MH17, the airline could not continue as a stock-market-listed company. Passenger numbers were down. Morale was low. The losses were mounting. The airline would need to be completely restructured or it would continue losing money for years.

Within six months of MH370, the plan was announced. Called "Rebuilding a National Icon," the recovery strategy was dramatic, drastic, and necessary. The national fund bought out the remaining shareholders in late 2014 and delisted the company from the stock exchange. Malaysia Airlines was then fully privatized. In the next six months, a new CEO, Christoph Mueller, joined MH from Aer Lingus. His restructuring plan announced in 2015 involved shrinking the airline by losing six thousand jobs, around 30 percent of the workforce, and shedding unprofitable routes. A new holding company, Malaysia Airlines Berhad (MAB), replaced MAS, Malaysia Airlines Systems. Now, at least for the time being, the airline is in the private sector, and its financial workings are being restructured out of the glare of constant publicity and the obligation to report results.

None of this had taken place, of course, when we went to Malaysia to film CNN *Business Traveller*. At that point, the airline and its financial performance were very much under scrutiny. Chief executive Ahmad Jauhari Yahya had already introduced a turnaround plan, cutting routes and making the airline more efficient.

Now Malaysia Airlines wanted to tell the world why it should survive and it was prepared to give us almost unprecedented access to do so. The plan involved me; my producer, Pamela Boykoff; and cameraman Scott Clottworthy flying from Hong Kong to Kuala Lumpur on MH9185 and filming on board the flight. The airline's intention was to show us their business class and how they were improving service. Best of all, we were expecting to film the pilots in the cockpit during the flight. In the post-9/11 world, getting to film in a cockpit while a plane is in the air is just about unheard of without special permission, which takes ages to get.

Before 9/11, passengers visiting the cockpit during flight was always a possibility on non-US airlines. Pilots were often agreeable to inviting young children (and their #avgeek parents) to the front of the plane to see them at work. I well remember as a child that one of the best things about our holiday flights to Spain was asking to go to the front and the flight attendant (we called them stewardesses in those days) coming back and saying, "Yes, the captain says please come up and say hello." I would walk nervously into the cramped, noisy cockpit of those older planes, looking at the dozens of switches and knobs (many more than in today's computer-driven flight decks) and gazing out of the front windows at the fluffy white clouds below and the glorious blue sky in front. Perhaps that's where I felt my first love for aviation. In the US, even before 9/11, the FAA always had much stricter rules forbidding nonairline personnel from visiting the cockpit in flight. Occasionally one would be allowed to do it for filming purposes, yet 9/11 made it just about impossible to get into the cockpit, sometimes even on the ground.

The only time I can recall being allowed in the cockpit of a US plane during flight was on a Boeing 777-300LR, when it attempted the longest flight in the world. A few dozen journalists were flying from Hong Kong to London, "the long way around the world." We flew eastward, crossing the Pacific, the US, and the Atlantic, covering 11,664 miles. The flight time was twenty-two hours twenty-two minutes, still in the record books as the longest passenger flight ever. As the flight was classed as "experimental," it was not covered by normal FAA rules and we were all security cleared, so access to the cockpit was available.

Cockpit access rules in parts of the world other than the US are frequently more accommodating, even today. Airlines and regulators will give permission for cockpit filming if you ask in advance and they obviously know who you are and what you're about. Malaysia Airlines was keen to pull out all the stops to make this visit go extremely well and it seemed everyone was prepared to do whatever was necessary.

When we boarded the 777 in Hong Kong, I asked the purser if I might say hello to the captain as a courtesy. If we are expecting to film on the plane, it is polite to let the pilots know our intentions, especially when we hoped to use our low-powered radio microphones during our filming. I was brought to the cockpit and met Captain Andrew Liu and First Officer Fariq Hamid. Captain Liu had been briefed about our project and was expecting us. He could not have been more charming and welcoming, making it clear the crew would help us in any way they could. And he offered up a bonus: Would I like to be on the flight deck for takeoff from Hong Kong? I became that nervous kid again, relishing the prospect of being in the cockpit for takeoff of this 777! Of course I said yes. With my colleagues filming our departure out of the passenger cabin window, I went back to the cockpit for takeoff.

Pilots take turns flying the plane. One of the problems we had in covering MH370 was that my colleagues kept calling the two men at the controls pilots or copilots. Normally this wouldn't be significant, but here, it was crucial to the story. Time and again I had to remind them to be more precise: The captain always sits in the left-hand seat and is always the pilot in command of the aircraft; the copilot, who is usually a first officer, sits in the right seat. One will fly the outbound sector, while their colleague does the return leg.

As we prepared for departure, Liu and Hamid were joined by a third pilot, which was unusual for such a short flight. Captain Liu explained to me that the extra pilot was a check pilot because First Officer Hamid was new to the 777 fleet. He had spent most of his time at Malaysia Airlines flying either the single-aisle 737 or, more recently, the bigger Airbus A330, and had spent the past few months in the simulators, training to fly the bigger, wide-bodied 777. Pilots are licensed to fly only certain types of aircraft at any given time. While the license will cover a range of planes from a particular family of aircraft (A319 pilots, for example, can fly the A318, A320, A321), a pilot must retrain to go from a narrow-bodied jet like the 737 to a much bigger, wide-bodied aircraft like the 777. Even though both aircraft are made by Boeing, they have very different cockpits and systems, and several months of training in the simulators are required to make the transition. I was astonished to learn that this was Hamid's first or second flight "on metal" rather than in the simulator.

Captain Liu is a very senior captain with training responsibilities at MH and therefore was permitted to supervise the newbie Hamid, who would be flying the leg to Kuala Lumpur under his supervision. The third pilot was there to oversee the whole operation, just in case. I assumed that Liu had flown the outbound leg to Hong Kong.

In an interesting quirk of procedure, it is normal policy at Malaysia Airlines for the captain to taxi the aircraft out to the runway, regardless of which pilot's turn it is to fly the plane. This is a throw-back to the days when there was only one wheel for steering a plane on the ground, and it was next to the captain's seat. While today's 777 have tillers for both pilots to steer on the ground, apparently the "Only Captains Taxi" rule has been preserved. Also, I am told, because taxi-ing can be tricky in congested airports, the feeling remains that the more experienced pilot should always drive the plane on the ground. This has always struck me as a bit odd; it means the captain does all the hands-on work taxiing the plane out, then gives the controls of the aircraft to the first officer, who has not yet handled the plane, just before the takeoff roll. Many airlines have this rule, but it seems to be often skirted around.

We reached the runway, and Liu formally gave the controls to Hamid. They performed their final checks and clearance for takeoff was given. Hamid put his hands on the double thrust levers and pressed them forward just a bit. Almost instantly, the electronic dials came to life as the Rolls-Royce Trent 800 engines spooled up their phenomenal thrust and the plane began to move. Once Hamid saw that the engines were responding, he pushed the levers all the way forward to get to takeoff power. With the power dramatically increased, the aircraft started to pick up speed.

Takeoff is exhilarating in the cockpit. For pilots, it may all be in a day's work, but for someone who doesn't experience it that often, it requires a leap of faith that the plane will get to flying speed before reaching the end of the runway. I was once sitting in the cockpit of a fully fueled Qantas 747 taking off from Auckland, New Zealand, bound for Los Angeles, when I asked the captain if he ever had a moment of doubt that the laws of aeronautics wouldn't apply that day. He looked at me as if I was mad.

As the speed increased, Liu made the standard speed callouts to

Hamid, who was staring straight down the runway: "One hundred knots," followed ten seconds later by "V1," the last moment they could decide to abort the takeoff. After V1, whatever happened, they had to take off. Now, with the plane reaching flying speed, Liu called out, "Rotate," the signal for Hamid to pull back on the steering wheel, bringing the aircraft nose off the ground, increasing the angle of attack of the wings, and giving the aircraft the extra lift to get into the air. It was textbook.

With the plane in the air, the autopilot was engaged and the departure checks completed. Then we were able to chat, and I got my first good look at Fariq Hamid, a man who had all our lives, literally, in his hands. He had been with Malaysia Airlines since 2007. He had around 2,700 flying hours, most of it on the 737 fleet, which made him a reasonably experienced first officer. With the exuberant and very senior Captain Liu next to him, Hamid didn't talk much, unless he was spoken to. Not that he was overawed; rather he was being respectful and concentrating on flying the plane: after all, it was one of his first flights in a "real" cockpit. I asked him why he was making the change from the 737 to the 777 fleet. He told me he had always loved flying, and moving to the 777 fleet would allow him to fly to more interesting destinations, like Sydney and London. He also said flying the 777 was much easier than the 737—the plane handled beautifully. I was curious to know how different it was flying a real metal plane compared to the training he had done in a flight simulator. He said the simulator was more difficult than the real thing, which was very easy to fly.

Leaving the pilots to their job, I returned to mine: back to the cabins to film the material we needed for *Business Traveller*. Filming on planes is always a bloody nuisance. Novice producers and reporters love the idea of doing it, but frankly it's nothing but hassle and trouble. You are usually getting in the way of the cabin crew trying to do their job, often waking up fellow travelers trying to sleep, or, worst of all, enraging a passenger who sees what you're doing as a gross invasion of their privacy. There's always one truculent passenger who complains and makes a fuss.

When I first did in-fight filming in the late 1980s, carriers like British Airways had a quaint rule that you couldn't film passengers' faces. We always had to film from the rear of the plane looking forward, only getting the backs of heads. The reason was, of course, that there might be people on board who were traveling with people they shouldn't be with, or they had told the boss they were doing something else and shouldn't be there at all. This rule has greatly relaxed in recent years and now all you have to do is make sure no one objects. Of course, there is always one person who does, even just to be difficult, and we have to film around them.

On this flight, Malaysia had made the necessary announcements to the passengers and we had carte blanche to film what we wanted. It was the easiest on-board filming I had done in years. I even managed to eat a meal and take a snooze halfway through.

About an hour or so out of Kuala Lumpur, the purser returned to take us back to the flight deck for landing in the Malaysian capital. This time I was joined by cameraman Scott Clottworthy, who was going to film our arrival from the pilots' viewpoint. We had reached the top of descent, and Hamid was to begin the initial procedures to take us back to land—but not before he had to navigate around some very nasty-looking storm clouds. This was entirely normal for this time of the year in Southeast Asia. The cumulonimbus clouds build up in the late afternoon, fueled by hot temperatures, rising humidity, and shifting winds. Liu discussed with Hamid the best way he should fly around this large weather system.

I am a nervous flyer, even after all these years. The sight of these giant clouds ahead set me wondering what would happen if we just barreled our way through them. Liu showed me the weather radar screen, which had a large patch of red in the middle indicating the clouds ahead. The 777 is a large plane and flying through the clouds would not cause it any physical harm, though it might well be very uncomfortable for the passengers in the back. Since flying passengers smoothly is part of an airline pilot's job, Hamid knew he had to fly around the clouds if he could. He executed long, gentle turns using the heading select on the autopilot as the plane continued its descent. All in a day's work for the pilot.

I had spent part of the flight wondering whether filming Hamid while he landed the plane was such a good idea, considering his inexperience on the 777. Of course, Hamid was qualified to land the aircraft, and he certainly knew the airport, since he had landed 737s there hundreds of times. For me, however, his flying competence wasn't the issue. Doing this complicated task in the privacy of your own cockpit is one thing; doing it with a TV camera from CNN behind you is something else. After thirty years of working in television, I can confidently tell you people become much more nervous when the watching eye of the camera lens is on them. Novice reporters often ramble nonsense, new CEOs suddenly become incoherent, and some people just freeze.

For Hamid, who was landing the new, bigger plane under the watchful gaze of senior colleagues, it would have been daunting enough on an ordinary day, but now he had the extra pressure of a camera from CNN sitting behind him, recording his every move. I wasn't being overly cautious. The TV world is full of examples of projects that "seemed like a good idea at the time" and ended up as disasters on the front pages of newspapers. Here, any incident didn't even have to be serious or life-threatening. A slow or delayed descent, a missed approach requiring a go-around at KL . . . anything out of the ordinary could cause us problems. I knew from long, bitter experience that if something went wrong, it would soon become known that CNN was in the cockpit, and even if we were there with permission, we would become part of the story and get the blame.

I wanted the footage badly, but I also knew I didn't want an incident on my hands. So I gingerly asked Captain Liu whether it was wise for us to be putting Hamid under more stress by filming his landing the plane. My hope was that Liu would decide to land the aircraft himself. Instead, his answer was immediate and unequivocal: Hamid was one of the best young pilots at Malaysia Airlines. "Exceptional" was how Liu described him; there was nothing to be concerned about. Still, I freely admit that as the plane began its final approach to KL, I was more than a little nervous.

Takeoff is exhilarating; landing is terrifying. The tension in a cockpit goes up several notches; pilots become much more focused; radio calls are terse; knobs are twiddled, levers are pulled, and the aircraft shudders as it's reconfigured to return to land. The cockpit visitor spends ages looking out of the window for the strip of concrete that's supposedly out there before finally spotting the bright approach and runway lights in the distance. One pilot describes doing a good landing as more art than science. You want the aircraft gently but firmly to kiss the runway. With the plane now well into its descent, I paused to look around the cockpit and wonder at the marvel that is modern aviation and the pilots at the controls.

While Scott was filming the landing using the big professional TV camera, I decided to film it on my iPhone. I'm not sure why—it seemed like a good idea, and I thought it might give us an extra angle we could use in the show. Hamid, steady as a rock, one hand on the thrust levers, the other on the yoke, eyes never leaving the runway, calmly brought the plane over the threshold as the automatic voice called out the minimum heights. Finally, touching the aircraft down, right on the center line, before the spoilers and reverse thrust engaged, slowing the aircraft to taxiing speed.

At this point, Liu announced that Hamid should do the taxi into the terminal to gain experience in steering the much larger aircraft on the ground, which he did effortlessly. When I asked the captain how Hamid had performed, he answered without hesitation that the landing had been "textbook perfect."

With the plane parked at the gate, we prepared to say our goodbyes. There were the inevitable photos taken with the crew. They had been so very kind to us, the least I could do was smile for a quick selfie . . . including the one with Fariq Hamid that would be widely shown weeks later. Today I am relieved that I didn't do my usual joke when taking these photos. Sometimes, when I'm wearing a suit and tie and people ask for selfie photos, I try to make the shot more interesting, so I hold up my tie as if the other person is strangling me. You can see in the photo as I grab the tie, and then think better of it. Thank God I did. It would have been horrible to have such a picture being shown around the world at such a tragic moment. Hamid put that photo onto social media, and as I sat before a studio camera three weeks later, it was very quickly being distributed around the world.

Now came the moment at CNN when we had to decide what we would do or say, if anything, about this photograph and remarkable coincidence. We had content that gave us a different perspective, and that material was exclusive, including video of one of the pilots flying a plane. This video was on a server in Hong Kong, so the call went out to get it all transferred as soon as possible to the CNN servers in

Atlanta, along with anything, and I mean anything, we had from that trip.

Sitting in a small, dark flash studio in the middle of the night, I had an awful feeling about how this coverage might develop. In the vacuum of twenty-four-hour news, as you wait for more details, overzealous producers might start to inflate this small portion of the story, and I would rapidly become part of it. I would be questioned and pushed to say more and more about what had happened on that short flight to Kuala Lumpur. No one intends for this kind of thing to happen; it's just the way it is, and I needed to stop it as soon as I could, but at the same time I had to be realistic. As a network on the biggest story of the night, we had something no one else had. At that point we had no idea how big this story was going to get, or how long it would last. We were dealing with a plane crash, an event that happens several times a year. These stories typically lead the news for a week or two, depending on the airline and where in the world the crash happened. We did not know we were going to be dealing with aviation's biggest mystery.

I sent an email to Mike McCarthy, our senior vice president of CNN International, expressing my reservations and enclosing a draft email I wanted to send to the whole network. "Please use this sympathetically," I suggested we tell producers. "You are looking at the pilot involved in this accident, flying a 777 three weeks before he probably perished at the controls." Mike immediately agreed and sent out a network-wide email, adding his own comments that it was "important we give the context around the video."[2] He noted that while the video was important for our coverage, there had to be "sensitivity in how it is written to."

The video of Hamid flying the plane was used sparingly. Obviously the *Business Traveller* show from Kuala Lumpur could not be broadcast either that month, or indeed at all. All the material shot in the cockpit, except for a very short clip of Hamid flying the plane, would be shelved. To show more of the material would be a gratuitous intrusion into grief, without adding anything to the understanding of the story.

There were other moments from that visit to Malaysia Airlines that would also be important to me as I covered the story in the days ahead. After we left Zahari and Hamid in the cockpit, we were due to film in the airport and interview the chief executive of Malaysia Airlines, Ahmad Jauhari Yahya, whom everyone called AJ. The interview would be done in the new first-class lounge. MH was proud of its new facility and its enhanced service and comfort. They wanted to show it off to us, as another example of how the airline was changing. It was a good place to talk to the CEO.

AJ is not your typical airline CEO. He is much quieter, less assuming than many of the larger-than-life, boisterous men who tend to make it to his position. As I will discuss later, this different style and temperament, and a lack of experience in running an airline, may have made a difference to the way Malaysia Airlines handled this crisis. For the moment, though, everything I was learning about the airline, and AJ's plans to turn it around, would, eventually, significantly help me in the coverage of the story once MH370 vanished.

One incident from that February 2014 trip to Kuala Lumpur soon became embarrassing. As Malaysia Airlines was to be featured so prominently in CNN *Business Traveller*, I agreed to be interviewed by *Going Places*, the airline's in-flight magazine. It was a standard feature in which each month someone is asked the same set of questions. I had completely forgotten that I had done this interview, until in the midst of the crisis I started getting emails from readers wanting to know why I was in the airline's magazine when I was all over CNN covering the missing plane.

I read the magazine and didn't know whether to laugh or cry. In the end, I cringed. The last question I was asked, "What did you most enjoy about Malaysia Airlines' famous Malaysian hospitality?" I answered, "Being invited into the cockpit was the highlight by far." I went on to gloat that it was "a rare treat in this security-conscious day and age . . . It was phenomenal to see two talented professional and experienced pilots handling this magnificent machine."

All of this was true, and I stand by every word; it just looked in horribly bad taste and was very poorly timed in light of what had just happened and the accusations being thrown about. The magazine interview was the last thing I wanted to have going around while I was front and center of covering this story. It fed the conspiracy theorists who were determined to believe CNN and I were somehow involved in whatever had taken place and had behaved disreputably. We had a short discussion at CNN about this article, and, of course, there was nothing we could do about it. We just had to be ready to answer any questions that were raised. It was out there, on the planes, and that was that.

So on March 7, 2014, I found myself in the studios on that Friday night, broadcasting about something that had just happened, about which I had more than a bit of background and in-depth knowledge.

Like many other aviation correspondents and pundits, I had little doubt that the story tomorrow would be "daylight and the first debris from the missing Malaysia plane has been spotted in the South China Sea . . ." This would then flow into the rhythm that these stories assume. I was wrong. The morning would bring no debris, and the story was about to take some extraordinary turns.

As for that video I took of Hamid landing in Kuala Lumpur, it is still in my iPhone. I can't delete it. In the days and weeks after MH370 was lost, I would watch it frequently, looking to see if I had missed anything, as if this one-minute ten-second piece of video might give me the answer to what had happened. I studied Hamid's face, looking at the runway ahead, wondering if he was involved in what happened that night in March. Then I looked at his hands on the thrust levers and wondered if they were the ones that had turned off transponders, reset autopilots, and sent the plane off deep into the south Indian Ocean. Ultimately, I watched the videos we shot on that Hong Kong–to–Kuala Lumpur flight and wondered, Hamid, what *did* happen on that flight to Beijing?

I have racked my brain to recall all the inconsequential chatter we made in the cockpit, and whether there was anything significant, a hint, a scintilla of importance. Something that in hindsight might give a tip-off that he was not in his right mind or was planning anything untoward. Of course, nothing has come to mind, which made listening to all the criticisms of the pilots in the days after all the more difficult. There is, at the moment, not a shred of reason to believe that this young pilot took over the plane, flew it to the south Indian Ocean, and murdered all those on board. Not a shred. To me, he seemed a charming, unassuming young pilot who loved flying and who was looking forward to visiting new, exciting destinations.

CHAPTER TWO

KUL TO PEK

Good night Malaysian Three Seven Zero.

—ZAHARIE OR HAMID

O n the night of March 7, 2014, passengers began arriving at Kuala Lumpur International Airport to check in for MH370, the overnight red-eye flight to Beijing. The 777 aircraft, with two classes of service, could carry up to 282 passengers; tonight there would be at least fifty empty seats, busy but by no means full.

The passenger mix was exactly the sort one might expect to see on this type of flight. Business travelers making their way between the capital cities after a long week's work, families returning home after a relaxing holiday in Malaysia, groups of workers from the same company who had been at a conference, and wanderlust lovers who were heading for an adventurous vacation in Beijing. The oldest passenger on board was seventy-nine-year-old artist Lou Baotang, a calligrapher who had been attending a convention in Kuala Lumpur. The youngest was Weng Moheng, aged just twenty-three months. Reading the passenger manifest, one realizes the passengers, from fourteen countries, clearly came from every walk of life. Old and young, they were the passengers we see every day in the world's airports, weary from long hours of traveling, excited by the adventures ahead or simply happy to be heading home.

In fact, there was nothing remarkable about MH370. It was your typical red-eye flight between two major destinations, the sort of flight that is the backbone of any airline's route network. Connecting Kuala Lumpur with Beijing, this flight (and its successor flight MH318) was an essential route for Malaysia Airlines. MH370 carried passengers who were traveling point to point between the two capital cities, as well as valuable transfer passengers (known as sixth-freedom traffic) who were using Kuala Lumpur as a hub, transferring from other destinations. The plane also carried tons of lucrative cargo for the growing electronics industry as well as an assortment of other goods. On paper, MH370 was an important flight for Malaysia Airlines, but otherwise there was nothing that would draw attention to it.

The very timing of the flight, leaving late at night and returning to Malaysia in the afternoon of the next day, was chosen so that passengers could make convenient connections over Malaysia Airlines' Kuala Lumpur hub. In the battle of aviation under way in Asia, Kuala Lumpur prides itself on being one of the fastest-growing hubs, promising speedy connections, where passengers from Europe and Australasia can connect.

The flight was crucial for Malaysia Airlines as it built up its business with Chinese travelers. To do this, the airline would often discount tickets in the Chinese market, attracting Chinese passengers who wanted to connect through Malaysia to other domestic destinations as well as regional flights in Southeast Asia, and, of course, on to Europe. More than 65 percent of the passengers on board the

March 8 red-eye were Chinese nationals. There were also passengers on board using MH370 to get to Beijing, where they would transfer on to other airlines. So the flight carried passengers who had either just come from Europe or were heading to Beijing to go to Europe on Chinese airlines. MH370 was a perfect example of how passengers use flights in today's complex global aviation industry.

By the time the doors were closed, there were 227 passengers on the aircraft. But all was not as it might seem. In the post-incident chaos, there was a great deal of confusion over exactly who was on the plane and who was not. There were claims that some passengers had decided not to travel at the last moment and their luggage had been taken off; there were passengers who had supposedly not checked in at all for the flight; there were passengers who had been added as standbys at the last minute; and of course there were the passengers who were not who they said they were, traveling on stolen passports.

This lack of immediate certainty about who was on the flight came as a surprise to many people, but to those of us who have covered airline crashes, it was normal. The passenger list is supposed to be 100 percent accurate, but frequently it isn't. We saw this again a few months later with MH17, which was blown out of the sky over Ukraine. It took the authorities days to confirm who was on that plane. As the MH17 report says, "the fact that it is not possible to establish who is on board an aeroplane at a simple press of a button is well-known and generally accepted in the aviation sector."[1] This is a large gray area that can cause initial confusion. All passenger lists are imperfect in some way because of the way they are compiled, with information from different airlines and computer systems. Sometimes foreign names get transposed. Often family names get confused for given names. Then there are passengers transferring from code-share flights and other airlines as well as those passengers who miss the flight or decide not to travel.

In the final hectic moments before an international flight leaves, gate agents are incredibly busy, trying to get everything sorted out so the plane can depart on time. They are changing seat assignments so families can sit next to each other, upgrading elite passengers to premium cabins, removing transfer passengers who are delayed on incoming connecting flights, reallocating empty seats to standby passengers. Next time you fly, just watch the supervising gate agent standing behind the podium, furiously typing away, making sure he or she can get as many people on the plane as want to fly. Always trying to make sure the plane leaves as close as possible to its scheduled time so it can make its takeoff slot. As the Dutch report makes clear, the final list of names on board can never be relied upon in an emergency.

In the hours and days after MH370 went missing, numerous cases of glaring anomalies in the passenger list came to light. There was a level of confusion about who was on the plane that should never have been allowed to happen. For instance, on March 10, 2014, Dato' Sri Azharuddin Abdul Rahman, the director general of civil aviation, admitted, "Yes, there are issues about the passengers that did not fly on the aircraft—there are five of them . . . We have to remove the baggage that they checked in on the aircraft. We have done so."[2]

Twenty-four hours later, he was contradicted by Inspector General of Police Tan Sri Khalid Abu Bakar, who said, "There was no five passengers who checked in and did not board. Everybody who booked this flight boarded the plane."[3]

Unfortunately, this statement was not accurate either. By March 12, the defense minister, Hishammuddin Hussein, was saying there were four passengers booked on the plane who did not show up at check-in. "Everyone who checked in to flight MH370 boarded the plane. Four passengers did not show up at check-in. No baggage was offloaded."[4]

This level of confusion about something as basic as who was on the plane was quite detrimental to the Malaysian authorities in those first crucial days as they sought to build confidence in their handling of the investigation. Journalists, myself included, were puzzled about these four or five missing passengers, and the way the authorities were distinguishing between being booked on the flight and checking in. In the heat of the moment it seems likely that the officials simply got the two mixed up, but this is not a luxury you enjoy when dealing with plane crashes. In the world of the twenty-four-hour news cycle, people are watching what you say in real time and putting it together with what your colleagues or other journalists are saying elsewhere. Knowing who was on the plane was crucial at a time when there were very few details. Right from the beginning, officials confused facts, muddied issues, and created doubts about what was happening. The way Malaysia Airlines handled the passenger manifest was sloppy, a point reinforced by the MH17 experience four months later, when it also took the airline days to confirm the names of those on board. They should have gotten it right or said nothing at all.

What was accurate was that there were four passengers who had bought tickets for the flight but did not check in. Hishammuddin said they were replaced by passengers on the standby list. We have never heard another word about these no-shows, which means somewhere in the world there are four people who daily must be counting their blessings that they didn't make MH370.

A far more serious problem with the passenger manifest was the fact that two people on the plane were using stolen passports. This discovery came about within hours of the plane's going missing, as the Malaysian authorities began notifying governments around the world that their nationals were on board. One can imagine the surprise when they received an extraordinary reply, first from the Austrians and then the Italians, that they were wrong. The names of Kozel Christian and

Luigi Maraldi had shown on the manifest as being on board the plane, but Christian was still in his native Austria, while Maraldi was on vacation in Thailand, where he was questioned by the police.[5]

The authorities in Vienna said Christian's passport had been stolen in Thailand in 2012. The Italians said Maraldi's passport had been stolen in Thailand in 2013. Hours later, on Sunday, March 9, the international police agency Interpol confirmed that the documents had been reported missing and they were listed in its database containing millions of Stolen and Lost Travel Documents (SLTD). All of which begged the question, If they were in the system, how come the passports had been used to travel and accepted as valid documents to enter and leave Malaysia?[6]

The reason the passports were not flagged as stolen was ridiculously simple: Malaysia never checked passports against Interpol's lost and stolen database. According to the country's immigration authority, "The immigration officer verified the bearer and the image on the biodata page in the produced passport were matched . . . additionally, the officer posed relevant questions to the subject including the reason for his travelling into the country."[7]

Attention was focused immediately on the stolen passports and Malaysia's failure to do full and proper checks. To those of us covering the story, this was a smoking gun, too good to be ignored. It seemed the crash would turn out to be some form of hijacking or terrorism. At CNN and elsewhere, the security analysts and pundits came out of the woodwork to opine that this was the breakthrough. After all, how else do we explain two passengers traveling on stolen passports on a plane that subsequently goes missing?

The media was urgently seeking any and all information about the men who had used the passports, who they were and what they looked like. It all led to one of the lowest points in the early days of the search for MH370. On Monday, March 10, in the third news conference to be held that day, Dato' Sri Azharuddin Abdul Rahman, the director general of civil aviation, announced, "We have looked at the footage of the video and the photographs. It is confirmed now they are not Asian-looking males."

Rahman was then asked, "If they are not Asian-looking males, what are they looking like?"

He gave a startling reply. Having gotten the name wrong several times, he said, "Do you know a footballer by the name of Balotelli, he's an Italian? Do you know how he looks like? They are not Asians."

A reporter asked, "Meaning he is black?"

"Yes," Rahman replied. "I don't want to dwell on that. But they are not Asian."[8]

I Googled Balotelli and, seeing the black Italian footballer, immediately assumed that Rahman meant the men were black. It was a bizarre moment. One second he is talking about how two men had gotten onto a plane with stolen passports, and the next he's talking about an Italian footballer. Watching the video, it is cringing to hear the reporters laughing at Rahman's efforts to get the name right.

When I met Rahman during my visit to Kuala Lumpur in the summer of 2015, I asked him what the Balotelli reference had been about. According to the director general, he was not saying the men were black. Rather he was trying to tell the reporters not to make assumptions just because of someone's nationality. One of the stolen passports was from Italy, but the man using it, he told me, was "unlike a face of a Caucasian." The reporters had pushed him, arguing that in the case of the Italian, he should look Italian. He had responded with the Balotelli comparison because "a person's image or appearance does not mean that they come from a particular country," he explained to me. Rahman has no regrets for the Balotelli remark. "I am very clear what I said at that time," he said, "but if they choose to report otherwise . . ."[9]

Photographs from the closed-circuit cameras at the airport were released showing two men going through airport security. Within twenty-four hours the Iranian police had the answer about who the men were, and told Interpol. They were identified as two Iranians, Pouria Nour Mohammad Mehrdad, aged nineteen, and Delavar Seyed Mohammad Reza, aged twenty-nine.

After viewing the photos, I could see what Rahman was trying to say: the Middle Eastern men did not look typically Italian. But they also looked nothing like Balotelli. Whatever Rahman intended to say or mean, he had created a mess. It added another searing moment that would be referred to many times in the future, as evidence mounted on how Malaysia was mishandling the crisis. The whole incident was awful.

Interpol now had chapter and verse on these Iranians. They had left Iran on different dates, using their legitimate Iranian passports. They had flown via Doha, Qatar, to Malaysia, where they had entered and left the country using the stolen passports. The men were flying to Beijing, scheduled to connect to a KLM flight to Amsterdam, after which they would go their separate ways. Pouria would fly on to Frankfurt, where his mother was waiting for him, while Seyed was to end his journey in Copenhagen. The two men had traveled incredibly circuitous routes to get to Europe: from Tehran to Doha to Kuala Lumpur to Beijing to Amsterdam and their final destinations, and with the exception of the first flight out of Iran, all would have been done using stolen passports.

As to their motives, Interpol was clear: these men were not terrorists. They were more like refugees traveling to Europe to seek asylum. Pouria's mother had been waiting in Frankfurt for her son. She contacted the police almost immediately once she heard the Beijing flight had gone missing.

So much for these men being terrorists. Now the heat turned up on the Malaysian authorities to explain how these men had been allowed to enter the country, then board an international flight using stolen documents. The Malaysians responded with a long statement on March 11, setting out the nuts and bolts of what had happened. There was not a word of regret or explanation about how this could have taken place in a post-9/11 world, far from it. The statement was almost belligerent in its defense of the indefensible. The statement from the head of the immigration authority said, "All the Department's standard operation procedures have been followed and strictly adhered to by the Immigration officers."[10]

Unsurprisingly, far from explaining matters, this generated more distrust. In effect, the Malaysians were telling us that everything had been done as it should have been. They were unable or unwilling to explain how this lamentable breach of passport security had happened. The justification was a breathtaking example of bureaucratic insouciance, which went on to disparage those of us who dared to question how this had happened.

By the end of the first day, we knew something odd was taking place. There was a plane incident, the plane was still missing, and there were passengers on board who had used stolen passports. The very fact that this had happened was troubling enough, yet it added insult to injury that the authorities were suggesting the immigration officers on duty at Kuala Lumpur International Airport had conducted the clearance properly.

The root problem was that Malaysia didn't check passports against the Interpol Stolen and Lost Travel Document database. If they had, both documents would have flashed up as stolen. If all this was grim, the authorities made the situation worse. The country's interior minister was quoted as telling parliament that the Interpol database of forty million passports was too large and that to check "may slow down the process of immigration checks at counters."[11]

Within hours, Interpol's secretary general Ron Noble went ballistic at this statement. Having interviewed Noble several times during the years when he was head of the global police body, I can attest that it is usually a challenge to get him to say anything controversial or negative about an Interpol member country. The man is a diplomat as well as a policeman. Now he was furious. The stolen and lost list is something of which he is rightly very proud. It is used millions of times a day by dozens of countries, and here the Malaysians were telling the world it was slow and would take too long.

Interpol blasted the Malaysian minister, saying they had no idea why he had chosen to make this "unjustified" accusation. The statement pointed out that the US consults the database more than 230 million times a year, the UK 140 million times, Singapore more than 29 million. "Not one of these countries, or indeed any INTERPOL member country, has ever stated that the response time is too slow," the press statement declared.[12] The statement pointed out that Malaysia did not conduct a single check of passengers, concluding, "If there is any responsibility or blame for this failure, it rests solely with Malaysia's Immigration Department."[13] For Interpol to attack like this was just about unheard of, and it's a measure of how out of control things were getting. It was only day three.

Added to the Balotelli misunderstanding, this passport and Interpol issue raised more questions about Malaysia's ability to handle the crisis with integrity and transparency. To be fair to Malaysia, the country was doing a good job of getting a huge number of countries involved in the search. But whatever might have been happening behind the scenes, the public face was dreadful.

I still wince at how we were all so quick to condemn these two passengers for blowing up a jet when the truth was actually tragic. They were two men who, seeking a better life, had used stolen passports to get to Europe. We know where the passports were stolen and we know where the tickets were bought and paid for. To this day, we haven't been told any details about the criminal ring behind the stolen passports, how the two men got them, or how they fit into the very real problem of stolen documents that flood the world. All we know is that the two men whose names were tossed about as the possible culprits for the loss of MH370 were as much victims on that flight as every other passenger.

While the passengers were checking in on March 7 in the main departure hall, in another section of KLIA, the flight crew was arriving for duty. Sitting in the left seat of 9M-MRO was to be fifty-three-year-old Captain Zaharie Ahmad Shah, a veteran pilot who had been with Malaysia Airlines for thirty-two years. Captain Zaharie had 18,400 flying hours, including more than 8,600 hours on the 777. He was, by any definition, extremely experienced. His first officer was very much at the other extreme. Fariq Hamid, age twenty-seven, the pilot I had flown with a few weeks before, had been with Malaysia Airlines for six and a half years. Having been promoted to the 777 fleet four months earlier, he was brand-new to flying the aircraft and had accumulated only thirty-nine hours "on type." This was to be his first flight without a third pilot in the cockpit to supervise.

As is usual, the pilots would take turns to fly the plane. One of them would be described as the PF, or pilot flying, and would actually fly the plane to Beijing; the other would be the pilot not flying or PNF (also called the pilot monitoring). The pilot not flying's duties include communicating with air traffic control, preparing and reading out the checklists, and generally doing all the work in the cockpit not involved in handling the controls and flying the aircraft. On the return leg, the pilots swap duties. One important point to remember: in aviation, it doesn't matter who is the pilot flying at the controls; the captain in the left-hand seat always remains the pilot in command.

By late into the evening, passengers and crew were now on board the 777 and the plane was ready to depart. Shortly before half-past midnight one of the two men in the cockpit requested permission to push back and start the engines. Who was the pilot flying? We have never been officially told, but we can make various assumptions: normally whoever is the pilot not flying does the radio calls.

The Factual Report concludes that while the plane was on the ground, it was the first officer, Hamid, who made the radio calls. Once in the air, it was the captain who operated the radios.[14] The fact that the pilots on the radio changed is not at all suspicious; it makes perfect sense. As I pointed out, at Malaysia Airlines there is a rule that captains always taxi the aircraft to the runway. This means Zaharie taxied the plane while FO Hamid made the radio calls. Hamid then took the controls and flew the plane into the air and toward Beijing, so now Zaharie did the calls. It also makes perfect sense that Hamid, as the new 777 pilot, would be asked to fly the plane on the outbound leg to Beijing.

Air traffic control recordings of the exchanges between the ground and the plane were analyzed, including the final words, "Good night Malaysian Three Seven Zero." During the investigation, these tapes were played for family members, colleagues, and friends of both men to help identify the voices. Those listening were taken to a room, unable to bring any phones or recording devices, the door was locked, and they were asked to listen to the tapes. It has been accepted that the voice that said the last words was Zaharie's. That would mean Hamid was the pilot flying, or that he was out of the cockpit.

I tested this theory with a senior training Malaysian captain during my visit to Kuala Lumpur, and he agreed. He said he too would have gotten the new first officer, Hamid, to do the down leg so he would gain experience in and familiarity with landing in Beijing, which would have been a new airport for him. It is safe to conclude that the pilot flying the plane that night was First Officer Hamid and operating the radios was Captain Zaharie.

Anyway, does it matter who was flying? Regardless of who was physically flying the plane on the first leg, Captain Zaharie was the much more senior officer and was the pilot in command. The very junior first officer, Hamid, would do what he was told.

Lumpur Delivery gave the pilots clearance to fly that night to Beijing. They were told the route they should follow after takeoff to exit the airport. They were given a number and told to set the plane's transponder to "squawk two-one-five-seven." This "squawk" would be the way MH370 was identified on radar screens along its route network.

A few words about transponders are required, as the device would become an important part of what would happen in less than an hour. Even though planes today have many complex communication tools, the transponder remains fundamental to an aircraft's identification and safety in flight.

Transponders (the word comes from transmitter-responder) are part of a plane's secondary radar system. A radar beam is sent up from the ground station and hits the aircraft. In primary radar, the beam is returned as just a blip. The ground controller knows that something is there, but not much more. When radar was first used in the Second World War, this very basic level of information proved to be lifesaving over the English Channel. In the crowded skies of today's world, merely having blips on radar screens would be downright dangerous; the controller needs to know much more information to ensure safe flying. Typically the transponder also sends details of the height, speed, and type of aircraft that is being flown.

In the cockpit, the transponder switch is located on the center unit between the two pilots. The pilot monitoring the aircraft that night would have dialed in 2157, the squawk number given by Kuala Lumpur ATC, and engaged the system. Now the aircraft would be visible to all radar operators and would show that number and flight details—that is, until it stopped transmitting.

All these last-minute adjustments in the cockpit were made as the plane continued its short taxi from the terminal to the active runway. MH370 was told to "line up" on Runway 32 Right, the longer of Kuala Lumpur's two runways. Two minutes later, at 00:40, MH370 was "cleared for takeoff"; the aircraft's twin Rolls-Royce Trent 800 engines spooled up to takeoff power and within minutes the plane was on its way to Beijing.

The departure from Kuala Lumpur was routine. When a plane is flying, altitudes over ten thousand feet are usually described by lopping off the last two zeroes. So over the next twenty minutes MH370 was instructed to climb to Flight Level One Eight Zero (eighteen thousand feet) then up to Two Five Zero (twenty-five thousand) before it was allowed to reach its cruising altitude of Flight Level Three Five Zero (thirty-five thousand feet). The plane was also given permission to proceed directly to its first waypoint, IGARI. A huge fuss would be made about waypoints once the plane went missing, so it's worth explaining them now.

Just as there are named roads on the ground that meet at junctions, so there are virtual highways in the sky. They are given names and numbers, and pilots follow them to get from A to B. The route to Beijing is fairly simple. The route MH370 was following took it northeast from Kuala Lumpur across the South China Sea, heading toward a waypoint called IGARI, which is located in the middle of the waters between Malaysia and Vietnam where the South China Sea meets the Gulf of Thailand. After IGARI the plane would fly to BITOD, then cross Vietnam and head to Beijing.

As the plane moved farther away from Kuala Lumpur Airport, the airport tower controller handed the flight over to an en route operator known as Lumpur Radar, who controlled much of the airspace around Malaysia. Lumpur Radar was now responsible for MH370's safe passage until it left Malaysian airspace and was handed over to controllers in Vietnam. It was the Lumpur Radar who directed MH370 to climb first to FL250, then to its initial cruising altitude of FL350 (thirty-five thousand feet).

The time was 00:50. What happened in the next thirty minutes are the events about which we know absolutely nothing, but are at the heart of the missing plane's disappearance.

At 1:01 a.m., the cockpit made a radio transmission to Lumpur Radar Control saying, "Malaysian Three Seven Zero maintaining Level Three Five Zero," basically telling the controller that the plane was at its altitude and was staying there. This is slightly unusual since the controller hadn't asked MH370 to advise when they had reached their altitude. Unless requested, pilots don't normally tell ATC when they have reached their altitude; there's no need. ATC can see a plane's altitude from the transponder information, and anyway, reaching altitude is what is expected. A pilot tells them only if requested, or if something has gone awry. To make such a call is unusual, but not abnormal. Not surprisingly, ATC just acknowledged the transmission by reading back the flight's call sign, "Malaysian Three Seven Zero."

Then, seven minutes later, the pilots did it again: "Malaysian Three Seven Zero maintaining Level Three Five Zero." The radar operator, probably a bit nonplussed about why this pilot kept reminding them of his altitude, acknowledged again by reading back the call sign, "Malaysian Three Seven Zero."

Eleven minutes later, at 01:19, the plane had just about reached the end of Malaysian-controlled airspace, ready to transfer over to the next controller in Vietnam. Kuala Lumpur radioed the plane, "Malaysian Three Seven Zero, contact Ho Chi Minh, one two zero decimal niner [120.9] good night."

The pilot, believed to be Captain Zaharie, acknowledged this with "Good night Malaysian Three Seven Zero." Those are the last words we ever hear from the plane.

What happened after the plane signed off at 01:19 is purely a matter of deduction coupled with rampant speculation. The only thing we can say with any certainty is that whatever took place on board that aircraft was happening about now.

Two minutes after "Good night Malaysian Three Seven Zero" was spoken, at 01:21, the plane's squawk, 2157, disappeared from radar screens in both Malaysia and Vietnam. Air traffic controllers have never spoken publicly about what happened, except for some newspaper quotes from Siti Sarah, the controller handling MH370. She noticed that the plane had disappeared from the radar screen and commented that in eighteen years on the job she had never seen such a thing.[15] Unfortunately, for everyone concerned, as later transcripts would show, she didn't do much about what she described as a "total communication breakdown."

The transponder was no longer sending its signal. One week later, the prime minister of Malaysia said, "Near the border between Malaysian and Vietnamese air traffic control the aircraft's transponder was switched off."[16] The plane was still visible as a blip on the screen to the most basic primary radar systems, but in the modern world of aviation and air traffic control, it had become almost invisible.

From now on, all information about the plane's position came from basic blips on military radar, and from "handshakes" on the satellite system.

In total, the Boeing 777 had six different ways to communicate with the ground. There were three VHF (very high frequency) radios, two high-frequency radios, a satellite communications system (SATCOM), and two air traffic control transponders. The radios had been used to communicate verbally with the ground all the way up to "Good night Malaysian Three Seven Zero." The transponder had sent out the squawk until it was switched off. The satellite system or SATCOM was used primarily for data transfers between the aircraft and the ground. It made the connection and sent the information through a very sophisticated system called ACARS—the Aircraft Communication and Reporting System.

Today's aircraft and flights are enormously complicated in engineering, technology, planning, and information requirements. Using both radio frequency and, when not available, SATCOM, the ACARS system sends and receives all sorts of information between the aircraft and the ground: everything from the position of the plane, including speed and height, to the amount of fuel on board and the way the plane is being flown. ACARS is also used for flight planning, rerouting, to receive weather data, even for exchanging information about connecting flights.

Companies other than an airline also tap into the ACARS system to receive valuable data. For instance, the plane's engine manufacturer, Rolls-Royce, can receive data telling them how the engines are performing and when they are likely to need maintenance. The airline's operations department will be able to follow the progress of a flight and tell whether the plane is being flown according to the standard operating procedures, and maintenance on the ground will be alerted when something goes wrong; if it's not urgent, sometimes the engineers know before even the pilots are aware of the fault.

Radio and radar transmissions are the minute-by-minute way planes are directed in the air, and ACARS is the unseen backbone of planes' communications with the ground. The information sent via ACARS is often vital: on June 1, 2009, Air France 447 from Rio de Janeiro to Paris went missing over the South Atlantic in the middle of the night. The plane had crashed into the ocean, killing all 228 people on board. It would be six days before the search teams were able to locate and recover any wreckage. It took a further two years and many weeks of searching deep underwater to find and retrieve the black-box flight recorders in order to confirm to investigators what had gone wrong.

During the first few hours of searching for the doomed plane, Air France engineers back in Paris had received ACARS data sent in the aircraft's last moments. The ACARS system on board the A330 had automatically sent messages reporting that the plane's systems were beginning to fail. More messages, seconds apart, over a four-minute period. One of the first warnings said the plane's pitot tubes, which measure how fast the plane is flying, had failed; there were alerts that the autopilot and auto throttle had switched off; the pilots were getting speed warnings in the cockpit display units. Long before any significant wreckage was found, Airbus, Air France, and the investigators knew that there had been a serious problem with the speed information the pilots were receiving and that was likely part of the cause of the crash.

Within two months, the Bureau d'Enquêtes et d'Analyses, the French investigators, were able to release an interim report. Although the BEA didn't know why the plane had crashed, they had been able to identify that the initial problem lay with the aircraft's pitot tubes. So they knew the reason for the crisis, if not the reason for the crash. It would be two more years, with the recovery of the black-box data and voice recorders, before the investigation could explain how the plane was being flown and the role played by the pilots. In the early days of the inquiry, ACARS messages had been the only information to go on.

MH370 was fully equipped with ACARS and it had been transmitting since the engines were switched on. Unless it was sending requested information, it was programmed to transmit updates to Malaysia Airlines roughly every thirty minutes. The data was uplinked from the plane to one of several geostationary satellites owned by the London-based satellite company Inmarsat. The latter downlinked the data at one of their ground stations and sent it on to a third company, SITA, which organizes the ACARS systems for many airlines. SITA is constantly receiving information from hundreds of aircraft from dozens of airlines. Just like a telephone exchange, SITA takes the right data and sends it on to the right airline. It sounds complicated but it is being done automatically thousands of times every hour.

As MH370 flew northeast toward Beijing, the plane was logged onto Inmarsat's Indian Ocean Region (IOR) I-3 satellite. The plane sent its last ACARS transmission at 01:07. The content of that transmission was finally released on March 8, 2015, the one-year anniversary of the plane's going missing. It was pretty normal stuff, including a regular position report showing MH370 flying at thirty-five thousand feet at Mach .82 with 43,800 kilos of fuel remaining.[17] Then nothing else. The next transmission from the plane should have been at 01:37, but that never happened. The only ACARS data after 01:07 were the messages being sent from Malaysia Airlines to the aircraft saying, "Pls contact Ho Chi Minh ATC ASAP. They complain cannot track you on their radar."[18] The logs showed as "failed." There were no warnings indicating aircraft failures sent from MH370, as had happened in Air France 447.

It is worth pausing here for a moment to consider that this was one of the most modern pieces of aviation technology, with six different systems on board for communicating, all of which worked independently, and there was not a word from any of them. The pilots weren't responding on radio; the transponder had been switched off; ACARS was either disabled or not working.

By 01:22, MH370 had gone silent.

With the plane's automatic communications tools now no longer transmitting, we get to the part of the story that is the hardest to understand. MH370 made a slight turn to the right and headed toward waypoint BITOD. A few moments after that, according to official reports, at 01:25, it made a major deviation, taking a sharp turn left, to the northwest, followed by another left turn. MH370 had now made a U-turn and was flying southwest. It was heading back the way it had just come, toward Malaysia.

What happened after this U-turn remains extraordinary and frankly very worrying for anyone who flies frequently on commercial planes. For roughly the next hour, MH370 retraced its route, crossing the Malaysian peninsula until it exited off the western coast by Penang. It then made another northwest turn and flew along the Strait of Malacca, through the Andaman Sea, and around the tip of Indonesia before making a final turn, this one to the south. For much of this unauthorized, unorthodox flying the plane was being tracked by radar both in Thailand and Malaysia, especially the Malaysian primary military radar based at Royal Malaysian Air Base at Butterworth.

According to a variety of sources, a young air force officer noticed a blip on the radar screen as the plane flew back across the country and out the other side. The final detection of MH370 came at 02:22, roughly an hour since "Good night Malaysian Three Seven Zero," and the switching off of the transponder.

Now for the most awful part: The radar operator did not report what he was seeing. The military didn't send up any fighter jets to investigate. No one called to find out what was happening—even though air traffic controllers in both Malaysia and Vietnam were asking questions about MH370's whereabouts. When the assertion was made that fighters had, in fact, been scrambled, the chief of the Royal Malaysian Air Force, in a statement on April 11, 2014, called it "totally false." What was the air force doing? Having seen an unidentified plane flying across the country, didn't they go and at least take a look?

The official explanation for why nothing was done, and a large plane was able to fly across the country unchallenged, was given to me by the prime minister of Malaysia, Najib Razak, when I interviewed him in Kuala Lumpur in April 2014. He said, "I believe there was a man who was monitoring the radar screen." No planes were sent up to investigate, he said, "because it was deemed not to be hostile . . . it behaved like a commercial airline following a normal flight plan."[19] This is a deeply unsatisfactory reason for not investigating what was going on. First, it is hard to see how this could be viewed as a commercial plane following a flight plan: the plane was flying without a squawk, the radar operator could only see blips, and there was no flight plan. In the US or Europe it is inconceivable that an unidentified aircraft, with no flight plan, would be allowed to fly across the country. In the post-9/11 world, if the radar operator was not immediately reassured what the plane was up to, air force jets would be sent up to investigate, fast.

Would it have made any difference if the controller had sent up planes to see what was happening? Obviously while we will never know, a look back at previous incidents gives us an idea of what could have happened if planes had been sent up. In the case of Helios Airways, in August 2005, a Boeing 737 was flying from Larnaca, Cyprus, to Athens, Greece, when the crew became incapacitated following an error in operating the oxygen system. There were frantic ATC radio calls as the plane made its way across Europe. The Greek air force was informed about forty-five minutes after the plane lost contact. Two F-16s were scrambled and made visual contact with the plane less than two hours after the plane stopped responding to calls. The military pilots flew so close to the stricken 737 that they were able to see the captain's seat was empty, the first officer was slumped over the controls, and the oxygen masks had deployed in the passenger cabin. Ultimately they saw a flight attendant enter the cockpit, look out the window, and acknowledge their presence, before the plane ran out of fuel and crashed.[20] Sending up the planes did not change the outcome in Helios, but it proved that you could gain valuable information. This never happened with MH370.

In the subsequent commotion over the failure to alert anyone, the Malaysia authorities had no real explanation for their lack of action. In April 2014, they announced an internal investigation into what had happened, but we have heard nothing more about this, let alone any findings or conclusions.[21] Any questions to officials about the progress of these inquiries are met with a standard response: nothing can be said until the final report . . . which since there is no plane to report on, is unlikely to be published anytime soon.

We are left with the stark fact that a major airline's large, widebodied jet was allowed to fly for hundreds of miles without any flight plan, and no one did anything about it.

So when did the military finally admit what they had seen that

Friday night? The Royal Malaysian Air Force (RMAF) did not reveal what they had seen until many hours after the plane went missing and the search had begun. According to a little-known and rarely read report presented by Malaysia entitled "MH370 Search and Rescue Operations and Lessons Learnt," which was prepared for an Asian regional meeting on search and rescue:

> The KL ARCC [Kuala Lumpur Air Rescue Co-Ordination Center] was informed by the Royal Malaysian Air Force (RMAF) of a possible Air Turn Back by MH 370 on 8 March 2014, at 10:30pm (1430 UTC). The RMAF also mentioned that the area towards the West of Peninsular Malaysia was the last known position observed on the military radar.[22]

There we have it: at 10:30 p.m. on March 8, twenty-one hours after the plane had gone missing and seventeen hours after the Kuala Lumpur rescue coordination center was activated, the very first formal acknowledgment that the plane may have turned back.

This exposed a stunning lack of coordination between the military and the civilian controllers and the various radar systems in Malaysia. While MH370 was flying way over Malaysia, and was seen by military radar, civilian air traffic controllers in Kuala Lumpur and Vietnam were beginning to ask each other questions about the plane's whereabouts. The confusion of the night can be seen in the log of communications among the controllers released on April 1, 2014, and in the several hundred pages of ATC transcripts released as part of the official report on the first anniversary of the disaster in March 2015.[23]

Normally, when an aircraft has been told to contact the onward air traffic controller, the pilots make the call within seconds. We know that Lumpur Radar had instructed the plane to contact Ho Chi Minh on

120.9 at 01:22. The controllers in Ho Chi Minh had received the flight plan and were indeed expecting to hear from MH370. It was sixteen minutes later when the Ho Chi Minh controller contacted Kuala Lumpur to say they hadn't heard from MH370, and the plane had been last seen over waypoint BITOD. Over the next few hours the numerous calls between the various air traffic control centers reveal a bizarre series of events that show how badly the crisis was being managed.

Throughout the night, civilian air traffic controllers seemed to be completely confused. For several hours the two air traffic controllers in KL and HCM went back and forth, repeatedly asking each other if they had heard from the plane or knew anyone who had. They tried different frequencies and even got other aircraft in the area to try to contact MH370. In the time period from when the plane deviated, 1:22, to when the last-known military radar position was noted, 2:22, there are at least fourteen communications between the air traffic controllers, airlines, and other aircraft. No one thought what was happening was urgent enough to call it a crisis.

The confusion was made much worse when Malaysia Airlines' operations department said MH370 was flying in Cambodian airspace and they'd been able to exchange signals with the flight. It would be a further fifteen minutes before someone remembered that MH370's flight plan didn't involve flying through Cambodian airspace. An hour later, Malaysia Airlines admitted the information had been based on projected tracking data, not real-time positioning. In other words, the airline had been looking at screens showing where the aircraft should be, not where in fact it was. It almost beggars belief that this mistake was made and not rectified sooner.

The time gaps in communications among the various air traffic control centers are staggering. For instance, at 04:25 there is a forty-four-minute gap between Ho Chi Minh and Kuala Lumpur checking on progress, and the next communication asking whether anyone had heard from Singapore. This went on for hours, with air traffic controllers in Malaysia, Vietnam, Cambodia, China, and Singapore all being haphazardly quizzed to see who had heard what. Seemingly no one recognized a crisis.

Keep in mind that throughout all of this, there was a radar operator, sitting in Malaysia, watching the radar blips as the plane crossed the country. This person apparently had no idea that everyone was looking for it because he didn't have access to the civilian data or communications. The military sightings wouldn't be revealed to the civilian authorities for more than eighteen hours. It is mind-boggling. No wonder the conclusion of the Malaysians themselves was to recommend "closer civil military airspace coordination and communication."[24]

The real problems of Malaysia's air traffic control were buried deep in the Factual Information Report released on the anniversary of the disappearance. It is now clear that Malaysia's air traffic control system was understaffed. There is legal authority for a fixed number of controllers, and they only had half that number working for them.[25] The level of staffing on the overnight shift was half that of the daytime so that the workers could "have breaks."

What is worse, it seems the air traffic controllers were breaking their own rules about when they should issue official warnings. The first and lowest level of warning is INCERFA, the uncertainty phase, when there is concern about the safety of an aircraft. One notch up is the ALERTFA phase, meaning there is now apprehension about the safety and failure to communicate with the plane. Finally the most serious: DETRESFA, when there is now real possibility of grave and imminent danger.

The rules say ATC is supposed to check if the plane has not been heard from within three minutes of an expected time to call in. In the case of MH370, the expected waypoint was IGARI. So the first call should have been IGARI plus three minutes. However, on that night, it would be IGARI plus thirty-eight minutes before Ho Chi Minh issued an INCERFA. Malaysia's rules say a distress phase or DETRESFA should be issued within thirty minutes of a plane's failure to make contact. The DETRESFA was not issued until IGARI plus seven hours and twenty-one minutes.[26]

I wish I could say that the MH370 delay was an aberration, but it is not. There have been other cases where a plane has gone missing in the middle of the night and it has taken hours to get a rescue operation under way.

In the case of AF447, from Rio to Paris, the last radio transmission of the aircraft was at 01:35. Over the next four hours, there were many calls between Dakar ATC, Atlantico ATC, Sal ATC, and Air France headquarters in Paris, all trying to see if anyone had heard from the plane. The thrust of the communications was usually the same: Have you heard from AF447? What time was the plane due at TASIL or POMAT waypoint? Or what time was it due in your airspace? Any idea if anyone else has heard from the plane? Nothing would happen for fifteen or twenty minutes and then the whole thing would be repeated all over again.

Hours after AF447 was supposed to check with various controllers and failed to do so, they were still trying to get in touch. It was not until 05:50, four hours and fifteen minutes after the last radio transmission (and three and half hours after it crashed), that Air France alerted the Search and Rescue Satellite tracking center to see if they had received any emergency transmitter alert. At 8 a.m. (six hours and thirty minutes after the last radio call), Brest Center wondered if it would be appropriate to launch an alert. Finally, the emergency alerts of INCERFA, ALERTFA, and DETRESFA were issued around 8:15, telling the aviation world that a plane was missing, likely in grave danger, and everyone needed to start looking for it. (Ironically, this is roughly the time the plane should have been getting ready to land in Paris.) It takes time to get things moving, so the first search plane didn't take off until 12:14, nearly twelve hours after AF447 went missing.

Now with MH370, hours had passed with seemingly pointless, repetitious requests for information about a plane that everyone seemed to know was missing but no one was doing anything sensible to find. It would be ages before senior staff seemingly saw the whole picture, realized that the situation was very badly wrong, and this was a crisis.

With MH370, the evidence of incompetence by air traffic control is everywhere. The Factual Information Report released in March 2015 gives the chapter and verse of what went wrong, but, astonishingly, it does not draw any conclusions or make any recommendations. For that we must go back and look at the ICAO review of the search and rescue.[27] "The time lapses . . . [indicate] there was probably not enough resources utilized and/or urgency in responding."

The 370 pages of air traffic control transcripts are the evidence of the true scandal of MH370: the way the plane was handled on the night of its disappearance. As I will show later, all the other criticisms of Malaysia can largely be seen as failures of PR and presentation. But it is the failure to recognize that the plane was missing, coupled with the fact that the military didn't alert the air force that a rogue plane was in Malaysian airspace, that remains at the heart of the issue.

There were plenty of opportunities to discover something was wrong on that night. A combination of incompetence, poor decision making, and bad operating procedures denied us the chance to gain valuable information. These mistakes set the scene for what was to follow in the months ahead.

CHAPTER THREE

CHAOS AND CONFUSION

"Any news for Malaysian 370?"
"Negative, sir."

—AIR TRAFFIC CONTROL[1]

B y the early hours of March 8, it certainly should have been clear that something was seriously wrong. Hours of communications among air traffic controllers across Asia had failed to contact MH370. As a frequent flier, I would hope that if my plane had been missing for so long, someone would by now be looking for it. Certainly most passengers would like to believe that if their plane went missing, the alarm would be raised within minutes, not hours. Yet even though ATC had no idea of MH370's whereabouts, and hadn't heard from it for hours, they just kept going back and forth asking the same questions. Nothing speaks more tellingly to the failure of ATC on that night than the last three entries in the controllers' log:

0530   The Watch Supervisor activated the Kuala Lumpur
        Air rescue Co-Ordination Center.

0541   Ho Chi Minh query for updates.

0614   Kuala Lumpur queried Ho Chi Minh if the search
and rescue had been activated.

By the time of that last entry, 06:14, the plane was supposed to be
about to land in Beijing. Here the air traffic controllers were still dith-
ering, asking anyone and everyone if they had heard from or seen the
plane.

When the plane failed to show up in Beijing on time, rumors
started almost immediately. An hour later, at 07:24, Malaysia Airlines
put out the press release confirming the fact that they were missing a
Boeing 777.

> Malaysia Airlines confirms that flight MH370 has lost contact
> with Subang Air Traffic Control at 2.40am, today (8 March
> 2014). Flight MH370, operated on the B777-200 aircraft,
> departed Kuala Lumpur at 12.41am on 8 March 2014. MH370
> was expected to land in Beijing at 6.30am the same day.

We already know the timing mentioned in the press release is
wrong; the loss of contact came at 01:21 after the "Good night Malaysian
370" communication. When the press release was published, no one
knew about the military radar showing that the plane had turned back.

Having been instructed to get to the bureau as soon as possible,
and armed with the basic knowledge of the plane's history, the route,
and background on the airline, I arrived at the CNN bureau in New
York and got to work.

Reporting during the early hours following a plane crash, I always
draw on my previous experience and try not to speculate too much

about what might have happened. Nothing infuriates the viewer more than a correspondent or pundit sitting comfortably in the studio, waxing on about facts about which we can have no knowledge—I know this because I get the emails and tweets telling me to shut up and stick to what we know! It may be fine for critics to go on websites like airliners.net and speculate to their hearts' content, but when you're broadcasting and friends and family of those involved are watching, you have a duty to make sure you don't cross the line. (For the record, I use airliner.net and PPRune.com quite a bit in the early hours because they contain loads of useful, informative facts from experts who do know what they are talking about.)

As someone who has been covering aviation for two decades, I always draw upon certain fundamentals. The first and most important is to consider in what phase of flight the incident occurred. According to a Boeing survey, 61 percent of accidents take place during takeoff and landing. Landing, incidentally, is far more risky, with 47 percent of accidents taking place then, compared to 14 percent on takeoff.[2] These statistics are not surprising. Takeoff and landing are the hardest phases of flight, requiring the most concentration, when the aircrew and aircraft are under the most stress. With takeoff, unless there is a power failure or incorrect flap setting, the plane is likely to fly. Landing is always the most difficult, as the aircraft is rushing toward the ground and any mistakes or failures are usually unforgiving.

Boeing's study shows that only 10 percent of accidents happen en route, or "in the cruise," when the plane has reached its cruising altitude. Incidents of major plane crashes during this phase are often the result of explosives. In 1983, Korean Airlines 007 was shot down by the Soviet air force while flying over the Sea of Japan near Sakhalin Island, killing 269 people. In 1985, Air India AI182 was brought down by a bomb off the coast of Ireland, killing 329 people. In 1988, Pan Am

PA103 crashed over Lockerbie, when a bomb on board exploded. Most recently, in 2014, Malaysia Airlines MH17, flying over the war zone in eastern Ukraine, was destroyed by a surface-to-air missile. The warhead was a 9N314M carried on the 9M38 series of missiles installed on the Buk system.[3] The warhead detonated off the left side of the aircraft, just above the cockpit, spewing molten metal pieces into the plane. All 298 people on board died. When I am covering a plane that has crashed during the cruise phase of flight, my first thought is to the possibility of explosives, placed on board, or missile attacks. The most recent example is, of course, Metrojet 9268. On October 31, 2015, the Russian-operated Airbus A321 was flying from Sharm el-Sheikh to Saint Petersburg when it broke up in midair over the Sinai Peninsula, twenty-four minutes after taking off. All 224 people on board died. At the time of this writing, the plane is believed to have been brought down by a bomb placed in the aircraft cabin by Islamic militants. The authorities say that there is a very short unexplained noise on the cockpit voice recorder, which experts believe is the sound of the explosion, before the power was lost. Otherwise, there is no evidence of any mechanical problems. Bombs and missiles are always high on the list of possibilities when planes fall out of the sky during the cruise.

If terrorism or military action is discounted, usually an extremely unusual set of circumstances is to blame for bringing down a plane during the cruise. For instance, in the case of Swissair 111 in 1998, a fire sparked in the in-flight entertainment system ignited flammable materials used in making the aircraft. Flames and smoke in the cockpit overwhelmed the crew, causing the plane to crash near Halifax, Nova Scotia; 229 people died. Then there was JAL 123, in which the 747 suffered a catastrophic structural failure that blew off the rear of the aircraft. The cause was a faulty repair to that plane's tail, made seven years earlier. Because it is so rare for planes to crash while flying en route, these cases always garner huge amounts of attention.

My fundamental point is that planes are designed and built to fly, and don't fall out of the sky for no reason. Certainly not when cruising along at thirty-five thousand feet. Where my thinking has shifted in recent years has been the result of a series of crashes in the cruise that had nothing to do with nefarious actions. Air France 447 went down in the cruise phase of flight because of the pilot's actions after a failure of the aircraft's speed monitoring. More recently, in the case of AirAsia 8501, the A320 fell out of the sky over the Java Sea for no apparent reason, except perhaps bad weather. However, the final report from the Indonesian authorities said the cause of the crash was a technical fault on the aircraft, which led the captain to switch off a crucial computer. That made the plane unstable, and the pilot flying lost control of the aircraft, which stalled and crashed. Another case of a crash in the cruise phase of flight caused by the way the plane was flown in a crisis.

Far more typical is the recent case of the Asiana 777, which crash-landed in San Francisco when inexperienced pilots brought the plane in to land too low and too slow, plowing the aircraft into a seawall. Or the Spanair crash in Madrid in 2008, where the pilot's failure to set the flaps meant the plane attempted to take off, couldn't gain height, and crashed back onto the runway. Even the case of TransAsia in Taiwan in 2015: after takeoff, there was failure of the right engine, but the pilot then switched off the left, good engine. All of these happened at critical points of flight, and in such cases answers are usually quick to appear.

When covering a plane crash, I am not trying to be an amateur aircraft investigator determining causes. Experience has shown me that whatever the final cause of a crash, the chain of events usually began with something quite unimaginable or unknown in the first few hours. After all, who would have thought it was accrued ice, blocking the fuel lines, that brought down British Airways 38, a 777 flying from Beijing to London Heathrow, in 2008. In the first few hours, we had reports from the first responders that the engines didn't appear to be running when it crashed, which had everyone thinking it had run out of fuel.

Inexperienced pundits tend to go on-air and opine away about causes. All too often they have to eat their words. In the case of MH370, on that Friday night I sat in the studios and immediately logged into the various websites where those who might have facts or knowledge of the plane, the flight, the passengers, the air traffic control system—anything—would start to leak the information.

I knew what time the plane had left Kuala Lumpur and how long it had been flying when it went missing. Therefore I knew we were in one of those rare situations when an accident occurs in the cruise. My colleague Aaron Cooper, who works in our transportation unit, wrote in an email, "We don't know much about what to put in the graphic, breakup explosion etc."[4] We all knew it was going to be something dramatic.

My fellow presenters immediately wanted possible explanations, and of course this requires speculation about the role of terrorism. Malaysia is a devoutly Muslim country, and given the current state of Muslim extremism, there was no shortage of theories that a bomb might have been involved (which it very well might have been, bearing in mind the unusual nature of plane crashes at altitude). I swatted these questions back with the usual caveat "far too soon to say"—but this is the rub: I am being paid to say something. Merely repeating "only time will tell," "we must wait for the investigation," and "we don't know yet" won't cut it. I am paid to be the correspondent who goes through the various options. If I continue to stonewall, it eventually leads producers to seek out the more outlandish pundits who will say more than they should, leading our coverage off into the beyond.

Thankfully, at CNN we have a cadre of the most experienced aviation experts, including Mary Schiavo, the former inspector general at the US Department of Transportation, and David Soucie, a former FAA investigator, who has written his own excellent book, *Malaysia Airlines Flight 370: Why It Disappeared—and Why It's Only a Matter of Time Before This Happens Again*. I keep reminding my CNN colleagues that these experts have a different role from those of us who are paid staff correspondents. Experts answer questions to the best of their knowledge, but staffers have to keep the coverage going as trained journalists. Doing that requires experience, so that anchors can keep throwing everything at us during hours when nothing is happening. Having spent most of my career in twenty-four-hour news, I was very familiar with this territory.

A plane crash story has a certain rhythm to it, even more so when it happens at sea: there is the initial announcement of a missing plane, followed by the launch of search and rescue boats and planes . . . then hours, usually days, of waiting until the first bits of debris are spotted from the air or wash up on land. With AF447, five days passed before the first debris was spotted in the South Atlantic. In the cases where the crashes occur in more remote areas, there may be a long wait before the first debris sightings. In AirAsia 8501, the A320 went down on December 28. The search and rescue operation was activated immediately, and it was two days later, the thirtieth, before the first debris was spotted in the Java Sea. Part of the airframe and the emergency slide were recovered and brought ashore, followed by the first bodies, which had been floating nearby.

For the rest of this chapter, I want you to forget what we eventually discovered about MH370: how it turned back and flew south for six more hours. Instead, to understand those first hours and the decisions that were made, the actions taken, I must avoid being clever with hindsight. I believe the only way to view the facts is to look at them as they appeared *at the time.* If you just stop and think about what was known at the time, much of what took place looks very different than it looks with the advantage of hindsight.

At this stage, it was believed the plane had been flying across the South China Sea, between Malaysia and Vietnam. Sightings of MH370 debris would depend on how quickly the search and rescue crews got there and how the 777 had fallen out of the sky. If it had blown up, or come apart at altitude, then pieces would be spread far and wide, like MH17. If the plane had essentially crashed into the water intact, then the debris field would be smaller, more akin to Air France 447. It's awful to use such harsh terms, but that is what I, as a broadcaster, am paid to do.

I sat through the coverage hour by hour. I saw and reported on just about every minute detail of what was being revealed. It is only as I put this picture together that events come into perspective and things begin to make sense.

By Saturday morning, ships and planes from Malaysia, Vietnam, and China were on their way to what was then determined to be the last known position of MH370, over the South China Sea, somewhere between Malaysia and Vietnam. It was there where the plane had been handed off between the two air traffic controllers between waypoints IGARI and BITOD at around 01:20. It was the obvious and logical place to begin searching.

Within twelve hours of the missing announcement, the false sightings of debris began. Vietnam Emergency Rescue Center was reported to have heard an emergency locator signal from the plane, southwest of Ca Mau province off the coast of Vietnam. The *People's Daily* in China said it crashed 153 nautical miles off the Tho Chu Islands, in the Gulf of Thailand, not a huge distance from the original route. There was a report that the plane had landed at Naning, which was rebutted by the Malaysian acting transport minister, Hishammuddin Hussein, at one of his early press conferences. A Vietnamese pilot said he had found an apparent oil patch in the South China Sea; supposed wreckage was spotted near an island off Vietnam; there were reports of oil slicks and columns of smoke rising from the sea all around the southern tip of Vietnam. On and on it went. Of course all of these reports had a ring of legitimacy about them because they all came from the plane's last known position. They had to be investigated and discounted, which would take days; incidentally, the oil slick found in the South China Sea was analyzed as bunker oil from a ship, not the much lighter aircraft oil.

Within forty-eight hours, there were thirty-four planes and forty ships from ten countries scouring the South China Sea as the search zone widened up into the Gulf of Thailand. "We have not found anything that appears to be objects from the aircraft," said Azharuddin Abdul Rahman of the Malaysian Civil Aviation Department. "For the aircraft to go missing just like that . . . as far as we are concerned . . . we are equally puzzled."[5]

Puzzled they certainly were, because while they were busy searching off the northeast coast of Malaysia, near Vietnam, indications that things were most definitely not as they seemed began to appear. As reported in the last chapter, the military had spotted a plane flying back across Peninsular Malaysia and did nothing about it. They only alerted the Kuala Lumpur rescue coordination center of this development late on Saturday night, March 8, at 10:30.[6]

The Malaysians never mentioned publicly that the military had reported seeing the plane, although they appear to have acted upon the news straightaway. They shifted the searches and started deploying planes and ships to the Strait of Malacca in the west almost immediately without ever saying why. At the time I was so preoccupied with so many strands of the story that I didn't notice this subtle, yet very important shift in the searching. Despite what the critics say, it is clear that Malaysian officials did start searching both in the east and the west of Malaysia as early as Sunday morning, March 9.

In the first of three press conferences on Monday, March 10, the director of civil aviation, Rahman, made the following statement:

> We also conducted search in the areas north of the Straits
> of Malacca as we do not want to discount the possibilities
> of the aircraft turn-back to the Straits of Malacca.[7]

Let's be clear: this is sixty hours after the plane has gone missing and it's the first time we ever hear an official use the words "turn back." But Rahman buries the reference, describing the situation as an "unprecedented missing aircraft—a mystery as you can put it." None of the reporters picked up the comment. There was no questioning as to why the Malaysians were now looking in the west. The Malaysian authorities just slipped the information into the briefing, and none of the journalists, myself included, gave much importance to the fact that the search was now taking place in the opposite direction.

This was followed by a second press conference, also on the tenth, when the acting transport minister, Hishammuddin Hussein, makes no reference to the new search zone, instead becoming defensive, saying, "We have nothing to hide."[8] He was referring to various allegations from the Chinese relatives of passengers who were becoming ever more distressed, holed up in a hotel in Beijing, claiming that they were being kept in the dark. Questions were raised concerning the stolen passports and how they had been used, as well as the four missing passengers and the ever-growing number of inaccurate sightings of debris. The number of issues was growing, and with no sign of the plane and an increasing clamor for facts, Hishammuddin stated, "I would like to make a plea to the media and the public at large not to spread and disseminate unverified and false news."[9] Unfortunately, he was hiding something—by Monday, the Malaysian authorities had evidence that the plane had turned back, and there had been a shift in the search zone to the west.

Finally, at the third press conference on Monday the tenth, AJ, the CEO of Malaysia Airlines, made an almost offhand reference to the new search zone. "We are also conducting searches on land and also west coast of Peninsular Malaysia and we already covered part of north of Sumatra."[10] Again, these comments were glossed over by most of us because we were obsessed by the stolen passports and the fact that the oil slick wasn't caused by a plane. It was also at that press conference where the dreadful Balotelli footballer comments were made. With so many issues on the table, no one picked up on the fact that the Malaysians were now searching in the west. Those who claim that the Malaysians delayed starting the search in the west haven't read the record. It is abundantly clear: the military told the authorities on that Saturday night (too late, to be sure, but still . . .) and they shifted the search almost immediately, but they chose not to draw attention to it.

I believe that the Malaysian authorities should have been far more open about what they knew and what was now taking place—even allowing for the fact that the information required further analysis and verification. If the information was considered credible enough to divert "a large number of assets, aircraft and vessels" to search these areas, it should have been revealed to the public and the families at the earliest opportunity.[11]

The failure to do this created the impression of a lack of transparency. You can't claim you are being open and then, when it's shown that you have not revealed everything you could have, expect to be believed in the future. The fact the military told them on Saturday night about the turn-back, but they didn't draw attention to it publicly, must color everything the authorities would subsequently say.

It's not surprising that the leaks started quickly. There were several military sources who were now openly telling of an unknown plane being traced on military radar back to Pulau Perak in the Strait of Malacca until 2:40 a.m.—an hour and twenty minutes after the "Good night Malaysian 370" handoff.

By the time the officials openly discussed the turn-back, the full-scale feeding frenzy was under way, and by Wednesday confusion ruled the day. It got so bad that the chief of the Royal Malaysian Air Force publicly quoted himself from an earlier press conference on Sunday, March 9, where he had said, "The RMAF has not ruled out the possibility of an air turn back." Again, this proves that the authorities knew about the turn-back very early on; they just didn't draw attention to it.

By Wednesday, March 12, it was time to come clean. The Malaysian government said:

> When the PM ordered the search area expanded on Saturday 8th and no trace of the aircraft had been found, we examined our military radar records for the new search area. We discovered the possibility that MH370 had passed over to the Strait of Malacca.

I was sitting in a studio when this was announced. I remember thinking, What on earth are they talking about?

Minister Hishammuddin said they were now searching 12,400 square miles in the Strait of Malacca, *and* 14,000 square miles in the South China Sea. A veritable armada of forty-two ships and thirty-nine aircraft had been deployed to the east and the west.

As the search in the Strait of Malacca picked up, critics began questioning why searchers were still looking in the South China Sea when the evidence now suggested that the plane had gone in the opposite direction. The reason is simple: there was still supposed evidence of debris being discovered in the original place. For example, ABC News Australia and the *New Straits Times* published photos showing potential life rafts found in the South China Sea. Half the story was about the new western search zone, but the other half was still about potential wreckage being spotted in the east.

Then, on Wednesday the twelfth, the Chinese released three satellite images that they said had been taken the day after the plane disappeared, showing possible wreckage in the South China Sea. The Chinese authorities gave chapter and verse on the time, the location, and the size of the objects.

When the news of these images was released, there was a general feeling that this was probably the plane. I immediately sent an email to our senior editors titled "My Guess? This is the plane." "The Chinese wouldn't risk getting this wrong," I told them. This was the consensus: "Agree," wrote back one, who went on to suggest that the images were probably deliberately blurred. "Likely they have higher resolution images they are not publishing," he said. It seemed inconceivable that the Chinese would risk making total fools of themselves by releasing pictures of debris they weren't sure came from MH370; in fact some went so far as to suggest the delay in releasing these photos was because they'd probably been there, seen the wreckage, and verified it, so keen were the Chinese to appear to be at the center of this investigation. Malaysian planes were dispatched on Thursday the thirteenth to see what could be located. Nothing was found; we were wrong.

On Friday the fourteenth, the Chinese admitted that the satellite images had been put out by mistake, stating, "The publication of the satellite image is an accident. The image is not confirmed as connected with the plane."[12] Forty-eight hours after it appeared, the first hard evidence of the plane's breakup had come to nothing. One can only wonder what happened to the poor scientist at the Chinese satellite agency who released the photographs in error. Meanwhile, oil slicks in the South China Sea were still being sighted, searched, and sampled. None would prove to be from the missing aircraft.

I have gone into great detail because I believe it is important to understand what was going on during that first week of confusion. On the one hand, there was the unconfirmed report of a turn-back and of searches taking place in the west. On the other, numerous reports of wreckage, oil slicks, and satellite images of debris were coming in from the east. Both possibilities had to be accounted for. If the Malaysians are to be criticized, it is for not being open and clear about what they were doing and what was taking place.

Meanwhile, another controversy was brewing: What were the exact last words spoken from the cockpit, and which pilot said them? We saw in chapter two that eventually the transcript showed the words to be "Good night Malaysian Three Seven Zero." That transcript was only released weeks later, after an enormous amount of fuss, most of it unnecessary.

During the first week of confusion, various officials from Malaysia stated that when the plane was passed from Malaysian to Vietnamese airspace, the last words from the pilots were "all right, good night." The first reference to this appears to have been made by the Malaysian ambassador to China at a meeting with Chinese relatives in Beijing.[13] Subsequently, a Malaysian civil aviation official confirmed to my colleagues that indeed, the last words heard from the cockpit were "all right, good night."[14] Then again the following week, these supposed final words were repeated by the director of civil aviation, Azharuddin

Abdul Rahman, at a press conference. "I can confirm that it was at 1:19 when we got the last transmission from the cockpit and it says 'all right, good night.'"[15] There seemed to be no doubt: the final words from the cockpit were "all right, good night." But this was wrong. As the transcript that was released two weeks later, on April 1, would show, the final words were "Good night Malaysian Three Seven Zero."

Many have asked me, Why does it matter what the final words were? After all, there is not a huge difference between "All right, good night" and "Good night Malaysian Three Seven Zero." It matters because the last words from the plane were spoken at a crucial moment, and whatever took place subsequently either had begun, or was about to.

Pilots are trained to be very precise when they answer radio calls from the ground so that there is absolutely no confusion about the requests they are making or the instructions they are being given. It is called read-back and it has to be correct. When an air traffic controller gives an instruction, the pilot usually repeats it word for word and then finishes with his call sign; that way there can be no confusion for the ground, the pilots, or any other aircraft in the area. I have heard air traffic controllers have arguments with pilots who have not done a precise read-back, and heard the controllers keep calling them until they had done it correctly. Accurate read-backs are an essential part of aviation safety.

The significance here is that the read-back of "all right, good night" was improper. It included neither a last instruction nor the aircraft's call sign. It led to widespread speculation about what might have been happening when the call was made. Saying only "all right, good night" without giving any further details could have been an indication of all sorts of things going wrong in the cockpit: the pilots may have been making the call under duress; it may not even have been the pilots saying the words. Here we had an experienced captain and a newly minted 777 first officer, both of whom knew the correct procedure and would have been expected to get it right. The last communication is anything but standard.

In many of my live reports, I had to discuss why this might have happened, how often pilots do not do a correct read-back, and what all of it meant. Of course, many were perhaps hoping that I would say this was evidence that the plane had been hijacked, or there was a crisis taking place on board, or the pilots had gone mad: anything but the basic fact that the read-back was improper, but we had no knowledge of why this was so. The "all right, good night" speculation grew by the hour and every network and newspaper found pilots and pundits who were able to pontificate that it was obvious evidence of major malfeasance by the pilots. It was nothing of the kind.

For days the Malaysians allowed this controversy to fester and grow. They obviously knew that the interpretation that was being put upon the words was wrong. Hishammuddin and Rahman had plenty of opportunities to set the record straight, but instead of doing that, they fanned the flames. For instance, on March 22, Minister Hishammuddin said in his daily press statement, "The original transcript of the conversation between MH370 and Malaysian air traffic control is with the investigations team, where it is being analysed. As is standard practice in investigations of this sort, the transcript cannot be publicly released at this stage. I can however confirm that the transcript does not indicate anything abnormal."[16]

The minister's words were very carefully chosen. In using the term "standard practice," he was cloaking himself in an international treaty known as ICAO Annex 13, which I will discuss later. He was right: the treaty does say, normally, air traffic control transcripts should not be released other than for the purposes of accident prevention.[17] But that same chapter also gives the investigating authority the power to override this provision if they feel it's necessary. In other words, Hishammuddin could have said, "We have a major crisis brewing here, the transcript reveals nothing, and I need to release it now."

If there was ever a moment for him to correct the record, this was it. He chose not to and can hardly complain about the consequences. As the firestorm grew, the minister once again tried to dampen it down a couple of days later, saying, "As far as the transcript is concerned, the technical committee is considering releasing it and we will keep you informed about the decision."[18]

Finally, on April 1, twenty days after "all right, good night" surfaced, the transcript was published with the only explanation for its delay being that it was "initially held as part of the police investigation."[19] The statement said the police were working to confirm that it was Hamid who said the words. (It wasn't.) The communications were, as we'd been told, entirely normal. The final exchange was:

01:19:24 ATC:	Malaysian Three Seven Zero contact Ho Chi Minh one two zero decimal niner Good Night
01:19:29 MAS370:	Good Night Malaysian Three Seven Zero

Now, pilots will say this read-back was not entirely correct because it didn't include the next frequency. The correct read-back should have been along the lines of "Contact Ho Chi Minh on 120.9, Malaysian Three Seven Zero, good night." But as everyone pretty much agrees, aircrew who are familiar with flying in this part of the world can hardly be blamed for resorting to a bit of shorthand in the middle of the night. It might be regarded as a case of sloppy read-back, nothing more. It certainly felt a great deal better than just "all right, good night." As the minister had indeed said, the transcript looked entirely normal. There was no smoking gun here.

Before we leave this subject, where did the phrase "all right, good night" originate? The answer appears to be a classic case of "double whispers." At some point, the original transcript of the air traffic communications had been translated from English into Mandarin. It was then translated back into English, where the final words were paraphrased into "all right, good night." In the process of these translations it had become mistranslated. A look at the translated document shows several other examples: for instance, the takeoff instruction that we know was "370, 32 right, cleared for takeoff, good night" was translated back and forth and ended up as "position 32 right. Runway ready. Permitted to take off MH370 copies that. Thank you. Good night."

Should the authorities have released the air traffic control transcript sooner? Transcripts of conversations between pilots recorded on cockpit voice recorders are usually officially released many weeks or months into an investigation. Publication of cockpit transcripts without the context of the final report is generally frowned upon by the ICAO Annex 13 treaty. But today, communications between the pilots and air traffic control must be viewed differently. These broadcasts are over the public airwaves, and there are many private services where you can listen to air traffic control talking to pilots in real time. In fact, United Airlines even makes listening to ATC possible during a flight with its popular Channel 9, which allows passengers to listen in to air traffic control talking to the pilots. One of the most popular apps and websites for aviation enthusiasts is LiveATC.net. Avgeeks the world over are listening to control towers from New York to Sydney.

Take the crash of Asiana 214, the aircraft that landed short of the runway in San Francisco on July 6, 2013. The audio of the tower talking to the plane's pilots was recorded by one of these third-party services. It was posted on YouTube within hours. It would be more than five months before the NTSB published the official transcript of all recordings. Since there is no hard and fast rule on all of this, there is no reason why the Malaysians could not have made a much earlier decision to publish the words (not release the audio) and correct the "all right, good night" mistake.

With the story well and truly bogged down in confusion and chaos over the issue of the turn-back and the question of the final words, we were suddenly faced with a new and far more significant development: the fact that the plane kept flying for many hours after it went missing. On Thursday, March 13, this bombshell came in a report in the *Wall Street Journal* that said that the plane's satellite ACARS system had continued to send monitoring data back to Rolls-Royce, the engine manufacturer. The *Journal* report said the plane had apparently flown west for at least four hours after it lost contact on radar. If true, this was about to blow the story wide open. Words failed all of us who read the article and contemplated its implications.[20]

I contacted several sources who all flatly denied that Rolls-Royce had received any information from the engines. Hishammuddin also denied the accusation, stating, "I would like to refer to news reports suggesting that the aircraft may have continued flying for some time after the last contact. As Malaysia Airlines will confirm shortly, those reports are inaccurate."[21] He concluded, "As far as Rolls Royce and Boeing are concerned those reports are inaccurate."[22] The minister would come to regret these comments—or at least, in hindsight, he should. The CEO of Malaysia Airlines added for good measure, "The last ACARS transmission was done at 1:07." He said, "It did not run beyond that."

The authorities were technically right, but they were very

misleading. There was indeed no data from Rolls-Royce that showed the plane continued to fly; nor indeed were there any ACARS messages after 1:07. But they were absolutely wrong in denying the core of the accusation: that the plane had continued to fly. The data did not come from Rolls-Royce, but from the satellite company Inmarsat, which owned a satellite sitting high above the Indian Ocean. In the next chapter I will explain exactly what Inmarsat is, what that data was, how it was used, and why it was so crucial; but for the moment all that's relevant is that the rumor the plane had kept flying was now leaking everywhere. No one could get a straight answer from the Malaysians on whether it was true.

Within a few hours the *Journal* reframed their story, tweeting, "We've corrected our story to note that satellite not engine data indicated MH370 flew for up to 4 more hours."[23] It was obvious that the story was true: MH370 had continued to send some sort of signal proving the plane continued flying, and probably did so for many hours.

Rereading the transport minister's statement that it was inaccurate to say the plane had kept on flying, I am left wondering how on earth he managed to say such a thing. He knew what the question was—did the plane keep flying or not?—when he made this statement; experts in Malaysia, Australia, the UK, and the US were working to interpret the Inmarsat data, and he knew it.

By Friday the fourteenth, Hishammuddin changed tack. He no longer said the story was wrong or inaccurate. Instead, he started being vague: "The investigation team will not publicly release information until it has been properly verified and corroborated."[24] A classic stonewall. This has been rightly held up as an example of the Malaysian government's lack of transparency.

By the time one week had passed, the level of confusion concerning MH370 had reached epic proportions. We had some passengers who were missing, others using stolen passports; we had an acknowledgment that the plane had turned back, but regardless, the searching continued over swaths of Southeast Asia; we had rumors that the plane had kept flying, but no one knew where, and there were weird suggestions about the final words from the cockpit. Broadcasting hour after hour over several days, I had an overview of the situation and could see that there was seemingly no sense to any of it. Shows were asking me, what does this mean, or that mean, and frankly we had absolutely no idea. (Of course it didn't stop some people from continuing to spew whatever was the theory du jour.)

Finally, on Saturday, seven days after the plane went missing, the prime minister of Malaysia, Najib Razak, spoke, and no one could disagree with his statement: "This has been a situation without precedent."[25] He admitted that the Malaysian air force had seen an aircraft flying across the country to an area north of the Strait of Malacca. And then he added new facts: First, that the ACARS system "was disabled just before the aircraft reached the east coast of Malaysia."[26] Second, that "the aircraft's transponder was switched off" and that the plane was being flown in a way that was "consistent with deliberate action being taken by someone on the plane."[27]

The PM said, "Based on raw satellite data, we can confirm that the aircraft shown in the radar was flight MH370."[28] What's more, the other international bodies—the FAA and the NTSB from the US and the AAIB from the UK—all agreed. So now we had it officially. The plane being tracked by the Malaysian air force was MH370. There was a turn-back. The plane had flown back over Malaysia and across the Strait of Malacca.

I was sitting in the studio, listening to all of this live, getting ready to give some analysis along with other colleagues. All of it on its own was incredible, but something even more extraordinary was about to be revealed.

The Malaysian prime minister admitted that "according to the new data, the last confirmed communication between the plane and the satellite was at 8:11AM Malaysian time on Saturday 8th March."[29] As he said these words I remember thinking, Hang on, if that's right, it means the plane kept flying for . . . I grabbed a nearby timeline sheet and looked. The plane kept flying for nearly seven hours after the "Good night Malaysian 370." This was more than incredible: it bordered on the unbelievable.

The raw satellite data had enabled the authorities to work out two potential directions in which the plane could have gone after the turn-back. The first was to the north, the second to the south. These became known as the two corridors, and they covered a vast area of the world. As Mr. Razak described the options, "The northern corridor stretching approximately from the border of Kazakhstan and Turkmenistan to northern Thailand; or a southern corridor stretching approximately from Indonesia to the southern Indian ocean."[30] Searching this huge area of land and sea was going to be more than a Herculean task. Even with all the countries being invited to join in, it would be nigh impossible.

The authorities were so sure of their new information on a turn-back and a westerly flight that they were abandoning the search in the South China Sea and focusing all their efforts on these new corridors. This was extraordinary: But where to start, on such a vast enterprise?

Sitting in the dark studio, my colleagues and I just looked at each other. It was difficult to comprehend what we had been told. Having been through a week of rumor, confusion, and chaos, we had just been handed a treasure trove of information that completely altered everything about the story we were working on. No more were we concerned about flaming oil rigs off Vietnam, or satellite photos claiming to show two boats together drifting. Now we had to get our heads around the startling revelation that the plane had flown for many hours through one of these two new corridors.

In that first week, we can break down the serious communication snafus as follows:

1. The inaccurate passenger manifest list

2. The passengers traveling on stolen passports

3. A delayed search of the pilots' homes

4. Failure to reveal the turn-back

5. Correcting "Good night Malaysian 370"

6. Mistakes regarding debris

7. Searching the east and west zones

8. The fact that the plane kept flying

As these errors mounted, they created the impression that the Malaysians were being secretive and less than transparent. There was no shortage of critics who laid into them, not least the Chinese official news agency, which described the search in the South China Sea as a "huge waste of valuable time and resources."[31]

Frankly, this statement is ironic coming from the Chinese, who were conveniently forgetting how unhelpful they had been with their own irrelevant discoveries of debris and their inaccurate satellite photos. It often seemed the Chinese were far more concerned with entertaining the domestic audience than in actually doing anything useful, as would certainly be the case, as we will see, when the real water searches began. Many of my colleagues and fellow pundits were looking for any excuse to blame the Malaysians. It is easy to criticize the ineptitude of the officials who handled the unfolding crisis, but it is also important to be evenhanded and recognize the difficulty of the task they faced. There are two major criticisms to deal with here. One, the Malaysians were slow to respond to the turn-back, wasting days searching in the wrong place. And two, they failed to acknowledge the fact that the plane kept flying for hours, and in doing this, they hindered the investigation.

As for the first accusation, I am convinced the record shows the opposite. As I have proved, statements made at the time of the disappearance show that the Malaysians were responding to the possibility of a turn-back from the very start. The air force chief says it on the first Sunday. The press conference on the following Monday refers to turn-backs three times. The prime minister admits it in his statement on Saturday the fifteenth. Within ten hours they became aware of the military radar evidence and the whole question of a turn-back was considered. To suggest otherwise doesn't tally with the facts as they unfolded.

So why did they continue searching in the South China Sea? Because they had to. The radar data was unverified and umpteen reports of potential debris were coming in. They had no choice: as expert after expert would say, the military radar was just a series of very indistinct blips—we have seen pictures of what this looked like— and until proved otherwise, it would have been criminal to stop searching in the most likely place, which remained the waters between Malaysia and Vietnam. Where I think the Malaysians were wrong is in their failure to reveal the turn-back on the Sunday when they had started to redeploy the assets.

Then there is the fact that the plane kept flying. Should the authorities have revealed this sooner than they did? Yes. By midweek there was ample evidence to say "this is what we are looking at, and this is what we think has happened."

These are fine judgments that have to be made in the heat of the moment, which is why I urged that we look at the situation as it was unfolding at the time, without the knowledge of hindsight. In week one, the authorities were dealing with the following facts:

1. A plane had gone missing.

2. There were reports of all sorts of debris in the area where it was reasonable to expect it to be found; all were unconfirmed.

3. It was known that two people on board were traveling on stolen passports: How had that happened?

4. There were four passengers who never boarded the plane.

5. There were early, unverified reports from military radar showing an unidentified plane flying in the west instead of east, across Malaysia: Was this MH370?

6. There was a confusion over the last words of the pilots, and what did this mean?

7. There was the extraordinary, almost unbelievable report that the plane had kept flying for hours after contact was lost; this, however, was based on untried and untested science.

8. Oh, and don't forget: there was no sign of the plane.

Now, I challenge any air investigator to deal with this set of circumstances in a better fashion. The sheer enormity of what had taken place would overwhelm the most sophisticated systems. (Let's not forget, the US was overwhelmed in building a website for its health care system, and that country had years to get it right and billions of dollars at its disposal.) There were moments when Malaysia's communications were seriously inept and statements that later proved to be false were presented as truths. But as I shall continue to argue, the evidence does not show that the actual investigation was delinquent. The mistakes were largely limited to those that happened on the night of the disappearance.

I realize that this conclusion is at odds with the prevailing view that the Malaysians made a cock-up of the whole investigation, that they were unreasonably secretive, and that they set out to mislead. It is an easy accusation to hurl given the lapses in communication, but ultimately, it does not stand up.

Before we leave this first week of chaos, I ask you to pause and quietly remember: when Malaysia Airlines put out their statement at 07:24 saying the plane had lost contact, MH370 was still in the air, flying south.

It would continue to fly for at least another forty-seven minutes.

CHAPTER FOUR

HANDSHAKES AND CORRIDORS

Clearly the search for MH370 has entered a new phase.
—Najib Razak, Malaysian prime minister[1]

A late-night announcement by the Malaysian prime minister shifted the entire direction of the search and gave the unfolding story an entirely new perspective. The plane had turned back, first heading northwest, then making another left turn and flying back across Malaysia and into the Strait of Malacca. Once it passed the northern tip of Indonesia, it continued to fly for six more hours. The question was: In which direction?

The raw satellite data to which Prime Minister Razak referred offered two possible corridors: northward up over China, toward Kyrgyzstan, Kazakhstan, and Uzbekistan, or southward, deep into the south Indian Ocean. The size and scale was enormous. Transport Minister Hishammuddin said, "From focusing mainly on shallow seas, we are now looking at large tracts of land, crossing 11 countries as well as deep and remote oceans."[2] The number of countries involved had increased from fourteen to twenty-five—including Kazakhstan, Uzbekistan, Kyrgyzstan, Turkmenistan, Pakistan, Bangladesh, India, China, Myanmar, Laos, Vietnam, Thailand, Indonesia, and Australia—so it was perhaps an understatement to describe the search area as "significantly expanded."[3] But what was this new information upon which these corridors were constructed? What was the prime minister talking about? He said it was all "based on new satellite information."[4] He was talking about the raw data provided by the London-based satellite company Inmarsat.

Inmarsat's name is an abbreviation of International Marine Satellite Organization, which was set up in 1979 by the United Nations maritime division to provide reliable satellite communications for ships at sea. Most commercial satellite companies positioned their satellites over land where people lived, watched television, and made phone calls, meaning the world's seas and oceans had almost no satellite coverage. Inmarsat was set up to fill in the global gaps, giving coverage pretty much across the globe.

Privatized in 1999, Inmarsat rapidly grew its business, introducing a host of new services, including those to airlines as well as to broadcasting companies and their journalists. The Inmarsat network is the backbone of the satellite phones my colleagues and I use when reporting from remote parts of the world, as well as the BGAN small satellite dishes we use to send back our video. Today, Inmarsat operates twelve satellites.

Though designed to be used by ships crossing the oceans, with a bit of tinkering, the Inmarsat network proved perfect for the aviation world. A new and very profitable form of business quickly arose. The Inmarsat satellites allow airlines to keep in contact with their planes as they cross oceans, where radar coverage is nonexistent and high-frequency radio transmissions are of poor quality.

MH370 was equipped with an Inmarsat Classic Aero terminal. The various pieces of technology were located halfway along the plane's body, behind the wing, above Door 3 in the roof of the plane. Wherever the aircraft flew, it was able to send and receive data by connecting to Inmarsat satellites. The information would be downlinked from the satellite at one of Inmarsat's ground stations, and the data forwarded on to SITA, the company that handled the information on Malaysia's behalf.

On March 8, from the moment the plane was powered up in Kuala Lumpur, its satellite dish had connected to the system, transmitting to the Inmarsat 3-F1 satellite.[5] The satellite was launched in 1996 and sits 22,236 miles above the Indian Ocean. At the other end of the link was the ground station in Perth, western Australia. The plane's SATCOM dish would be used to send all sorts of information from the moving aircraft to the airline: everything from the moment its parking brake was disengaged to its engine performance, its speed, height, and fuel consumption. In return, the airline could alert the crew of any changes to the flight plan, send them internal messages, even give them connecting gate information for passengers. The data would always travel along the path, from the plane to the satellite to the ground station, and vice versa. The SATCOM is a crucial part of the ACARS system, which I explained in the last chapter. ACARS uses the satellite communication link to send enormous amounts of data to the ground. It is especially useful when there is a technical fault. Sometimes, when less important pieces of equipment fail, the ACARS system will alert the airline's maintenance department to the problem before the crew themselves might even be aware of it. Certainly any major problems

MH370 would have faced, such as an in-flight fire or massive decompression of the plane, would have immediately been telegraphed to the ground. As confirmed by the prime minister, the last ACARS message was sent at 01:07, and thereafter nothing more was sent or received. In Mr. Razak's words, ACARS was disabled, and the transponder switched off.

If ACARS and the transponder—everything, in short—were either disabled or switched off, what was this satellite data that was suddenly so important? The answer to this question changed the course of the whole investigation. It was something both simple and complicated at the same time. Even though it wasn't sending any data, the plane's satellite unit remained connected to the satellite network. Think of it like your computer modem remaining connected to the phone modem or broadband line even if the computer itself is switched off. In this case the satellite dish on the roof was switched on, powered up, and connected to the satellite. It was logged onto the Inmarsat system, though the various terminals on board were sending no data.

Whenever a plane crash or aviation incident occurs, Inmarsat staff are trained to check if the aircraft or airline involved is one of their customers. On that first Friday night/Saturday morning, they established immediately that Malaysia Airlines was indeed a customer, and that the Indian Ocean Region satellite had been handling transmissions from MH370. Now that the plane was missing, Inmarsat's engineers in Perth rushed to their computer terminals and accessed and retrieved the logs of transmissions for 9M-MRO to see what the plane had been transmitting and if there were any reports of technical faults. I am told this is an entirely normal process whenever there is an incident involving one of its customers' aircraft. When they checked, what they discovered was anything but normal: the logs showed no data had been sent from the plane after it went missing, but the plane and the satellite system had remained in contact for many hours. During this time, the aircraft and the satellite had performed a so-called digital handshake every hour—and these handshakes had occurred seven times, long after the plane had effectively disappeared.

This "handshake" is easy to understand. Basically, once logged onto the system, Malaysia's planes were programmed to send data at least once an hour, though usually, of course, they did so more frequently. However, if a plane was logged in and did not send any data for an hour, then the satellite automatically checked that the connection was still operational.[6] This is known as the log-on interrogation. The plane, if still connected, would reply "log-on/log-off acknowledge." No data would be transferred, but the two sides would have performed a digital handshake. In simple terms, think of it as the satellite saying, "Are you still there?" and the plane answering, "Yes, I am."

What Inmarsat engineers discovered in the case of MH370 was that this handshaking had taken place, at the expected hourly intervals, for seven hours after the words "Good night Malaysian Three Seven Zero" were uttered from the cockpit. MH370 could not have crashed if it was still sending signals to the satellite at 02:25, 03:41, 04:41, 05:41, 06:41, 08:11, and 08:19. There is one extra wrinkle with the handshakes that requires understanding. Of the seven handshakes, the first (02:25) and the last (08:19) were different from the others. These handshakes were not acknowledging a connection but rather were the plane itself logging onto the system, and this would become very important later on . . . There were a couple of periods in which it appears that the plane was not logged onto the system at all, and these raised even more questions.

This discovery of the handshakes was immediately sent to Inmarsat's headquarters near London's financial district, in an office building on City Road where the lobby of the building has models of satellites hanging from the wall. The heart of the operation is the control room, the perimeter of which is wrapped around by giant screens showing maps of the world and the position of Inmarsat's satellites. These screens can be programmed to show what is happening with any of the satellites in real time. At any moment the control room staff can tap into their computers and get a readout of who is on the system. It is quiet and efficient. When I went to visit Inmarsat, I was fascinated by the thought of those satellites many thousands of miles in space, being controlled from this room.

It is here that the vice president of satellite operations, Mark Dickinson, is based. Dickinson was given the task of assembling the team of engineers to interpret the MH370 data that Perth had retrieved from the satellite database. Two months after the incident, I met and interviewed him. I was shown around the control room and saw the sort of information they had received from MH370. Dickinson admitted that what had happened with MH370 was exceptional. He told me "having messages six hours after the plane is lost is probably the biggest disbelief in terms of what you have." It was his job to try to find out what these handshakes and bursts of data meant and to use this data to find out which direction the plane had taken.

The satellite team in London worked through the British air accident regulator, the AAIB, which would be the point of contact to Kuala Lumpur. Since Inmarsat staff members were now part of the investigation, they were bound by the ICAO treaty rules on privacy and so could not issue any statements themselves. Initially, we heard almost nothing from Inmarsat other than that they were working on the problem.

To make sense of the data retrieved in Perth, Inmarsat used a technical piece of mathematics known as the burst time offset and the burst frequency offset and applied it to the handshakes. A detailed explanation of what these are is unnecessary to understand what Inmarsat did. For the moment, all we need to see is the basic principle, which then allows us to decide if we think the Inmarsat data is credible; after all, the entire search operation would be based on its findings and remains so to this day. I can't say it often enough: everything rests on the Inmarsat data.

Let's start with the "burst time offset," or BTO. Every time a plane or the ground station sends a transmission, the length of time it takes to be received by the satellite can be measured in very small quantities called microseconds. Obviously the ground station doesn't move, so the time it takes for the transmission to go from ground to satellite remains pretty constant. The same is not true for the plane, of course, flying many hundreds of miles an hour either toward or away from the satellite, which is thousands of miles above it. Thus the time a transmission takes alters depending on which direction the plane is flying. If the plane is flying away from the satellite, then the transmission time gets minutely longer; if it's flying toward the satellite, the time is shorter.[7] In essence, to use the burst time offset, you measure the microseconds it takes for the signal to be received between the plane and the satellite. Once a series of these timed differences is examined, investigators can work out how far the plane must have been from the satellite.

To start with, Inmarsat engineers studied the satellite timings from points where they were absolutely certain of the plane's location—for instance, when it was waiting to take off on the runway in Kuala Lumpur; also the last ACARS transmission at 1:07; even the basic radar position over the Strait of Malacca. In all of these cases, they took the timing of those small satellite differences, and because they knew the exact location of the plane, they could compute the BTO. Once they knew those numbers, they could work out where the plane should have been at each of the handshakes.

The use of BTO data in satellite transmissions is a fairly recent development, prompted by the Air France 447 incident. After that crash, satellite engineers realized that ACARS signals could be enhanced with BTO data, which would help geo-locate a plane in an emergency.[8] In the case of MH370, by looking at the BTO for each of the seven handshakes, Mark Dickinson and his team in London were able to work out how far the plane was from the satellite. That enabled them to draw a circle on the earth showing the likely position in relation to the satellite at that time.

Obviously, when you look at the circle drawn by this data, half of it is on a side of the world where it would have been impossible, either in time or amount of fuel, for the plane to have reached. The half remaining creates the two corridors that show the locations where the plane might have gone: one corridor going north from the last known position, up toward Kazakhstan and China, while the other goes in the opposite direction, to the south, deep down into the Indian Ocean.

For each handshake, an arc was created, showing where the plane could have been to generate that particular BTO. It sounds complicated, but for our purposes, all we need to know is that the BTO data allowed the men in London to create the seven arcs. The plane had to pass across each of the arcs, with the final resting place being somewhere along the seventh. It was that last arc to which the prime minister of Malaysia referred when describing the northern and southern corridors.

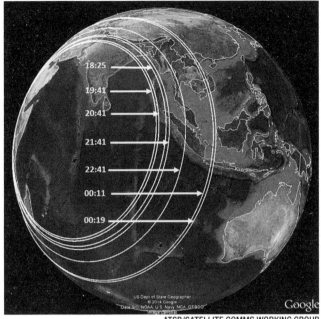

18:25
19:41
20:41
21:41
22:41
00:11
00:19

US Dept of State Geographer
© 2014 Google
Data SIO, NOAA, U S Navy, NGA, GEBCO

Google

ATSB/SATELLITE COMMS WORKING GROUP

The seven arcs as constructed from the Inmarsat data. The arcs show the timings in Coordinated Universal Time—UTC—at which MH370 must have crossed each position. These rings form the backbone of the entire search for MH370.

It is important to realize here that the arc is not a "route" along which the plane is flying. Rather, the plane is flying between the arcs, so that it crosses each of them at the designated time when the handshakes occur. When it got to the seventh arc, the fuel had run out and that is where the flight ended. Thus Inmarsat was able to say there were "two corridors"—one to the north and one to the south—and MH370 had ended up in one of them.

The Malaysian prime minister's announcement of the corridors was progress of sorts. Yet if the Inmarsat experts had potentially solved one problem, they had most definitely created another: the arcs that the prime minister showed were absolutely huge, covering millions of square miles of both land and sea.

As a journalist, covering these events and having to broadcast immediately about what I and my colleagues were hearing, I knew I was way out of my depth. The concepts being bandied about—of arcs, corridors, burst time offsets—were mind-bogglingly difficult to understand and get across. First of all, I am not a satellite engineer. In fact my knowledge of math and physics is abysmal. Nevertheless, sitting in the studios hour after hour and listening to all of this, I realized I had to get a handle on it and what I didn't understand I needed to quickly find someone to explain. Many of our experts were certainly knowledgeable on the subject, but some were unable to get the information across in layman's language. Time and again I saw my fellow anchors' faces crease in confusion, unsure whether what they were hearing was important or just simply technical gobbledygook. Sometimes I wasn't even sure myself. All I knew is that the prime minister of Malaysia had thought this vital enough to change the entire direction of the search. I am not ashamed to say, I had to get myself up to speed on all this stuff if I was going to be able to do my job properly.

One of the most important parts of the correspondent's job is to take highly complex information, understand it, simplify it, and then broadcast it. I know that leaves many experts feeling we have "dumbed down" a subject, but broadcasting is a mass-viewership business. There is no point in leaving the entire audience confused just to get in a minor bit of data. Of course, after thirty years, I have become very familiar with the process and its results: the experts think I'm an idiot because I want to simplify what's happening, while some in the audience think I'm trying to be clever and bamboozle them. Fortunately, at CNN we had some of the best brains in the business who came on-air and talked us through all of the science. Where they sometimes left the audience behind in their enthusiasm to explain satellite technology, I was brought in to make it understandable. I tried never to pretend that I knew or understood any more than I actually did.

I knew that this was an extremely volatile situation in which the facts could change in a moment. So I had to steer the middle ground. For instance, on the morning show *New Day*, I would be called in to make sense of all of this to a breakfast-show audience that didn't have much time but still wanted to know the latest. My philosophy has always been that it is far better for the viewer to grasp the basics than to dot every *i* and cross every *t* and lose them on the way. I know that some people thought my approach was unsatisfactory—and they happily told me so on Twitter.

With the prime minister's latest statement, one thing was clear and could be readily understood by everyone: the new search corridors were vast, and at this stage there was no debris or any sign of the plane. It would be sixteen months before the flaperon washed up on the shores of Reunion Island, confirming the plane had gone down in the southern Indian Ocean. Back in mid-March 2014, the searchers were facing a search zone that covered an area of 2.2 million square miles. There would be twenty-six countries involved in the search operation, each being asked to share its satellite and radar data with Malaysia, which was coordinating their efforts. Nothing on this scale had ever been done before. It was a gigantic logistical, diplomatic, and technical operation. Merely obtaining the cooperation from the countries involved was a major challenge. To get some countries to provide their detailed satellite and radar information, Malaysia promised them secrecy. They told us they were "not at liberty to reveal information from specific countries,"[9] which of course did little to enhance the appearance of transparency.

The search in the northern corridor would be led by Kazakhstan and China. Some countries quickly gave their results: "The Kazakhstan authorities have assured us that they have found no trace of MH370," said Hishammuddin Hussein at one of the daily briefings.

In the southern corridor, Indonesia and Australia took the lead. Other countries, including the United States, sent ships and planes. In hindsight, it was always a hopeless long shot. The truth is, with corridors covering enormous swaths of Asia and the south Indian Ocean, it was futile. The size of the search areas was simply too large: the authorities needed more information if this wasn't going to be a complete waste of time.

As the operation gathered speed, those of us covering the story knew where the planes and ships were being sent to search but very little of the behind-the-scenes work of the international experts who determined these areas. The experts never spoke. They never gave interviews. They never revealed what they were doing. The level of official secrecy seemed extreme. Some organizations, such as Britain's Air Accidents Investigation Branch, never said a word. Indeed their website still just stated baldly: "We are not able to comment further on this investigation, which is being led by the Malaysian authorities." Everyone hid behind the Malaysians, who in turn were hiding behind the broad secrecy curtain known as ICAO Annex 13 (which as I shall argue later, was used to excess).

From morning to night, our attention was firmly focused on the searching operation now under way along the northern and southern corridors. An astonishing number of search aircraft were taking to the skies from airports and military bases in Malaysia, Indonesia, India, Kazakhstan, and Australia. Ships were repositioning to western Australia to locate any debris: P-3 Orions, Poseidons, Hercules aircraft . . . all were being stationed in Perth, western Australia, to begin looking.

The search in the northern corridor was relatively straightforward by comparison. We knew, from the Inmarsat BTO, the location of the seventh arc, and that the plane had to have kept flying for six hours. Unless it went round and round in circles (which some people still think it did), it must have reached the upper end of the corridor, so there was no point searching the lower part. The plane had to have reached China or Kazakhstan. The searchers quickly got into the air to comb the huge, wide-open spaces: nothing was found.

In the southern corridor, it was much more difficult. The search zone was more than 1,500 miles off the coast of western Australia in one of the most remote parts of the world, and it was huge. The US National Transportation Safety Board estimated the area of ocean to be searched as 410,000 square miles, which the Australian Maritime Safety Authority described as the size of France.[10] Everyone was concentrating on one simple thing: search from the skies, spot debris, and see if it was from the plane. There were planes and ships from Australia, New Zealand, China, Japan, and South Korea, with more on the way. Hour after hour I sat watching the video feeds coming in from my colleagues in Perth, always hoping, and frankly expecting, that before long something would be found. After all, no commercial plane that had ever crashed did so without leaving a trace.

This searching experience was being repeated dozens of times and soon it started to feel as if the whole escapade was hopeless. Day after day, I tried to remind viewers that if history was any guide, debris would be spotted and it was just a matter of time before something was sighted. I wasn't just being Pollyanna. Experience had taught me that eventually something is either seen on the surface or washes up on the shores of nearby countries.

As if to prove my point, late at night, New York time, there was a news flash: Tony Abbott, then prime minister of Australia, was to make a statement in the House of Representatives in Canberra. CNN was already wall-to-wall with this story, and now we had to ramp up even further. Canberra is fifteen hours ahead of New York, from where I was broadcasting. Our regular evening show, *CNN Tonight*, would already be finished by the time Abbott spoke, so we were instructed to stay on the air. Around midnight, we watched as, across the globe, Mr. Abbott rose to speak. He at once had us riveted:

> New and credible information has come to light in relation to the search for Malaysia Airlines flight 370 in the southern Indian Ocean. The Australian maritime safety authority has received information based on satellite images of objects possibly related to the search. Following specialist analysis of this satellite imagery, two possible objects related to the search have been identified.

He then went on to say that planes were on their way to locate the objects, which were 2,500 kilometers (1,500 miles) west of Perth.

I had no hesitation in saying I believed that the Australians knew far more than they were letting on, and that they were probably bloody sure this was debris from the plane. In hindsight, it is difficult for me to overstate how important this development seemed at the time, and I said this on television. So, why did I tie my colors to the mast so foolishly?

First, we have the Malaysians saying there are these two corridors; then we have the search planes scouring the most likely place; now we have the Australian prime minister saying something may have been found.

Abbott is a very experienced politician, not someone who was likely to make such significant statements unless he was pretty sure of what he was saying. He was also making them to the Australian parliament. If he was wrong, he'd look like an idiot. What's more, he used the phrase "new and credible information." The use of the word "credible" added huge amounts of, well, credibility to what was being said. Finally, he talked of a "specialist analysis" of two possible objects. His caveat that "it may turn out to be unrelated to the search for MH370" was almost boilerplate throwaway, added just for the record. Mr. Abbott left us with the ringing words "I did want to update the House on this potentially important development."

Anyone who has spent time working in news and politics knows that most senior politicians are very circumspect in situations like these, for the very reason that they don't want to get it wrong. There were many less dramatic ways than speaking in parliament that he could have released this information, for instance just by coming out and making a press statement. Knowing how many advisers and spin doctors are employed by top politicians, I thought it inconceivable that Abbott would have made those comments to parliament without being pretty sure.

The announcement in Canberra was quickly repeated by the Malaysians in Kuala Lumpur after the two prime ministers had spoken: it seemed almost a done deal.

The consensus was: "they've found it." Now it was just a matter of waiting for the search planes and ships to locate the debris, which the satellites had seen some days earlier.

As we watched to see if the Australians' "highly credible" debris would prove to be from MH370, more resources were being rapidly dispatched to Perth. China was sending five ships, three planes, and several helicopters. The Japanese were sending some P-3 Orion search planes. The British had volunteered HMS *Echo* to the mission and Australia was preparing to send HMAS *Ocean Shield* out to sea. In the northern corridor, things were much quieter. Kazakhstan said there was no sign of any debris. The focus was firmly on the southern corridor, in which there were more sightings of potential aircraft remnants. On March 23, the French said their satellites had picked up something at sea, then the Chinese claimed their satellites had found something worthy of investigation. All in all, there were 122 potential objects. During this period, it was getting increasingly difficult to follow exactly what was being found and where. At the regular press briefing, Hishammuddin said, "We have now had four separate satellite leads, from Australia, China and France, showing possible debris. Some objects appeared bright, possibly indicating solid material."[11] It's not surprising everyone was convinced that this was the right area and the debris would soon be found.

Finding whatever had been spotted would prove to be a challenge, as Prime Minister Abbott had admitted in his statement to parliament. "I should tell the house that . . . the task of locating these objects will be extremely difficult," he warned. First, the satellite photographs were several days old, so merely going to the place where they were last seen would be useless, because the tides would have caused the debris to drift farther away. This is a well-known challenge for oceanographers, who use tidal charts to work out in which direction debris may have drifted. Unfortunately, each time the search planes reached the assumed locations, they found nothing.

On occasions when they did find objects, they turned out not to be debris from an airplane. The most notable example was when planes were sent to survey debris spotted by satellite, which turned out to be a dead whale carcass. Old wooden cable drums, parts of shipping pallets, and all manner of assorted rubbish were found swirling about over days of searching. The fact that the searchers were locating so much debris in the middle of such vast open spaces seemed to me unusual—that is, until our oceanographers explained that the search area was one of the world's natural garbage dumps. Known as the Indian Ocean Gyre, it is where the south equatorial current and the western Australia current meet, creating tides that move in a counter-clockwise circular motion. At the center of this circle is a patch of water several million square kilometers in dimension. Shipping debris caught up in the gyre currents ends up in this patch, swirling around and not drifting away. Consequently, it is unsurprising that so many sightings of potential debris occurred in this area. Searchers were combing through the exact part of the ocean where rubbish accumulates. Those same drift models would come back into play when the first, and at the time of this writing only, piece of debris, the flaperon, was found. Oceanographers used the models to reverse the item drift from Reunion to the primary search zone, confirming this area as the likely place where the plane went down.

All the false debris being seen merely proved that the searchers needed more and better information to help narrow the search area. In Kuala Lumpur and London, an international group of engineers was working on this problem. Having already used the BTO to set up the corridors, Inmarsat's engineers were now looking at ways to delve further into the handshakes.

They now concentrated on the "burst frequency offset," or BFO. As we saw earlier, the burst time offset was used to develop the arcs and set out the potential directions, north or south. The BFO could be adapted to work out where on the arc the plane might have crossed. But what is the BFO?

Imagine you are standing on a street and you hear a police car siren coming toward you. The siren appears to get louder and its tone changes as it gets closer to you. Once it has passed, the tone changes as it goes farther away. This is called the Doppler effect. The sound frequency is changing as the distance increases or decreases. Any sound-wave frequency has a given Doppler, and the thinking was, the satellite handshakes contained a limited amount of raw information and that information was being transmitted on a frequency that could be measured. The searchers would concentrate on the frequencies the satellite received and compare them to the frequency they might have expected. The difference would lead them to the position on the arcs.

The starting point was the same as with the BTO. The engineers looked at the frequencies received by the ground station on those specific occasions where they definitively knew where the plane was, such as on the runway at Kuala Lumpur. Then they examined the BFO data. This gave them a baseline from which to work out all the other BFO data received later in the flight. They were able to look at the frequency measurements actually received by the ground station from the handshakes and compare them to what was expected. Using this information, they were able to work out possible places on the arcs where the plane should have been. Of course, I have greatly simplified the process here because I am not a satellite engineer, and we don't need to fully understand exactly what they did or how they did it. According to a variety of satellite engineers to whom I have spoken, there was nothing new or revolutionary about the material with which they were working. What was different was the interpretation and uses to which it was being put. The timing and frequency data allowed Inmarsat to turn the satellite handshakes into a navigation tool, and in this way they were able to confidently say where they thought the plane had gone.

This new interpretation of the data was revolutionary. As Mark

Dickinson at Inmarsat told me, "Turning this communications system into a navigation system . . . it hadn't been done before."

Everyone in Inmarsat was aware that they were at the forefront of experimentation with this latest set of numbers. Dickinson made it clear that "we had to check and make sure we understood the system and double check and get other people to check for us. Validation is very important when it comes to making sure you have confidence in what you have done."[12] So now it was time to make sure everyone else agreed.

When the Inmarsat data first came to light and work began on its interpretation, the Malaysians put together an international working group based in Kuala Lumpur. It consisted of Inmarsat, the Air Accidents Investigation Branch, and Rolls-Royce from the UK; the NTSB, FAA, and Boeing from the USA; the Civil Aviation Administration of China and the Air Accident Investigation Division of China; and, of course, all the Malaysian authorities.

Inmarsat was careful to avoid "group think," where a theory takes hold and everyone becomes blind to its deficiencies. To prevent this, all those with the expertise were given the same raw data to see what conclusions they would come up with. They went away, made their own models, and came up with their own results. Dickinson told me, "It's very important this isn't just an Inmarsat activity. There are other people doing investigations, experts who are helping the investigation team who have got the same data who made their own models up and did the same thing and broadly speaking they got roughly the same answer."[13]

They tested all these theories against nine previous flights of 9M-MRO, the aircraft being used for MH370, and against eighty-seven other aircraft using the same equipment, flying at the same time. In each case, the results were clear: they were able to predict the route these planes took pretty accurately. Unfortunately, pretty accurately isn't accurately enough: in one case, using MH021, there was a 146-nautical-mile discrepancy in location at the seventh arc.[14] In another case, using MH009, the difference between the predicted and the actual flight path was 200 nautical miles.[15] These are sizable areas when it comes to searching the ocean, especially when you aren't sure exactly where to start in the first place.

So, did the plane go north or south? When they created graphs of the two possible corridors the plane might have taken, and then compared them to the data they had received, the research suggested that the plane had flown along the southern corridor. The predicted and actual reference data for both the time and frequency data showed there was a much better correlation for the southern option. No one disagreed.

The Inmarsat data is crucial to the whole search operation. There has been a huge amount of controversy over who knew what and when, and how the data was processed. Numerous allegations have been made that the Malaysians were slow in receiving the data from Inmarsat, accepting it as valid, and then acting upon it.

Little has been said about how the Inmarsat data was handled during this two-week period. No official account of this has ever been officially released. In the Factual Report published on the first anniversary of MH370's disappearance, there is just one paragraph on page 5 that deals with the Inmarsat data, saying "extensive work" had been done.[16] This is quite surprising since the report runs to 109 pages, and includes laborious details on everything from cabin-crew training to Malaysia's air traffic control structures, but almost nothing on the data upon which the entire search had been based. Then there is the Australian ATSB's report on the underwater search.[17] This exhaustively reviews the Inmarsat data, but says nothing about how it was handled by the authorities.

From those I have spoken to, and looking at the record, Inmarsat knew within twenty-four hours or so that the plane had kept flying. Word of this reached officials in Malaysia pretty soon thereafter. It is worth quoting Minister Hishammuddin Hussein, who said:

> The investigations team received the complete raw Inmarsat satellite data which included the six handshakes at approximately 15:00 on Wednesday 12th March . . . Upon receiving the raw data, the Malaysian authorities immediately discussed with the US team how this information might be used. The US team . . . then sent the data to the US where further processing was needed before it could be used. Initial results were received on Thursday 13th March at approximately 13:30, but it was agreed that further refinement was needed so the data was sent back to the US. The results were received at approximately 14:30 Friday 14th March and presented to a high level meeting at 21:00 Friday.

Six days from when the plane went missing, the Malaysians had the results, and during that period of the twelfth, thirteenth, and fourteenth of March, the Inmarsat data was whizzing back and forth between Malaysia and the United States, and not a word was being said publicly about it. Disingenuous at best were the minister's comments on March 13:

> I would like to refer to news reports suggesting that the
> plane may have continued flying for some time after the last
> contact . . . those reports are inaccurate.[18]

Clearly, throughout the week, everyone closely involved in the investigation knew that the plane had kept flying; they chose either not to announce it or to be obscure about it. Does this matter? Yes and no. No, because it frankly had no bearing on the outcome. The data was still being worked on, and until the experts were more certain about what it meant, it was a work in progress. Those who claim that this effort hampered and delayed the searchers from possibly finding debris in the water sooner are wrong. The searchers could not have been directed to a particular location any sooner because the information was not definitive: they risked being sent to the wrong places and wasting even more time. What does matter is that information was being withheld, and in some cases we were being misled, and this blows another hole in the Malaysians' claim that they were being transparent. They had obfuscated on the turn-back, now they were doing the same with the Inmarsat data.

I have consistently defended the Malaysian government's handling of the investigation, but this is one area where I cannot do so. During that first week, the Inmarsat data showing that the plane kept flying was not some minor point. It goes to the core of the event. Even in the fog of confusion caused by the unique, extraordinary circumstances, this was obviously central to all discussions. The defense that it had not been firmly verified doesn't hold up. It should have been publicly revealed. Since Malaysia was the investigating authority, it fell on them to reveal the information, and they didn't.

By way of contrast, in the case of Germanwings 9525 in April 2015, there was a leak of the contents of the cockpit voice recorder to the *New York Times* that revealed that the first officer, Andreas Lubitz, had deliberately crashed the plane.[19] This information was confirmed the next morning by the Marseille prosecutor, who went into great detail on what was on the cockpit voice recorder.[20]

Back with MH370, ten days after they started working on the Inmarsat data, everyone, it seemed, was in agreement. It had been reviewed by all the major investigators; the theory had been tried and tested against tens of other 777 flights in the air at the same time, and even run against previous flights of the MH370 aircraft, 9M-MRO. According to Inmarsat's Mark Dickinson, "No one has come up yet with a reason why it shouldn't work with this particular flight when it has worked with the others."[21] It seemed there was no doubt the plane had flown south and it was time to tell the Malaysian prime minister.

The pressure in Kuala Lumpur was now very high. The first week of searching had been fruitless as they came to grips with the fact that the plane had turned back and kept flying. The north/south corridors had been established, and while there were many reports of potential debris being spotted, nothing had been found. No debris, no sign of hijacking, no information at all, except for these weird satellite handshakes that had created vast corridors to be searched. There was a feeling that Malaysia was completely out of its depth and bungling the investigation. The level of international criticism was rising. The premier of China, Li Keqiang, was quoted by Xinhua urging the Malaysians to provide "more detailed information in its possession . . . in a timely, accurate and comprehensive manner."[22]

On Monday, March 24, the men from Inmarsat briefed the Malaysian prime minister on the results of their latest findings. The experts were unanimous: the plane had kept flying for hours and gone south. When Najib Razak received this information, he told me his reaction was to ask, "'Are you sure?' I asked them again and again, 'Are you sure?' And their answer to me was 'We are as sure as we possibly can be.'"[23]

The prime minister had to be sure, because if the evidence was solid, he would have to make an unpleasant announcement. Only a week previously he had publicly revealed that the plane had turned back, and announced a shift in the search. Now, armed with the new data from Inmarsat, the prime minister had to drop the next bombshell in the mystery of MH370. The official experts were unanimous: all the satellite data pointed to the fact the plane had flown south after making its turn around the northern tip of Indonesia.

Prime Minister Najib Razak was scheduled to speak at ten o'clock that night. In New York, it was nearing 10 a.m. as I sat in the studio, waiting, along with my colleagues, to see what he was going to say. We knew it had to be important, bordering on crucial; after all, the Malaysian prime minister only spoke about MH370 when there was something major to report.

Some of us assumed the prime minister would announce that debris had been found that could be verified as part of MH370, while others thought he would announce that the search was being called off. I didn't think calling off the search was possible at this stage, however desperate it had become. Shortly before the top of the hour, Razak spoke, flanked on the one side by Rahman, the director of civil aviation, and on the other by the acting transport minister, Hishammuddin. He started off telling us that Inmarsat had been refining the analysis of the satellite data, what we now know was adding the BFO calculations to the BTO they were already working with. In a massive understatement, the prime minister said, "Using a type of analysis never before used in an investigation of this sort, they have been able to shed more light on MH370's flight path." Inmarsat and the British accident investigators had concluded that "MH370 flew along the southern corridor, and that its last position was in the middle of the Indian ocean, west of Perth."

Then came the words the passengers' families dreaded:

> This is a remote location, far from any possible landing sites. It is therefore with deep sadness and regret that I must inform you that, according to this new data, flight MH370 ended in the southern Indian Ocean.[24]

It was a pivotal moment in the MH370 story: the official announcement that the plane had gone down in the ocean. To many of us, it was a statement of the obvious. Yet the prime minister's simple phrase "flight MH370 ended in the southern Indian Ocean" was about to cause even more controversy and pain. There was to be no closure.

CHAPTER FIVE

THAT TEXT

For the family members, this was a terrible moment.

—David McKenzie, CNN correspondent

While we were all digesting the prime minister's announcement that the flight had ended in the southern Indian Ocean, and were at the same time trying to understand the Inmarsat documents published by the investigators, there was another story brewing that proved to be just as controversial. Within moments of the prime minister's statement, we started seeing reports that a text message had been sent by Malaysia Airlines to the families—a text that, even today, boggles my mind.

An hour or so before Prime Minister Razak addressed the cameras, Malaysia Airlines sent out the text that must be printed in its entirety for its dreadfulness to be fully appreciated:

> Malaysia Airlines deeply regrets that we have to assume beyond any reasonable doubt that MH370 has been lost

and that none of those on board survived. As you will hear in the next hour from Malaysia's Prime Minister we must now accept all evidence suggesting the plane went down in the Southern Indian Ocean.

This text was sent to all those family members who had registered their mobile numbers with the airline so they could be kept informed on developments. Most of those who had made the trip to either Kuala Lumpur or Beijing were now being accommodated at the airline's expense in several hotels. As a swift means of getting in touch, Malaysia Airlines was using SMS (Short Message Service) to alert the families when briefings were being held. But no one ever thought for a moment that the company would choose a text message as a way to let them know that the plane had crashed and everyone on board had perished.

I clearly remember the moment when we saw the text. I was sitting in Studio 54, the newsroom studio on the fifth floor of CNN's New York bureau. Having heard the prime minister's statement, we were now deep into "pundit-vision." The usual suspects and I were parsing every line of the statement, analyzing the words he used and the timing, as well as coming to grips with a five-page document in which Inmarsat explained how they'd determined where the plane had crashed. We were suddenly alerted that our correspondent in Beijing was sending a copy of the airline's SMS message. Next thing, I see it on the monitor as the anchor is reading its contents. It was shocking. In the heat of the moment, I tried to find a good reason why it might have been sent, and came up empty. Moments later we started seeing video of family members in shock and hysterics. The criticism was pretty much universal: crass, insensitive, thoughtless, heartbreaking.

Malaysia Airlines defended its decision. At a press conference the day after the prime minister's announcement, Ahmad Jauhari Yahya said:

> Our sole and only motivation last night was to ensure that in the incredibly short amount of time available to us the families heard the tragic news before the world did. Whenever humanly possible we did so in person with the families or by telephone, using SMS only as an additional means of ensuring fully that the nearly 1000 family members heard the news from us and not from the media.

The explanation has a certain cruel logic: there were families in Kuala Lumpur and in Beijing, and most had been informed in person or told to show up at one of the places where they were given the news and would then watch the prime minister speak. It is admirable that the company wanted to ensure that the families heard the news firsthand rather than through the media. But by text? Furthermore, this important message was sent only in English, even to the Chinese families.

Many family members didn't understand what it said. Rough translations sparked rumors, and far from making the situation clear, this sent people into a panic. There was already an enormous amount of mistrust between the families and the Malaysians, both the government and the airline. Stuck as they'd been in hotels, the families had little confidence in either their own government or the airlines telling them the truth.

It didn't have to be this way. In the crash of Germanwings 9525, the news that the first officer, Andreas Lubitz, had deliberately flown the plane into the French Alps, murdering 149 people, was leaked to the *New York Times*, which published the story. Immediately the authorities held private briefing sessions with the families, confirming the awful news, before the prosecutor told the world the next morning. Of course, we don't know how many families were present at those briefings or how many did in the end hear the news through the media. But at least the French and German authorities reacted humanely to the developing crisis.

Unfortunately, in cases like this, it's inevitable that some family members will learn unpleasant facts from the media. In the Germanwings case, the announcement to the victims' families came thirty-six hours after the incident. In MH370, it was sixteen days.

In short, the decision to send this text was a very bad one, for which there is no justification. Whatever the rationale, common sense and decency should have kicked in and someone at Malaysia Airlines should have said, "No, don't send such details, just tell people there is to be an important announcement and give them a number or person to call."

Besides the text itself, there is another troubling aspect: the choice of words used. The phrase "beyond any reasonable doubt" is classic legalese, the kind of words used in criminal trials, where juries are repeatedly reminded they must be sure of the accused's guilt "beyond reasonable doubt." Why they would use such a phrase in telling someone about their loved one's death, I can't fathom. I don't understand the inclusion of these words unless they were trying to make their case. When you then add the phrase "we must now accept all evidence," we are left with a text that has all the hallmarks of a statement that was drafted by a committee. It immediately invites the reply "No, we must *not* now accept," as indeed, at the time, there was no physical evidence of the plane's crashing. In weeks of searching, not a single piece of debris had been recovered. Another sixteen months would pass before the first piece of the plane washed up ashore on Reunion

Island. There were no distress signals; the science upon which the entire ocean crash was based, the Inmarsat handshakes, was, by the authorities' own admission, novel and untested. To claim that evidence existed "beyond a reasonable doubt" that the family members "must now accept" was simply adding insult to injury.

Then there were the words "none of those on board survived." While obviously this is a logical inference given the circumstances, it was the kind of wording deliberately avoided by the prime minister in his statement on March 24. Mr. Razak was very careful not to say that the passengers had perished, so the text sent by the airline was directly contradicting the prime minister's statement. To the families involved and certainly to those of us watching, it created the impression that two sides of "official" Malaysia were sending out conflicting signals. Whether through lack of coordination or sheer obtuseness, the airline's text made a bad situation worse and inflamed the wrath of the families, many of whom would continue to claim, "How can you say this when there is no debris, no physical evidence?"

This is not just a matter of my being clever after the event or reading too much into a text message. This SMS wasn't just thrown together. I imagine many people debated the wording; if they didn't, they should have. Also, Malaysia Airlines' answer that there was a shortage of time doesn't bear much scrutiny either. The prime minister spoke late at night, and I am guessing it would not have made much difference if his statement had been delayed an hour or two while the airline ensured the families were properly informed. This infamous text marked one of the low points in the handling of this tragedy.

Three weeks after he made that statement, I traveled to Malaysia for an exclusive interview with Mr. Razak. We met at Seri Perdana, his official residence in Putrajaya, about an hour's drive from the capital, Kuala Lumpur. Our car proceeded down a long driveway lined with lush tropical plants. A mansion used for greeting foreign leaders and official functions, Seri Perdana is an extraordinary place. Official rooms are decorated with large chandeliers and big, overstuffed armchairs in bright colors. To do the interview we had to move some large and extremely heavy coffee tables.

Mr. Razak is an elegant politician from a family steeped in Malaysian politics. He is as comfortable in the salons of Western power as he is with Asian politics. As we set up for our interview, Razak was preparing for the imminent arrival of President Barak Obama, the first visit by a sitting US president in fifty years. The occasion was important in establishing Malaysia as a major player in diplomatic relations between the United States and Southeast Asia, especially as the two sides were negotiating the Trans-Pacific Partnership on trade. Razak's advisers were eager to make sure I also asked about these wider issues, even though they knew that my interview would focus on MH370.

Prime Minister Razak admitted that in drafting the March 24 announcement, his words had been "very carefully chosen." I wanted to know why he had not been more direct. After all, as the Malaysia Airlines text said, all the evidence suggested that the plane went down in the south Indian Ocean with all loss of life; surely he should have said the same thing. His answer surprised me:

> At the time there was that remote possibility that there could be survivors, a very remote possibility. So I didn't want to exclude that, therefore I chose the words "the flight ended." I didn't say everybody died on board. I didn't say the plane crashed into the sea and everybody died in that process, but I said the flight ended in the southern part of the Indian ocean.[1]

No doubt, while the prime minister was being diplomatic in his statement, everyone knew what he really was saying. I suggested his carefulness with his wording was neither helpful nor useful to the families. Even now, more than a month since the plane had disappeared, Razak would still not say that everyone on board had died.

> QUEST: Are you prepared now to say the plane and
> passengers have been lost?
> RAZAK: I would on the balance of the evidence, it would be
> hard to imagine otherwise, Richard.
> QUEST: But the significance is until Malaysia says the plane
> has been lost the compensation can't go ahead. So I ask
> you again, Prime Minister, are you prepared now to say
> the plane and passengers have been lost?
> RAZAK: At some point in time, I would be, but right now I
> think I need to take into account the feelings of next of
> kin. And some of them have said publicly that they're
> not willing to accept it until they find hard evidence.
> QUEST: Aren't you just delaying the inevitable and drawing
> out the process?
> RAZAK: Richard, the truth of the matter . . . as far as the
> government is concerned, we could say that, but it's
> simply out of respect of the next of kin and I think in
> due course and given the reality of the situation my
> sense is they will have to accept it. But let us give it a
> little more time.[2]

"A little more time" turned into ten months. The Malaysian government finally declared MH370 an "accident" on January 29, 2015.

The declaration by Azharuddin Abdul Rahman, the director general of the Department of Civil Aviation, was being made because "after 327 days and based on all available data . . . survivability in the defined area is highly unlikely." Mr. Rahman concluded:

> It is therefore with the heaviest heart and deepest sorrow that on behalf of the government of Malaysia we officially declare Malaysia Airlines flight MH370 an accident . . . and that all 239 passengers and crew on board MH370 are presumed to have lost their lives.[3]

Why did it take so long to make this declaration, when the first round of deep-sea searching had finished many months earlier? The decision formally to declare an aviation incident an "accident" is more than just stating the obvious. The word "accident" is used in the international treaty that governs aviation, known as the Chicago Convention, and specifically the famous Annex 13 to the convention: a veritable bible of air accidents. Annex 13 sets out the rules for handling aviation accidents, including which country is responsible for holding the investigation, who is involved, what needs to be done, when reports must be sent, and so on. Annex 13 sets out the duties and responsibilities of those involved and imposes strict confidentiality during accident investigations. The term "accident" is defined in chapter one of Annex 13, and includes those occasions when "the aircraft is missing or completely inaccessible." Obviously, under Annex 13, MH370 is an accident.

The standard answer for why it is important to formally declare a crash an accident is that it allows the passengers' relatives to start the process of claiming compensation, which is governed by another treaty called the Montreal Convention.[4] In the case of MH370, an interim payment of $50,000 had already been made in June 2014 to relatives of those on board.[5] In fact, the recourse to compensation as the main reason to declare an accident is not entirely accurate. There doesn't need to be an Annex 13 declaration of an accident to claim compensation because the Montreal Convention uses a different definition of an accident.[6] All in all, I am not sure why the Malaysians waited until January 2015 to make that declaration other than out of a desire not to antagonize the families any further, or indeed draw more attention to MH370, if that were possible. The choice of January 2015 seems entirely random; there were plenty of earlier dates when they could have done it—for instance, April 28, 2014, when the underwater search by *Ocean Shield* came to an end, a moment that arguably better fit the definition of "missing plane" under Annex 13. Or they could have waited only a few more weeks and done it on the first anniversary in March 2015. This was another of those odd events that have transpired during the MH370 saga that seem to have no obvious explanation.

In the grand scheme of things, it might well be argued, what does it matter when the declaration of an accident is made, or what was said in a text? The plane was missing. No one knew what had happened. Both of these events were only saying what everyone already knew. I think it does matter because it shows what was happening within "official" Malaysia at the time. Everything and everyone was under tremendous scrutiny and increasing strain, and for good reason: nothing like this had ever been seen before. The official systems in place were neither robust enough nor sufficiently tried and tested to withstand the glare of global attention, and I don't mean just in Malaysia. Everywhere governments and organizations seemed ill equipped to be dealing with this unique event. As an example, look at the immediate response and confusion of the families to the prime minister's announcement and China's reaction to the statement the plane had gone down in the ocean.

From the first days of the crisis, the families had been accommodated in several hotels in Kuala Lumpur and at the Metropark Lido Hotel in Beijing. Since the largest number of passengers on board the aircraft were from China, there was a sizable number of relatives staying at the Lido. Sequestering relatives like this is normal in any major accident. It makes it easier to provide assistance and keep them up to date on the latest developments. It also allows them to offer care, comfort, and emotional support to each other during difficult and dark days. Unfortunately, in the case of the Lido Hotel, this was far from the reality. The hotel had been turned into a circus. It was overrun by media and press, and families had to run the gauntlet of the media every time they went from one place to another, especially to the grand ballroom, where the briefings were held. Instead of creating an oasis of support, the Chinese had created a pressure cooker in which the inability of the Malaysians to provide much information—for good reason, since there wasn't any—was seen as dishonesty, incompetence, or both.

I sat and watched the pictures coming in to CNN from these hotels, and day after day it looked awful. Officials from Malaysia were holding briefings that turned into mudslinging matches. You could see the anguish and pain etched on the families' faces as they waited for any morsel of information. It is not surprising that this was a tinderbox, waiting to burst into flames. It was in this environment that the infamous text was received, with predictable results.

The arrival of the Malaysia Airlines text set off a wave of anguish among the relatives even before everyone was called together into the main room to hear Prime Minister Razak speak. No sooner had the prime minister finished than pandemonium broke loose. There were scenes of tears, screams, and hysterics as the families were told what they had feared: the plane had crashed. CNN's David McKenzie was there:

> You had people desperately crying, some of them were carried out on stretchers, unable even [to] walk, some of them lashing [out] angrily at the cameras assembled; there was this awful public moment that should have been very private for the family members but for them they wanted also to express to us how angry and upset they were because they wanted the world not to forget them.[7]

The video coming in from Beijing was heartbreaking to watch. Scenes of hysterics, people being removed by stretchers, screaming at the cameras, being carried from the room. I remember thinking, What on earth were the authorities doing allowing the massed ranks of the media to get so close to the room where the people were being told this information? Once it was clear what was happening, why didn't they find another way to get the people out of the ballroom, or at least put up screens to protect their privacy as they left? Of course, one has to question the members of the media themselves, who decided to record and show these pictures, my own network included.

In writing this chapter, I went back to watch the scenes again. The incident was badly handled from beginning to end: the airline and the government's lack of preparation for what they must have known was about to be announced, coupled with the decision to let the media be so close to the door through which the relatives would have to pass, and finally the decision to allow the grief-stricken relatives to walk past the cameras. Remember, this was not happening in an open field or in some uncontrolled environment: it was an entirely controllable situation. Other cases show how it might have been handled better. With Germanwings 9525, only two days after the plane crash the authorities managed to take families from Germany and Spain to the rescue center in the French Alps. The cameras were kept at a respectful distance as relatives visited the crash site, where the French authorities had set up a temporary memorial. It was calm, dignified, and, of course, very sad. Without doubt, in these cases there are always going to be pictures of tears and grief, but nothing like we saw with those Chinese relatives in MH370.

Within hours of hearing the news, which many refused to accept, the relatives in Beijing decided to march to the Malaysian embassy in protest. Such spontaneous action in China was just about unheard of. To this day, it is not entirely clear whether the Chinese government was stoking the anger or merely responding to it. Whichever it was, the Chinese got more than they bargained for when the families decided to take matters into their own hands. This reaction was hardly surprising. The Chinese government had spent the past two weeks repeatedly berating the Malaysians for their lack of information or openness, with veiled threats if things didn't get better. On March 24, faced with dozens of angry, anguished relatives marching through central Beijing to the Malaysian embassy, the Chinese authorities seemingly had little choice but to facilitate the procession. In a story that had already become like none other we had seen, suddenly we were getting live pictures, Skype video, and reports from the streets as the protesters marched the three miles from the hotel to the embassy. David McKenzie remembers this as one of the defining moments of his coverage:

> China is a country where if you go on the streets and protest you are going to get locked up. But the Chinese author-

ities knew that because of the emotional power these families had they couldn't just round them up and throw them in detention. And the family members just expressed that anger and frustration.[8]

At the embassy, protesters screamed for the ambassador, who agreed to meet them at the hotel. A few bottles were thrown before the Chinese officials herded the protesters onto buses to return them to the hotel. Finally a meeting with the ambassador took place. It was short, sharp, and acrimonious.

It was now sixteen days since the plane went missing. I had covered every twist and turn. There were many events, issues, and questions all competing for attention. Some, like the stolen passports, had seemed important at the beginning, only to evaporate into a sidebar to the main story. Others, such as the families' increasing anger at the way the matter was being handled, gradually took center stage. In my broadcasting, I was always trying hard not to be hypercritical of those who were having to deal with exceptional circumstances. I keep coming back to the fundamental point: the authorities didn't have any wreckage or evidence of the plane's location; for some reason, the plane had turned back and reversed its course; and it continued flying for six hours after contact was lost. Then there was the use of the weird data in order to geo-locate the route. I repeat: nothing like this had been seen before. Many have said that the search was like looking for a needle in a haystack. To which others have added that nobody had even found the haystack that contained the missing needle. Where I differ from other commentators is that I am a realist. In these conditions, it's not surprising that the confusion reached epic proportions. Governments move slowly. Militaries move with stealth. Corporations move with one eye on their business. Here, none of the facts turned out to be what they were originally thought to be. Nothing was working as it was meant to. It may be depressing to say this, but the search operation was as good as could be expected in the circumstances.

By now, wherever you look, the situation is starting to spiral out of control. In China, the relatives are bellicose and suspicious. In Malaysia, the government is beleaguered and being criticized on all sides; we have the Malaysian prime minister refusing to say the plane had crashed while the airline is saying all on board were lost. The search focus is now on a vast ocean, a zone so big as to be nearly useless. It is more than two weeks since the plane went missing and no one has the faintest idea of where it is, other than to point to a large ocean and say we believe it's somewhere in there, but we can't prove this. Into this maelstrom the Australians come riding to the rescue.

CHAPTER SIX

RACE TO THE PINGS

This search and recovery operation is probably the most
challenging one I have ever seen.

—Angus Houston[1]

Malaysia bore the legal responsibility for handling the search for MH370; on March 17, 2014, they delegated the task of running the daily search operation in the southern corridor to Australia. With a search area established, everyone agreed that the next step was to scour the region for the sound of pings emanating from the plane's underwater locater beacons, which would in turn lead searchers to MH370's black boxes.

All commercial aircraft carry two recorders. The first, called the cockpit voice recorder, or CVR, documents what is being said in the cockpit; the second, called the flight data recorder, or FDR, records what is happening to the plane's systems and what the pilots are doing to control the plane. Finding both is an essential part of an air-crash investigation. Robustly constructed and designed to withstand the force of most air crashes, they are especially crucial in accidents with no survivors, when physical evidence has often been destroyed beyond recognition. In such cases, the contents of these recorders can help investigators determine the causes of crashes. To solve the mystery of MH370, it was imperative to recover the black boxes. The question was where to search.

The Inmarsat data had established an area off Australia as being the most promising. The further analysis of the last handshake, pointed to the seventh arc, meant the plane's most likely final resting ground was roughly 1,500 miles off the coast of Perth. This area, 372,000 square miles, is part of Australia's flight information region for search and rescue, so initially the Australian Maritime Safety Authority (AMSA) was in charge.

The headquarters for the mission was RAAF Base Pearce in Perth. Immediately, the base became a hive of activity as planes from militaries around the world arrived to join in the search. Watching from the other side of the world, it seemed that the entire operation had taken on a new and more professional approach. This was confirmed within days when the Australian prime minister appointed the former chief of the defense staff, Air Chief Marshal Angus Houston, to take charge of the new Joint Coordination Centre (JCC). After two weeks of confusion between Malaysia and Australia over who was directing the operation, a single country was now in charge, on its own territory. Australia left no doubt of its intention to get the job done, but Houston was quick to emphasize how difficult this would be. "This will be a slow and painstaking process," he repeatedly reminded us.[2]

Angus Houston's arrival created a change in perception. At last a man capable of true leadership had taken command. In his early press conferences, Houston answered questions that Malaysian authorities had previously dodged. He didn't hide behind regulations or Annex 13. If a question went too far, or couldn't be answered, he bluntly said so.

After weeks of Malaysia's apparent bungling, the Australians gave form and cohesion, as well as confidence, to the search and rescue operation. Many officials also felt this way, while saying nothing against the Malaysians publicly.

Houston had huge amounts of experience in dealing with an aggressive, questioning media baying for information where none was available. Soft-spoken, yet with a firm voice that left no doubt about the authority he wielded, he was clearly a man who was used to giving orders and having them followed. So well did he perform in this crisis that in July 2014, after MH17 was shot down in eastern Ukraine, Prime Minister Abbott again called upon Houston to act as his special representative in recovering the remains of the Australians who had been on board. In Australia, when there's a knotty problem to be solved, the call is "Send for Angus."

Incidentally, in January 2015, Tony Abbott recommended Houston be knighted by HM Queen Elizabeth II for his work on MH370. While "Sir Angus" accepted the honor, he made it clear he wished to continue being called by his first name, telling ABC Radio, "It's a great honour to be recognised in this way. But I'd like people to still call me Angus. That's probably the way I am." So I shall defer, and leave off the knighthood!

So where were they going to search for floating debris? Every morning AMSA would issue a press release and a map telling us where the planes would be flying that day. The maps had color markings showing the more prominent zones in red and secondary areas in yellow. We would look at the maps in amazement, wondering what had caused AMSA to shift the area where they were looking. Usually the movements were a few hundred miles up a bit, down a bit, across a bit in large search boxes where they believed the most likely place to be.

On March 28, the search area shifted dramatically. Having been focused about 1,500 miles southwest of Perth, AMSA announced that the search would shift 680 miles to the northeast, considerably closer to the Australian coastline. The new area was based on updated advice from the Joint Investigation Team (JIT), which was continuing its work in Malaysia. The team was composed of experts from Inmarsat, NTSB from the USA, AAIB from the UK, ATSB from Australia, among others, who were still refining the data that could be gleaned from the handshakes and radar while the plane was being tracked. They had reviewed the data from the aircraft's turn-back and flight across Malaysia before heading along the Strait of Malacca. Their latest research showed that MH370 was flying faster than first thought; therefore it burned more fuel in the early part of the journey. This meant there would be less fuel after the southern turn for flight toward Australia. It all comes down to mathematics: we know the flight must have lasted until 08:19 (the time of the seventh handshake) and the team of investigators now had new speed information, so they had a better idea of where on the seventh arc the plane had reached. The consequence of all of this was the dramatic shift of the search zone nearly seven hundred miles to the northeast.

Just as before, authorities appeared to tinker with the location of this new zone day after day, moving it up a bit, down a bit, or to the side. Those of us watching on an hour-by-hour basis were never given the reasons for why they did this, leaving us with the impression that they were randomly searching around a particular patch of ocean on any given day. We were never given access to the people who were making these decisions, nor were we allowed to film the JIT at work in Kuala Lumpur (we asked many times). Every request was refused, usually on the grounds of the privacy and secrecy of the Annex 13 process. I believe this was a mistake. Briefings by politicians, civil servants, and military leaders are no substitute for observing the men and women who actually do the work.

How they determined the search zones was later described in great detail in the ATSB report "MH370—Definition of Underwater Search Areas" and a subsequent update.[3] Although extremely complex, this work basically boiled down to one question: If the plane flew this far with this much fuel in this amount of time, and turned at this point, how far south toward Australia could it have flown in six hours? The experts had some facts upon which to base their calculations:

1. They knew for certain what the BTO and BFO of the plane was when it was on the ground in Kuala Lumpur and when it started flying.

2. The amount of fuel on board was transmitted as part of the last ACARS transmission at 01:07.

3. They knew, from the military radar data, the route it took after it did the turn-back, then headed across Malaysia and out into the Strait of Malacca, so they could more precisely determine the speed at which it was flying.

4. They knew the times of the Inmarsat handshakes and of the unanswered satellite telephone calls, and they knew the range of the satellite movement in its geostationary orbit. Therefore they could construct the seven arcs.

5. They knew from Boeing and from Malaysia Airlines the range and endurance of the aircraft with a given amount of fuel and at various speeds and altitudes.

Putting it all together, and simplifying hugely: How far had the plane flown, and where on the seventh arc had it come down?

Related to this question was the knotty problem of working out what happened when the plane ran out of fuel, the engines stopped, and the aircraft started its deathly descent toward the water. How did the plane actually fall from the sky? Which way did it go? Did it head straight down, nose first, or did it glide, and descend in a gentler spiral? Knowing the path the plane took in descending from thirty-five thousand feet to the water was of the utmost significance in determining exactly where to search. At this point, we need to go back to the source of so much information about MH370's whereabouts: the Inmarsat handshakes.

You will remember that in total there were seven handshakes between the plane and the satellite network. But these seven were not all of the same exact type. Five of them involved the satellite initiating the handshake—putting out its hand first. However, two handshakes— the first and the last—were different. With these, the *plane* put out its hand first and tried to connect to the satellite, actions known as log-ons. The reason for this was not clear, and it meant the system received an unusual message. The Factual Report published on the first anniversary described the first and last handshakes as follows:

> During each of the two in-flight Log-Ons the GES (ground
> earth station) recorded abnormal frequency offsets for the
> burst transmissions from the Satcom.[4]

The experts had to work out why the first and last handshakes were accompanied by abnormal numbers. There were only a few possible reasons, the most likely of which was a major interruption in the power supply. If the satellite unit lost power, when it was restored the unit would reboot and try automatically to connect again to the satellite. The consensus was that this is what had happened. The plane had lost power, and when it came back, the units were attempting to log on. That only raised another crucial question: Why did the SATCOM lose power?

The first handshake was of particular interest because it occurred immediately after the air traffic control handover from Malaysia to Vietnam, just around the time the plane made its turn-back. Truth is, we know almost nothing about this particular power problem—except that it was not because someone switched off the unit in the cockpit . . . something "just happened."

In the case of the seventh handshake, at 08:19, the experts are pretty much agreed that this was when the plane's fuel ran out. Boeing and Malaysia Airlines did tests in their 777 simulators to discover how the plane would react when it ran out of fuel. First the right engine would fail, or flame out, as it is called in aviation. Shortly after, the left engine would stop.[5] Because the engines were generating the aircraft's electrical power, all the aircraft systems would stop working. Boeing had long determined how to deal with the eventuality of a plane having a double flame-out or losing all electrical power. To keep essential equipment working in a power emergency, a windmill-type device is installed on the 777, called the RAT—the Ram Air Turbine. This deploys from the right side of the plane, under the wing. Once in the airstream, the turbine's propellers turn, giving just enough electrical power for essential systems to control the aircraft, and this includes powering the satellite unit. The thinking was that when MH370 ran out of fuel, the satellite unit switched off until the emergency RAT generated enough basic power, then the satellite unit attempted to reconnect to the satellite. This was the moment when the plane was falling out of the sky. But which way was it falling, and how far and how fast?

The popular view is that once a big jet loses power, the nose goes down and the plane dives toward the ground. That is not the case. As I said at the beginning, planes are designed and built to fly. So provided a plane has some sort of forward motion to generate air over the wings, it will glide downward. The effect is that, contrary to what most people believe, large jets can glide for many miles if they have lost engine power . . . but with one crucially important proviso: the pilots must quickly make the right decisions and fly the plane very carefully. For the pilots, the trade-off is having to descend, in order to keep up the airspeed to generate lift. In general, a large jet will glide for roughly fifteen to seventeen miles for every thousand feet of altitude it loses— if its pilots do everything correctly.

There are two famous cases of modern jets having to glide after losing power. In the first, in 1983, on Air Canada Flight AC143, a 767 lost power flying from Montreal to Edmonton. Its fuel ran out because of an unbelievably basic miscalculation by the pilots and ground staff, who used the wrong formulae in converting fuel amounts between kilograms, pounds, and gallons. The incident became known as the Gimli Glider because the pilots were able to glide the powerless plane as many as thirty-nine miles to an old, unused runway at the Gimli Air Base. (Unused perhaps by aircraft—the 767's silent arrival certainly came as a nasty shock to the drag racers who were using the runway at the time. Luckily no one was seriously hurt.)

Then there was the case of Air Transat AT236, in 2001, in which an Airbus A330 was flying from Montreal to Lisbon. Because of a leak in the right tank, the aircraft ran out of fuel while it was flying at 34,500 feet. The pilots put it into a glide formation and managed to nurse it another sixty-five miles to land at Lajes Airport in the Azores. This case is all the more remarkable because the pilot made a 360-degree turn as well as a variety of "S" maneuvers to bleed off more altitude before landing—and all this in the early hours of the morning when it was still dark. In terms of MH370, these examples show that understanding how a plane can and will fly once it has lost power was crucial if searchers were to formulate a plan about where to search around the seventh arc. The difference of a degree or two in any direction would make the search zone much larger.

So, planes can glide, if someone is driving them. But what if no one is at the controls? In the Air Canada and Air Transat cases, the pilots did the best they could to put their aircraft into the optimum glide configuration, deploying slats and keeping the profile of the plane in the best position for greatest lift and least loss of height. In the case of MH370, we have no idea whether anyone was in the cockpit trying to control the plane when the fuel ran out. So while Air Canada and Air Transat cases show how pilots can continue gliding their planes after engine failure, the Australian investigators had to consider the case of a plane that ran out of fuel and everyone on board, passengers and pilots alike, was already dead. In the world of aviation they like to be a bit kinder in terminology and describe such a plane as having an "unresponsive cockpit." Understanding what happens when no one does anything to an aircraft after engine failure was essential to the search for the downed Malaysian plane.

Two well-known cases come to mind. A Helios Airways 737 that crashed in 2005, and the Learjet carrying the golfer Payne Stewart in 1999. Both of these cases involved failures in the oxygen supply to the aircraft. The Helios plane was flying from Larnaca to Prague via Athens when the air in the cabin ran out because the automatic pressurization equipment had been switched to manual by maintenance workers overnight. Once the work was completed, the workers forgot to switch the equipment back to automatic, and the pilots failed to notice this before takeoff. As the plane climbed, the air on board became ever thinner, eventually causing all on board, except, it is believed, a flight attendant, to perish. This flight attendant was seen at the controls by pilots of F-16 fighters who were sent up to intercept the aircraft. On the cockpit voice recorder you can hear two Mayday calls. When the fuel ran out, the plane started a descent, which increased in speed as both engines flamed out, and the plane crashed into a mountain.

It was a similar story with the Learjet carrying Payne Stewart. Here, for reasons never clearly established, there was a failure of the air supply and everyone on board succumbed to hypoxia. The plane flew for more than two hours before it ran out of fuel. When that happened, first the left wing dipped, then the plane went into a steep descent. A pilot in an F-16 from Oklahoma Air National who was flying alongside observed, "It's soon to impact the ground; he is in a descending spiral."

The Australians took these and other cases into account and decided that when MH370 ran out of fuel, the glide potential of the plane would have been up to a hundred miles. But since they don't believe anyone was at the controls, "the descent would develop into a spiral."[6]

The knowledge of previous crashes was valuable in determining where to begin the search for debris. Finding any floating wreckage would certainly validate that a crash took place, and would tell searchers they were in the right part of the ocean, but it most certainly would not mean that they had found the aircraft's crash site. In the time between the crash and the sighting of floating debris, the currents very likely would have moved the pieces some distance.

A whole new science has been developed that helps "reverse-drift" debris to the place where a crash was most likely to have taken place. I say "science," but those involved in doing the calculations would probably say that "reverse-drifting" is as much an art as a science. It involves knowing and understanding tides, currents, and winds, but it also involves the knowledge that only years of experience in determining crash sites can give. The longer the time between the crash and the discovery of the debris, the harder the task.

Take the case of Air France 447, which, you'll recall, crashed in the South Atlantic. It took five days to sight the first wreckage, which was about thirty-eight miles from the last known location of the plane. Experts reverse-drifted the movement and created a circle of forty nautical miles where they believed the A330 had come down. Despite the fact that the searchers picked up debris and knew they were in the right area, it still took two years and multiple searches of the ocean floor before they were able to locate the main part of the aircraft and retrieve the black boxes.

With MH370, it was much more difficult. By the time the experts agreed that the plane had gone south, more than two weeks had passed. Now the searchers needed debris: something from the plane that would show that they had found the farm, and could now start working back to find the haystack and then the needle.

An aircraft carries many items that will float, including seat cushions, life vests, clothing, luggage, even parts of the aircraft itself. But so much time had gone by that even allowing for reverse-drift techniques, it was likely that only a few items would be found, and they may have drifted many miles from the crash site. If there was anything left on the surface, it would be slim pickings. The lack of debris has been one of the major issues in this case; everyone keeps asking why nothing was found. The answer is that because it took more than two weeks to get to a likely crash zone, anything on the surface would have sunk or drifted away by the time investigators arrived.

Regardless, under the instructions of the Australians, planes and ships left Perth to search the likely zone. They were directed to two areas: first, the plane's most likely crash site; and second, farther afield, where any debris was likely to have drifted. It was seen as essential to try to locate some debris, to establish that the search operation was indeed in the right part of the ocean.

The search crews endured hours of flying in order to reach the locations, followed by intense moments of looking out of small windows at the ocean below. Because the search zone was so far from Perth, merely getting there and back used up most of the plane's fuel, leaving barely a couple of hours, if that, to search. My colleague Will Ripley, working as CNN's Tokyo correspondent, joined a US search flight that left from Malaysia. This was a ten-hour flight, seven hours of which would be taken up getting to and from the search zone. Once there, the pilots switched off one of the engines to conserve fuel and make the searching easier. The plane then descended to three hundred feet, with the eleven-member team either looking out of the windows, scanning the open ocean by eye, or studying radar screens sensitive enough to pick up a school of dolphins.

Ripley told me that while looking "after a while your mind starts to play tricks on you. You think you might see something then you realise it's a white cap on a wave."[7] He described the searching time as "pretty disappointing because there's part of your mind that hopes you are going to find something."

The search operation was formidable. In an area around 200,000 square miles, 1,100 miles west of Perth, ten aircraft and eleven ships swept the ocean, reporting potential sightings of debris by the dozen. Any debris that could be verified might lead investigators back to the most likely place where the plane went down. Only then could they start listening for "the pings."

What are these pings that became such an important part of the search for MH370, and that, as we shall see, ended up prolonging the search for the plane and the misery of the families? Attached to both the flight data and voice recorders is an Underwater Locator Beacon, or ULB, whose purpose is to help find the box if a crash occurs in water. A cylindrical device that sits at the end of the box, the ULB is designed to transmit a signal when it comes into contact with water. Unfortunately, quite often the ULB either gets ripped off the device during the crash, or simply doesn't work as intended. With our extensive coverage at CNN, I found myself on-air explaining again and again the workings of the CVR and FDR and the techniques for finding them underwater. Hour after hour I would go through the significance of the ULB, how far underwater you could expect to hear the signal, what the search team would be listening for, how long the battery would last once activated in the water, and so on.

The ULBs installed on MH370's voice and data recorders were made by Dukane. They were built to the required standard and could withstand water depths of up to twenty thousand feet, well within the limits of the southern Indian Ocean. After the beacon activated, it would transmit a pulse on a frequency of 37.5 kHz just about every second, which sounds like a click more than a ping.

Once the ULB was pinging, Dukane specified that its battery life would be a minimum of thirty days. Therefore the ULBs should have kept pinging until at least April 6, 2014. But so much time had already been lost just getting to the right search zone: grappling with the details of the turn-back, establishing the Inmarsat data, refining the data and establishing the corridors, deciding that the southern corridor was the place to search. The batteries could die in less than ten days.

News thrives on breaking news—add in a deadline, and you have a heady brew perfect for a twenty-four-hour news network. At CNN, we put on the screen a "countdown clock" timed to run out on April 6, thirty days after the plane was said to have "ended its journey in the southern Indian Ocean." I had seen countdown clocks used before at the network, usually for political stories—counting down to a possible US government shutdown, for example. In another case, involving the possibility of a debt default, the clock was used to count down the moments until midnight. I had never seen it used like this and I was concerned. I thought it risked creating the wrong impression.

Every show would start by reminding viewers of the number of days (or hours) left before the batteries on the pingers were due to expire. Yet, with the clock ticking down on one side of the screen, I would be broadcasting on the other side, saying how the deadline was not necessarily a deadline because batteries frequently lasted much longer than thirty days. The manufacturer guaranteed a "minimum" of thirty, but the CEO of Dukane happily came on our show to say the ULB pinger could last many more. As the armada set sail looking for debris, we began to get a good idea of how much of a shot in the dark this story was turning out to be. I said many times on-air that the searchers appeared to be making it up as they went along, and I still think this to be true.

The searchers were working in good faith with the best informa-tion they had, but that information was scant and of dubious accuracy. More resources were arriving all the time: the British Ministry of Defence announced that it was sending the nuclear submarine HMS *Tireless*. The location of Britain's nuclear submarines, part of the coun try's nuclear deterrent, is almost never revealed. That the UK was pre-pared to publicly announce where its nuclear sub was going would be just about unprecedented.

Days and days of searching on the surface had uncovered nothing, and time was running out for the ULB batteries. A sense of hopeless-ness was starting to build. It is no exaggeration to say that during those days in late March, the whole world was watching this steadfast, some might even say quixotic, attempt to find a plane that could have been anywhere. I went back and forth in my view on whether they would find anything. I simply didn't know and was getting exasperated being asked if they would.

Finally, Angus Houston made the decision that he could no longer rely on finding debris on the surface to lead him to the right spot. It was time to bring in more specialized equipment—in this case a device that is lowered into the water and towed behind a ship in order to listen for pings. The machine was called a towfish, and was known as a towed pinger locator, or TPL. A TPL had been put on board the Australian defense vessel *Ocean Shield*, which had arrived on scene from Perth earlier. The hope had been there would be verified debris from the plane that would reveal that the search team was roughly in the right place. Then they would launch the TPL to locate the black boxes. But there was no debris, and time was running out. On April 4, 2014, *Ocean Shield* deployed the TPL, and the search went under the waves.

Late on Saturday, April 5, the first reports came in that a Chinese ship had picked up the signal of a potential ping and held it for approximately fifteen minutes. The ship was the *Haixun 01*, and according to various Chinese media, it had heard a pulse with a frequency of 37.5 kHz: exactly that used by the underwater locator beacon. In the words of CNN's Beijing producer, the Chinese media were treating it as "basically confirmed to be the MH370 black box." Angus Houston was told about it, and immediately dispatched HMS *Echo*, which also had a TPL on board, to see if the ship could reacquire the signal. There were several promising signs, not least that the *Haixun 01* was in a primary search zone (albeit searching in an area it hadn't been tasked to search). Houston's statement at the time sounded promising:

> The characteristics reported are consistent with the aircraft black box. A number of white objects were also sighted on the surface about 90 kilometers from the detection area.

The next day, *Haixun 01* said it had heard the pings again in roughly the same location, but this time for a much shorter period, just ninety seconds. We were so desperate by now for any sign of hope that, once again, everyone at CNN leaped on this information. Then we had a reality check when we saw video of the equipment that the Chinese had been using. Instead of the high-tech, sophisticated TPL equipment, the sort being deployed on *Ocean Shield*, the Chinese were using a very basic Benthos handheld acoustic listening contraption, primarily intended for scuba divers. They had lashed the simple microphone to a pole, which was dropped over the side of a small rescue boat while the operator listening for the pings used a pair of earbuds. Technically, this piece of equipment had a listening range of more than a mile, but the depth of the ocean it was working in was at least two and a half miles. Worse, by using the device just under the surface, rather than thousands of meters below, the entire operation was likely to be contaminated by noise from the boats, the waves, and any other ocean disturbances. Even Justin Manley, a senior director at Teledyne Benthos, agreed that "holding the device over the side of a vessel may not be the best option."[8]

Sitting on the set, I watched the disappointing report of *Haixun 01* with a panel of experts, including David Gallo of the Woods Hole Oceanographic Institution. We were openmouthed in astonishment. Gallo was part of the team that found Air France 447 after others had failed. He had no doubt this escapade was a load of nonsense, but you didn't need to be an expert to recognize that the Chinese equipment was rudimentary and its attempts amateur. The whole thing was a joke.

In retrospect, Houston may have had an inkling of this when he said in his press conference:

> This is an important encouraging lead but one which I urge
> you to continue to treat carefully.[9]

There was one final piece of weirdness about *Haixun 01*'s finding. When the pictures of their search dinghy were released, it became clear that they also had an underwater locator beacon in their boat. If they heard anything at all, it was probably the pings from their own boat. Needless to say, no one else was able to reacquire the signal and pretty soon the whole thing was discounted. Months later, the ATSB's report on the underwater search summed it up:

> HMS *Echo* reported that the detections were unlikely due
> to the depth to the seafloor, surface noise and the equip-
> ment utilised.[10]

It was a polite way of saying that the *Haixun 01* ping reports were nonsense and a waste of time. To this day, I have no idea what the Chinese were up to. Some of my colleagues said that they thought the Chinese released the pictures to cover up the real searching equipment they were using, which they didn't want any prying Western eyes to see. I don't agree. I think it was either incompetence or something worse: there were journalists on board the *Haixun 01*, and it's possible the whole exploit was designed for the Chinese domestic audience. The Chinese knew that the home audience would simply eat up the story. Whatever the truth, it added nothing to the investigation and, in my view, was another example of China hindering the process rather than helping it.

At the same news conference at which Houston discussed *Haixun 01*'s reports, he revealed that *Ocean Shield* had, within the last few hours, reported hearing pings. This was far more important than the ham-fisted Chinese attempts. *Ocean Shield* had fully deployed its TPL eleven thousand feet underwater when it heard a ping. The very way Houston told us about it was like a jolt of electricity:

> This is late-breaking news. I thought it was important that we are totally transparent with you. I just want you to know that the search is a dynamic thing. Things are happening all the time and this broke this morning—what, an hour ago.

Weekends at CNN can often be relatively quiet, with news typically covered by a skeleton staff. Not so for these weekends. With the network's news-gathering force at full strength and with nonstop programs on MH370, we were following every twist and turn of this story. Now we were all waiting for more information about the pings. It's worth printing Houston's exact words, so you get an idea why everyone was so confident about the veracity of *Ocean Shield*'s report:

> I can report some very encouraging information . . . The Towed Pinger Locator deployed from the Australian Defence Vessel *Ocean Shield* has detected signals consistent with those emitted by aircraft black boxes.[11]

There were two separate signal detections; the first was held for two hours twenty minutes and the second was held for thirteen minutes, and they were up to two thousand yards apart. What's more, the location was very close to the seventh arc and the location of the last handshake, the one that occurred where it's believed the plane ran out of fuel. Houston was using phrases like "this is a most promising lead," "it's probably the best information that we have had," and "I'm much more optimistic than I was a week ago."[12] To be fair, Houston did give the usual caveat—"we need further confirmation. And I really stress this. It's very important"—but most of us weren't listening. This was day thirty-one since the plane would have entered the water, activating the pingers. The searchers were now working on borrowed time, and everyone was just relieved that something had been heard.

Ocean Shield kept going up and down the ocean grids in a regular formation that was described as being "like mowing a lawn." The goal was to try to reacquire the signal and narrow down the area. The more pings they heard, the easier it would be to determine where the boxes were on the ocean bed. Forty-eight hours later, more pings were heard by *Ocean Shield*. One detection lasted for roughly five minutes thirty-two seconds, and another for seven minutes. In total, *Ocean Shield* heard something on four occasions. But was it the pingers from the beacons?

Houston came close to saying yes in his press conference on April 9. He told us that the first two signals had been analyzed by the Australian Joint Acoustic Analysis Centre, what he called the Australian defense forces "centre of excellence for acoustic analysis."

> The analysis determined that a very stable, distinct, and clear signal was detected at 33.331 kilohertz and that it consistently pulsed at a 1.106 second interval. They, therefore, assess that the transmission was not of natural origin and was likely sourced from specific electronic equipment. They believe the signals to be consistent with the specification and description of a Flight Data Recorder.[13]

This was followed by extremely strong comments from the Australian prime minister Tony Abbott on a visit to China. Abbott had been unduly optimistic before on the question of debris. Now he was even more so:

> We are very confident the signals are from the black box.[14]

Short of saying "yes, we have the physical evidence," this was as close as you could get. It is not surprising everyone believed that *Ocean Shield* had managed to hear the black boxes pinging in the nick of time—before the batteries finally died.

There were, however, several problems with these pings, the most serious of which was the frequency with which they were transmitting. Dukane Underwater Locators transmit at 37.5 kHz, whereas these pings had been registered at 33.31 kHz. Since the frequency was different, did this mean that the searchers had heard something else? An intense debate began on whether the signal from the recorders could degrade to that level and, if so, what would cause it to happen. On CNN we interviewed numerous experts, including Anish Patel, the CEO of Dukane, all of whom agreed it was possible for the ping locator signal to degrade because of the battery's age, damage, depth, or time in the water. There was much discussion of the possible effects that aging batteries, depth and temperature of water, even the heavy silt of the ocean floor could have on the frequency. Angus Houston specifically addressed this at a press conference with the Australian defense minister:

> The advice from the manufacturer is that 33 kilohertz—or
> 33.2 kilohertz—is quite credible. The Air France battery
> from 5 years ago was 34 kilohertz.[15] So what happens,

Fariq Hamid and me in the cockpit of MH9185 sixteen days before he flew MH370. The picture was discovered on his social media pages and flashed around the world. I have spent hours wondering if, during our meeting, I missed anything in what he said or how he behaved.

First Officer Fariq Hamid landing MH9185 from Hong Kong to Kuala Lumpur, sixteen days before he was the copilot on MH370. This was one of his first times flying a 777. His landing was described by the captain as "textbook perfect."

© Cable News Network, Inc. A Time Warner Company. All Rights Reserved.

The international-arrivals board at the Beijing airport on March 8, 2014. It displays flight MH370 from Kuala Lumpur as "delayed" while relatives arrive to meet passengers from the flight. At the time, no one knew that the plane was still in the air and would continue flying for at least another hour.

Mark Ralston/AFP/Getty Images

Me appearing on *Anderson Cooper 360°* on March 7, 2014. It was the first broadcast I made on MH370, when we were getting the initial reports that the plane was missing. My aim in these early broadcasts was to give the few facts we knew, without speculating too much.

© *Cable News Network, Inc. A Time Warner Company. All Rights Reserved.*

Chinese schoolchildren hold a candlelight vigil for those on board MH370, two days after the plane went missing. It took place while Chinese authorities were saying the Malaysian government had to "step up" its efforts to find the missing aircraft.

Imaginechina via AP Images

Dato' Sri Azharuddin Abdul Rahman, director general of the Department of Civil Aviation Malaysia, and me. He is responsible for overseeing the official Annex 13 air investigation into MH370. He has no regrets over his "Balotelli" comments, which he says were misunderstood.

Courtesy of Richard Quest

Malaysian police hold up pictures of two Iranian men who traveled on MH370 using stolen passports. Pouria Nour Mohammad Mehrdad, aged nineteen, and Delavar Seyed Mohammad Reza, aged twenty-nine, flew from Iran to Malaysia and were now going on to Beijing and then Europe. Initial concerns that they were terrorists have been discounted by Interpol. They are not believed to have been involved in the disappearance of the plane.

Imaginechina via AP Images

Royal Australian Air Force sergeant Chris Platt looks out of an observation window from an AP-3C Orion patrol aircraft searching for floating wreckage from MH370 in March 2014. At the height of the search, ships and planes from twenty-five countries were involved in the hunt for debris from the plane.

Australian Government Department of Defence

MILITARY RADAR PLOT FROM PULAU PERAK TO LAST PLOT AT 02:22H

TIME - 02:22H
295R 200 nm from
Butterworth AB

PENANG

A military radar plot of MH370, showing the blips of the aircraft as it was tracked across Malaysia and out into the Strait of Malacca. The graphic was shown to the Chinese relatives at the Lido Hotel in Beijing in March 2014. It is the only formal evidence from the tracking of MH370 as it crossed the Strait of Malacca.

Kim Kyung Hoon/Reuters Pictures

Right: Launch of the Atlas IIA rocket carrying the Inmarsat 3-F1 satellite in April 1996. The satellite would sit over the Indian Ocean. It was with this satellite that MH370 performed seven "handshakes," which generated the data for the entire search operation.

Courtesy of Lockheed Martin Corporation

Below: Map showing the vast northern and southern corridors established March 15, 2014, following the discovery of the Inmarsat handshakes. The northern corridor was abandoned nine days later.

© Cable News Network, Inc.
A Time Warner Company. All Rights Reserved.

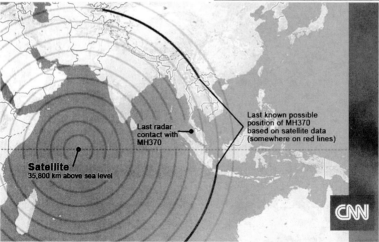

Last radar
contact with
MH370

Last known possible
position of MH370
based on satellite data
(somewhere on red lines)

Satellite
35,800 km above sea level

CNN

"It is therefore with deep sadness and regret that I must inform you that . . . flight MH370 ended in the southern Indian Ocean." Malaysia's prime minister, Najib Razak (second left), makes the sad announcement sixteen days after the plane went missing. Far left is Azharuddin Abdul Rahman, director general of the Department of Civil Aviation Malaysia; second right is Hishammuddin Hussein, acting transport minister. *Imaginechina via AP Images*

An anguished relative in Beijing collapses after hearing the Malaysian prime minister confirm on March 24, 2014, that the plane went down in the southern Indian Ocean. The treatment of the families is widely regarded as one of the poorest features in the handling of the MH370 crisis.

ChinaFotoPress/Getty Images

Chinese relatives march through Beijing to the Malaysian embassy on March 25, 2014, to protest against the lack of information about the search for MH370 and the whereabouts of their loved ones.

Lintao Zhang/Getty Images

Najib Razak, prime minister of Malaysia, giving me an exclusive interview during my assignment to Kuala Lumpur in April 2014. Despite being pushed, he refused to say that those on board the plane had perished.   © Cable News Network, Inc. A Time Warner Company. All Rights Reserved.

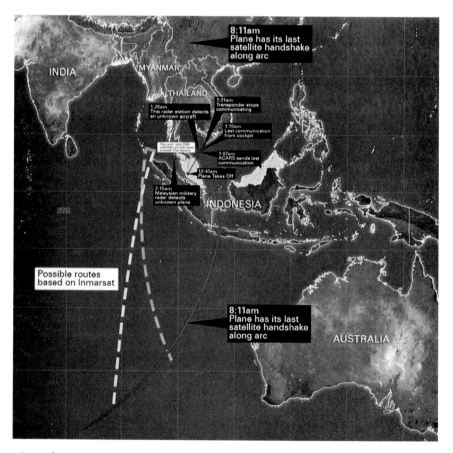

Timeline of crucial events in the moments after MH370 went missing. Huge amounts of time were spent at CNN refining the timeline to ensure accuracy.

© Cable News Network, Inc. A Time Warner Company. All Rights Reserved.

Listening for the pings. Australian defense vessel *Ocean Shield* at work in the southern Indian Ocean while a Royal Australian Air Force AP-3C Orion flies past dropping sonar buoys to assist in the search for MH370 in April 2014. They are hoping to hear the pings from the underwater locator beacons on the aircraft's black boxes.

Australian Government Department of Defence

A Chinese searcher from the *Haixun 01*, the vessel that claimed to have heard pings from the black boxes of MH370. The picture shows the rudimentary detection equipment that was used and gave people cause to doubt the results and findings. No one believed the attempt to search this way was credible. *AP Photo/CCTV via AP Video*

The Towed Pinger Locator on board *Ocean Shield*. The TPL was launched from the back of *Ocean Shield* to try to hear the pings from the plane's black boxes. Despite many days of searching, only false readings were ever received, and the TPL was abandoned in favor of an underwater search.

Australian Government Department of Defence

It's time to go underwater. The Bluefin-21 autonomous underwater vehicle is craned off the deck of *Ocean Shield* as it begins another five-thousand-meter voyage to the bottom of the southern Indian Ocean to look for wreckage from MH370. Weeks of searching revealed nothing in the most likely search zone, and eventually it was abandoned.

Australian Government Department of Defence

Air Chief Marshal Angus Houston (ret.) holds a map showing the search areas for MH370 after announcing that *Ocean Shield* twice detected signals in the past twenty-four hours that he says are consistent with aircraft black boxes. The signals are never heard again, and the conclusion is reached that they were false. So far, no reason has been given for the mistake.

Paul Kane/Getty Images

Ocean Shield, the main ship deployed with the Towed Pinger Locator and Bluefin-21, departs Fleet Base West to return to the search for the missing Malaysia Airlines flight MH370.

Australian Government Department of Defence

Me appearing with Chris Cuomo on CNN's *New Day*. The show built a massive floor map so we could demonstrate the latest search positions and developments. Chris constantly asks me, "Will the plane be found?" I still believe, "Yes."

© *Cable News Network, Inc. A Time Warner Company. All Rights Reserved.*

I'm answering viewers on the CNN Special Report "The Mystery of Flight 370" with Don Lemon when a viewer raises the question of black holes and psychics. This was one of the most controversial parts of CNN's coverage.

© *Cable News Network, Inc. A Time Warner Company. All Rights Reserved.*

Two prime ministers at the center of the search for MH370. Malaysia's prime minister, Najib Razak, says good-bye to Australia's prime minister, Tony Abbott, at the end of his visit in April 2014. Razak has been visiting Perth to see the MH370 search operation headquarters and to thank Australia for its support.

AP Photo/Paul Kane, Pool

Me with the Malaysian prime minister, Najib Razak, after our interview. Mr. Razak describes the loss of MH370 as "unprecedented" and says any weaknesses in Malaysia's performance will be investigated and published.

Courtesy of Richard Quest

Surveys of the ocean bed are called "bathymetric." This one shows the area around the seventh arc, the location believed most likely to be where the plane went down. The map reveals undersea mountains and valleys that have to be navigated during the search in the area known as Broken Ridge. The bathymetric study was conducted by the ATSB.   *ATSB*

A map of the seventh arc showing the ocean being searched, from June 2014. The zones are classified as priority search, medium search, and wide search areas. This map reflects the initial search area of twenty-three thousand square miles.   *ATSB*

The aft view of sea conditions from the *Fugro Discovery*, one of the four ships engaged in the detailed ocean-bed search for MH370. The long, deep underwater search begins in October 2014.
ATSB/ABIS Chris Beerens, RAN

Above: Brutal sea conditions experienced by the *Fugro Discovery* during the winter months. Frequently, searching is suspended because of high winds and rough seas.
ATSB/ABIS Chris Beerens, RAN

Left: Nighttime view from the stern of the *Fugro Discovery* as she sails across the southern Indian Ocean. Day or night, if the crew is able, the searching never stops.
ATSB/Chris Beerens, RAN

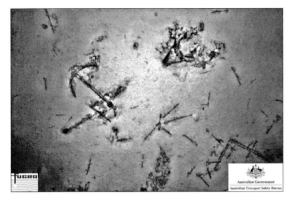

Previously unknown debris from a wooden shipwreck discovered on the seafloor during the search for MH370. This photograph was used by the authorities to demonstrate that the searching techniques and equipment were sophisticated enough to find small items, such as the anchor, on the seabed.

ATSB/Fugro

Above: The search area around the seventh arc was extended in 2015 to cover 70,000 square miles (120,000 kilometers). If nothing is found here, then the tripartite group of Malaysia, China, and Australia has said the search won't be extended any farther in the absence of new data. It is what the families fear: the search for MH370 will be over for now.

ATSB

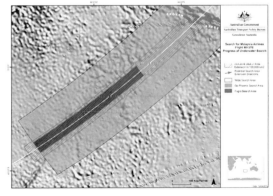

Right: A more detailed map showing the new, larger 70,000-mile search zone and how it is divided between Go Phoenix and Fugro companies.

ATSB

Sarah Bajc and I meet during my visit to Kuala Lumpur in April 2015. Sarah lost her partner, Philip Wood, who was a passenger on MH370. She has been one of the leading family members critical of the way the investigation has been conducted. Sarah is convinced someone is covering up something.

Courtesy of Richard Quest

Datuk Seri Hishammuddin Hussein, defense minister of Malaysia and, at the time of MH370's disappearance, also acting transport minister. Hishammuddin led Malaysia's response and was the public face of the crisis as he held the daily press conference. Criticized for how he responded to the crisis, the minister believes, "History will judge us well."

Courtesy of Richard Quest

French police remove the flaperon that washed up on Reunion Island more than sixteen months after MH370 went missing. It took more than six weeks before the authorities were able to say with "certainty" that this piece of wing had come from MH370. So far, it is the only confirmed piece of wreckage from MH370 to be found.   *AP Photo/Lucas Marie*

A sign at the Department of Civil Aviation headquarters in Putrajaya guiding people to the operation room for MH370/MH17. A sobering reminder of the twin tragedies afflicting Malaysia Airlines.

Courtesy of Richard Quest

KLIA—Kuala Lumpur International Airport. The human-sized distinctive sign stands outside the terminal building and is a popular spot to have one's photograph taken. *Courtesy of Richard Quest*

A Malaysia Airlines poster at KLIA: "On this journey of life, we're all travellers looking to make that great trip with someone." Since the tragedies of MH370 and MH17, Malaysia Airlines has gotten a new CEO and has been nationalized by the state and undergone a complete restructuring. *Courtesy of Richard Quest*

Left: A 2015 departure board at Kuala Lumpur International Airport. Missing is any reference to Malaysia Airline's late-night flight to Beijing. Having initially renamed MH370 as MH318, the airline ended the flight on May 1 because of commercial pressures.

Courtesy of Richard Quest

Below: A sand sculpture created at Puri Beach, on March 25, 2014, by Indian sand artist Sudarsan Pattnaik as a tribute to the passengers of Malaysia Airlines flight MH370.

Asit Kumar/AFP/Getty Images

there's a change . . . with the pressure on the ocean floor and the age of the particular batteries, the capacitance can change and you get changes in the transmission level.[16]

There were some who did not believe that this was the pinger. Jeff Wise, one of CNN's aviation analysts, went out on a limb and said, "I feel there's a lot of problems with this data."[17] He stated categorically that he didn't think it was the pinger. He believed the distance between *Ocean Shield*'s detections was too far, that the detections, once acquired, should have been held longer, and ultimately the frequency was wrong. Jeff was proved right. It became clear that the sounds that had led to so much hope and confidence did not come from the black boxes. Exactly what those noises were has never been properly determined. The Australian Transport Safety Report just says:

A review of the *Ocean Shield* acoustic signals was undertaken independently by various specialists. The analyses determined that the signals recorded were not consistent with the nominal performance standards of the Dukane DK100 underwater acoustic beacon. The analyses also noted that whilst unlikely, the acoustic signals could be consistent with a damaged ULB.[18]

To this day we have never learned what those pings or noises were. We know *Ocean Shield* was operating in total silence mode. It is a sad anticlimax to a chapter of the story that had showed such huge promise at the time.

I asked the commissioner of Australia's ATSB, Martin Dolan, what he thought of the ping escapade and where he thought things had gone wrong. He told me:

We have given a lot of attention to that. The two most likely
possibilities are actual interference on the pinger locator
equipment or another source of signals; ultrasonic devices
are used to track marine mammals and fish.

One year after the plane went missing, the release of the Factual
Report dropped another bombshell in regard to pingers.[19] It revealed
that the battery on the ULB attached to the flight data recorder had
actually expired fifteen months before the crash, and there was no
record that it had been replaced. Malaysia Airlines' engineering people
had failed to enter the current battery into its engineering computer,
so the system gave no warning in 2012 when it was time to be replaced.
All this despite the CEO of the company saying, "We can confirm
there is a maintenance program. Batteries are replaced prior to expi-
ration."[20] In the case of the battery on MH370's recorder, that was not
so. We don't, and probably never will, know what effect the age and
ineffectiveness of the battery had on the transmission ability of the
pinger. Opinion suggests it would have seriously degraded the battery's
performance, which would have shortened the thirty-day guaranteed
transmission time.

In thinking about the pings and the pingers, I have been left wondering about whether the media's unrealistic expectations actually created the situation. After all, the search was in the deepest of oceans in
the remotest part of the world, and the searchers weren't even sure they
were in the right place. Were we to blame for the fact that everyone
believed they were hearing the pings from the black boxes? No, I don't
think so. A review of Houston, Abbott, and the various experts' opin-
ions indicate they clearly believed these were pings from the underwater locator beacons. Although they qualified their comments, they still
left us with the impression that they were hearing the right noises.

Unlike others, I don't blame them for this. They had set as their goal absolute transparency. If they had followed the policy of the Malaysians and not revealed details until they were absolutely confirmed, they would have been rightly criticized. When they did release information, we chose to hear only what we wanted to hear, and ignored any warnings otherwise.

Whatever *Ocean Shield* heard, it was never heard again. Finally, on day thirty-eight, with everyone in agreement that the pinger batteries would by now have finally died, Angus Houston announced the next phase of the search.

We haven't had a single detection in six days.[21]

It was time to launch Bluefin-21.

CHAPTER SEVEN

SEARCHING DEEP

I guess it's time to go underwater.

—Angus Houston

When *Ocean Shield* set sail from Perth to begin her search using the TPL, the towed pinger locator, she also carried equipment that would help in a deeper underwater operation. On board was an AUV—an Autonomous Underwater Vehicle—called Bluefin-21. The towfish used until now had always remained tethered to the ship, whereas Bluefin-21 could swim, unattached, to the bottom of the ocean, guided by remote control. This extremely expensive, torpedo-shaped machine contained side-scanning sonar that generated a highly detailed picture of the ocean bed, hopefully picking up signs of any aircraft debris as it did so. Bluefin-21 was owned by Phoenix International, a company that works for the shipping and oil and gas industries and has a contract with the US Navy for search and recovery operations. It was the US Navy that instructed Phoenix to send Bluefin-21 to Australia, following a plea from Malaysia's minister in charge. Hishammuddin Hussein recalled the conversation he had with the US Defense Secretary, Chuck Hagel, when he asked if he could borrow Bluefin-21:

> I called him up. I said, "Secretary Hagel, you know we need this side-scan sonar to do this search." And he said, "I don't know what it is." And I said, "To be honest, sir, I don't know what it is that I'm asking for." The amazing thing [that] happened is that, without even calling me back, within two days the Bluefin 21 was on its way to Australia.[1]

Bluefin-21 is described by its manufacturer as "an efficient workhorse able to execute surveys with demanding requirements."[2] Few would disagree that the environment and circumstances in the southern Indian Ocean where it was now being sent met that definition. Unlike the towed pinger locator used so far, Bluefin-21 could roam above the ocean bed, untethered from the ship above, on a preprogrammed course guided by GPS. The device used side-scan sonar to sweep the ocean floor, creating a digital picture of any wreckage from the plane that might be there. The primary search area was more than a thousand miles from the Australian coast and the waters were, in parts, more than 15,000 feet deep. In fact the depths were greater than the safe operating limits of Bluefin-21, which has an operating limit of 14,700 feet. This would prove to be a problem in the early dives.

Also, very little was known about the floor in this part of the ocean. Previous surveys, done years before, had been scant. In short, if you were going to suggest one of the most inhospitable places in the world to do a detailed underwater search, you'd be hard-pressed to find a much worse spot.

. . .

The first job was to determine where exactly to deploy Bluefin-21. It was not easy: there was no floating debris to prove they were in the right place, and *Ocean Shield* had not heard any more pings from deep down since early April. So once again, the authorities did their best to make the most logical decision about where to begin. First, the location: on the seventh arc underneath the last Inmarsat handshake, where it was believed the plane had run out of fuel. This was also the place where *Ocean Shield* had "received transmissions from the deep," as Angus Houston called the series of erroneous pings believed to be from the beacons.[3] A combination of handshakes and pings all led the search team to this spot.

Using Bluefin-21 was a time-consuming business. Each full search cycle would take about twenty-four hours: two hours to deploy to the bottom of the ocean; sixteen hours of searching; another two to get the device to the surface and back on the ship; and then up to four hours to download the data from the recorders and begin the analysis. It was slow. The AUV would trawl above the ocean bed at a walking pace of two to three miles an hour. This meant only fifteen to twenty square miles a day would be covered: literally a drop in the ocean. Luckily the area that they were searching, part of the Broken Ridge Plateau, while deep, was known to be relatively flat. They would not have to worry about Bluefin-21 hitting underwater mountains or being lost in deep valleys. Those problems would be saved for later.

Watching and covering all of this, once again I was thrown into a world about which I had little or no knowledge; certainly nothing about the operation of these machines and the dangers involved in using them. Of course, we had experts like David Gallo, who was involved in finding Air France 447 in the South Atlantic and who guided us through these issues superbly. Even with these experts, however, the lion's share of the coverage is always the responsibility of the staff correspondent, who is a trained journalist and who has the task of pulling it all together and doing an elegant job of "on the one hand, and on the other hand." I frequently think this is the least understood part of the staff correspondent's job, sometimes even by my newsroom colleagues. Staff correspondents are not assumed to be instant experts on every subject. Our job is to take the facts, as they appear at that moment, turn them into digestible bites, and leave the viewer with a real feeling for what is happening and why it is important.

On April 15, Mission One began, as Bluefin-21 was lowered into the water and quickly ran into problems. The depth of the water in places was greater than the AUV's safe operating limit of 14,700 feet. After completing only six hours of searching, the built-in safety features activated and the machine returned to the surface. Since the waters around this area were roughly fifteen thousand feet deep, Bluefin-21 would be pretty useless if it kept bobbing back to the surface every time it reached 14,700. Yet the device was all they had, the only machine available on short notice. As the Australian prime minister Tony Abbott later said: "You do the best you've got with the equipment that you've got."[4] Finding a more suitable submersible and getting it delivered would involve tremendous delay, so it was necessary to see if Bluefin-21 could operate successfully at these greater depths. Advice was sought from the manufacturers, and on April 17, the Australians said:

> Phoenix International have assessed that there is a small but acceptable risk in operating the vehicle in depths in excess of 4500 [meters].

It was a relief to everyone. The machine's settings were adjusted and would now allow for searching across the area under investigation.

What were we doing at CNN during all of this? Examining every nook and cranny of the entire operation. We had brought in experts in all sorts of fields; we had even launched manned submersibles in the waters off western Canada, where my colleague Martin Savidge had swapped the cockpit of a 777 for hours underwater in cramped conditions. In order to explain the logistics, for the morning show *New Day* we created giant floor maps and large-scale graphics. No matter how hard we tried, we were still scrambling around with the same few facts we had learned weeks ago. Essentially, there was no new information with which to work. As *Ocean Shield* and Bluefin-21 got to work, the twelve-hour time difference between Australia and New York meant that we in New York were getting the results of that day's searching just as *New Day* was going to air; sometimes, if there were delays in the analysis, we wouldn't receive the results until evening, in time for the prime-time shows. When the results were announced, the press release always carried the same sentence: "Data analyses from the mission did not provide any contacts of interest."

With each passing day, the area remaining to be searched by Bluefin-21 was getting smaller and smaller. By the end of April, the search of the most promising 120-square-mile zone had finished and nothing had been found. Bluefin-21 then spent several days tidying up and searching the surrounding areas, just in case. In all, there had been more than eighteen missions, yet nothing was found. Finally, on May 29, all that was left to do was bring the whole *Ocean Shield* operation to a close with this disheartening announcement:

> The Australian Transport Safety Bureau has advised that
> the search in the vicinity of the acoustic detections can

now be considered complete and in its professional judge-
ment the area can now be discounted as the final resting
place of MH370.[5]

To say it was disappointing is a huge understatement. For a society
brought up with disaster movies that always have at least a conclusion,
if not a happy ending, this was bleakly frustrating. There was no result.
No conclusion. No closure. Naively perhaps, many of us had thought
that once the right piece of equipment went underwater, parts of the
plane would be located. Even though that would not be the answer the
families wanted, it would at least have brought about the closure they
needed.

Nor had things been any easier or more successful in the air. For
weeks, even while Bluefin-21 was searching under the waves, planes and
ships were still flying out from Perth, looking for any signs of debris.
This was truly a fruitless and thankless task. By April 28, with the
underwater search coming to an end, the Australians decided it was also
time to put a stop to the air and surface search. At a press conference,
Australian Prime Minister Tony Abbott recognized the inevitable:

> By this stage, 52 days into the search most material would
> have become water logged and sunk . . . and with the dis-
> tances involved all of the aircraft are operating at close to
> the limit of sensible and safe operation . . . Therefore we
> are moving from the current phase to a phase which is
> focused on searching the ocean floor over a much larger
> area.[6]

This was the moment everyone, most of all the families, had been
dreading. All avenues of searching had led nowhere. There was

nothing seen from the air and nothing had been discovered on the ocean floor. Worse, the most likely resting place, the spot where the (false) pings had been heard, had been discounted. All that was left to do was bring home the ships and decide what to do next.

Deciding on the direction of the search would require much thought and discussion. Since the discovery of the turn-back and the Inmarsat handshakes, there had been no new leads. The experts had certainly refined the existing information, making it more accurate, but there was no new data to work with, no new direction to follow. The search was still essentially based on the turn-back at 1:25, the military radar traces up to 2:22 on the night of the disappearance, and the seven Inmarsat handshakes, along with a couple of unanswered satellite phone calls. This information had been parsed a million ways, using many different models of aircraft performance to determine where the plane finally ended up. There was still much confidence in the seven arcs, but the bedeviling issue with them was where—along or to the side of that seventh arc—the plane had foundered.

The three countries with the most at stake met to decide what to do next. Malaysia bore the legal responsibility for the investigation, China had the largest number of its citizens as passengers, and Australia was the likely crash site, located as it was in the international search and rescue zone. At the press conference after this meeting, the talk was all about entering a "new phase," involving a detailed, slower underwater search over a much larger area. Prime Minister Abbott laid out the size of the issues:

> Essentially . . . what we are looking to do is conduct as thorough an undersea search as is humanly possible, if necessary, of the entire probable impact zone which . . . is roughly 700 kilometres by 80 kilometres.[7]

This is almost twenty-three thousand square miles, roughly the size of West Virginia. The authorities were now planning to do what they had hoped would not be necessary: start searching the entire area where the seventh handshake had occurred. It would be a deep-water search, which would be painfully slow and take many months to complete. Unlike Broken Ridge, where Bluefin-21 had searched, this part of the ocean floor was not flat and full of silt. Here there were large mountains and deep valleys and ravines. To make matters worse, there was very little knowledge of exactly what was down below.

The three countries formed a tripartite group to decide on the way forward. It was obvious that the extreme urgency of the earlier search was past. Angus Houston's Joint Agency Coordination Centre was being relocated from Perth to the Australian capital, though operationally it would remain in western Australia. Everything now would require more in-depth study, and more experts would be needed. The review would now take place out of the glare of publicity that had characterized the efforts of the previous seven weeks. The fear of the families was, of course, that the tripartite group was finding the whole thing too expensive and troublesome and was planning to wind down the search. Warren Truss, the Australian deputy prime minister, went to some lengths to scotch that idea, saying "we have committed ourselves to an ongoing, continuous effort."[8] But what did this actually mean?

Until now, everything had been done in a hurry. From the futile searches in the South China Sea, to the huge air operation off the coast of Australia, to the most recent undersea search by Bluefin-21 . . . it was all driven by the thirty-day deadline of the pinger batteries. Now that time imperative was past. With the passage of weeks, the chance of discovering any debris floating on the surface had become virtually nonexistent and the batteries on the pingers were long since dead.

Those responsible for the search could take stock, refine the data they had, and, hopefully, come up with new ideas on the best place to search. This would involve the International Working Group of satellite and computer experts based in Kuala Lumpur, who were still refining the Inmarsat handshakes.

So a new phase of the search operation began, one that would be based on longer, slower searches over much greater distances. There had never been any doubt that the seventh arc was the place to begin searching, but where along that arc continued to be an unknown. The general trend in thinking was changing, moving the search zone farther south within the primary search zone. The reinterpretation of the Inmarsat handshakes and satellite calls pointed to 9M-MRO having made the turn south sooner after passing Indonesia, to its having been traveling marginally faster when it was flying between Malaysia and Indonesia. Interestingly, the new search area was moving toward the zone that an independent group of experts had for months been advocating as the most likely crash site.

There was also the question of which type of search vehicle to use and what was available. These sophisticated vehicles are always in demand by industries from oil and gas to shipping and telecom, which use them for repair and monitoring undersea cables. Bluefin-21 had been fine for that first urgent undersea search, but overall it was probably not the right machine for a more detailed search over a much larger area. Bluefin-21 took too long, with each search cycle taking twenty-four hours from launch to recovery and data analysis. It was not financially sensible to do this over twenty-three thousand square miles (remember, the original undersea search had been only a couple of hundred square miles). Instead of an AUV (autonomous underwater vehicle), the preference was to go back to a towfish contraption run on a cable off the back of a ship. An ROV (remote operated vehicle) tethered to the back of a ship, would be able to search for much longer periods of time, constantly sending data along the cable back to the ship. Any time lost winding up the cable when the ship had to be turned would be offset by longer periods of searching and much greater control.

Once it was decided where and how to search, one very important question had to be answered: What was the ocean bed like where they were searching? If you are about to send down a machine, tethered to a ship, to roam a few hundred feet above the bed, you had better know the lay of the land to prevent the craft from getting lost in deep-sea ravines and valleys or snagged and caught up in mountains. This part of the southern Indian Ocean had barely been surveyed. With the earlier searches there simply wasn't the time to undertake such efforts. Now time was no longer of the essence, so the first order of the day was to undertake a bathymetric survey, as a study of the ocean bed is known. This is done with ships that have multibeam sonar mounted on their hull. The sonar sends out sound waves that bounce off the seafloor. The ship picks up the return signal and a picture of the seabed is created. The ship then goes back and covers the area in overlapping lines, to make sure it has captured the ground immediately underneath the ship itself. It was estimated to take three to four months to complete a bathymetric study around the seventh arc, the area deemed the most likely place where the plane crashed into the water.

Surveying began almost immediately with the arrival of the Chinese ship *Zhu*. The data it received was sent to Australia, where Geoscience Australia, the country's ocean experts, drew up a picture of the seabed. Now the operation was no longer looking for the plane itself; the searchers just needed to know what they were dealing with at the bottom of the ocean. What they discovered emphasized the difficulties of the task ahead. In an online video, Geoscience Australia described the surveyed terrain as including "large mountains and deep trenches some of which plunged more than 6000m [20,000 feet] below sea level, along with the mountain ridges, which measure 34 kilometers long [15 miles]."[9]

As the bathymetric survey was being completed, the Australian and Malaysian governments put out tenders for commercial companies to bid for the work of doing the actual searching. This would involve many primary and subcontractors. For instance, three Malaysian companies—Petronas, Boustead, and Detec—provided the high-tech sonar equipment for the search.[10] In August, the contract for the search itself was awarded to Fugro Survey Pty Ltd. Also contracted was Phoenix, which had been responsible for the earlier Bluefin-21 search. The ships being sent were the *Fugro Equator* and the *Fugro Discovery* along with the *Go Phoenix*. These were later joined by the *Fugro Supporter*. By September, the experts had a pretty good idea of what the ocean bed looked like. Enough research and bathymetric work had been done to allow the ships to start their real mission: the deep underwater work. On October 6, 2014, around five months after *Ocean Shield* terminated its search, *Go Phoenix* launched a towfish and began phase three of the deep-sea search, an operation that would take at least a year to complete.

For those on board the ships, the endeavor was and remains hard going. Sailing to the search zone from Australia takes about six days. Once there, the crew works twelve-hour shifts launching the towfish sonar on ten thousand feet of cable to the bottom of the ocean. The towfish sonar passes over the terrain about a hundred meters above the bed, carefully following the contours of the rough landscape that the bathymetric survey has revealed. The data from the sonar and cameras is sent back to the ship via an armored fiber-optic cable, as thin as a human hair. The ships maneuver up and down, along preplanned grids, "mowing the ocean" until an image has been created to one-meter resolution. Such detail is fine enough to see any debris that might be from the aircraft.[11]

For months the ships have been mowing the ocean, identifying anything picked up by the sonar. There are three categories being used: the lowest is Category 3, for those contacts that are of some interest, because they stand out from the surrounding area. Category 3 contacts have a low probability of becoming significant to the search. Next up is Category 2. These objects are of more interest but still unlikely to be significant. The highest is Category 1, for sonar contacts of high interest that warrant immediate further investigation. By March 2015, there were dozens of objects that were either Category 2 or 3, but nothing had been rated Category 1.[12]

In May 2015, there was a good example of how this system works in practice. *Fugro Equator* detected a cluster of small sonar contacts just twelve nautical miles to the east of the seventh arc: a prime area where debris from the plane could be. It was classed as Category 2, unlikely but worth another look, so they sent down a self-propelled AUV (autonomous underwater vehicle). They couldn't be sure what they were seeing, so several more AUV passes were made just above the surface. Surprisingly, it turned out to be a previously uncharted wreck of a wooden ship, recognizable by the anchor.[13] While it was disappointing that it wasn't the plane, the discovery did prove the searching protocols were robust enough to find something as large (or small) as pieces of an aircraft.

The sense of hopelessness that arose because nothing from MH370 had been found gave rise to a raft of criticism about the way the search was being carried out, and about those doing the searching. In late May 2015, three of the bidders who didn't get contracts for the phase three search went public with their concern. Essentially they believe that Fugro doesn't have either the experience or the correct equipment for such a difficult underwater search. According to a statement published in newspapers: "Fugro is a big company but they don't have any experience in this kind of search and it's really a very specialized job," said Paul-Henry Nargeolet,[14] who was involved in the search for AF447. "I have serious concerns that the MH370 search operation may not be able to convincingly demonstrate that 100 percent seafloor coverage is being achieved," said Mike Williamson, founder and president of Williamson & Associates.[15]

It is almost impossible for the victims' families to know what to make of these criticisms. On the one hand, the Australians continue to say they have total confidence that the entire area is being properly and thoroughly searched. On the other, you have these companies raising fundamental doubts about the competency of those involved.

I asked David Gallo how he responded to these criticisms based on his experience locating AF447. He said the remarks were "very similar to what I went through after our first 2 month search looking for AF447." Some critics complain about everything in deep-sea searching. Gallo reviewed much of the data from the MH370 searches and concluded:

> I'm impressed with the systems and with the operations plan. Now is not the time to quit. After our 2 months of nothing we spent months reviewing everything and fought to go back out. We were granted that permission and found the aircraft in 7 days. If the needle is in the haystack, they'll find it. To me that is the biggest issue: Is it there?

Is it there? The fundamental question that hasn't shifted a jot from day one of the search.

At the time of this book's writing, in the autumn of 2015, the searching had settled into a routine. The ships mow the ocean for several weeks, then head to Australian ports for resupply, after which they return to duty. With more than half of the original twenty-three thousand square miles searched, the concern has become what happens if nothing is ever found. Not unrealistically, the relatives feared the search would be called off. On April 16, 2015, the tripartite group of Malaysia, Australia, and China announced:

> Should the aircraft not be found within the current search area, ministers agreed to extend the search by an additional 60,000 square kilometers [23,000 square miles] to bring the search area to 120,000 square kilometers.[16]

The new, larger area is still based along and around the seventh arc. It marginally extends the search zone to the left and right of the seventh arc and at the southern end. The biggest change is a dramatic increase in the amount of ocean to be searched to the north, meaning the plane had not flown as far as they thought before running out of fuel.

By the end of May 2015, winter conditions in the southern hemisphere were worsening. Some vessels, such as *Fugro Supporter*, along with the AUV she carried, had already been released from assignment. The AUV remains in storage in Freemantle, Australia, in case it is needed to search inaccessible places or verify finds. Other vessels, such as *Go Phoenix*, have also been demobilized. During the worst winter weather, the searching is confined to the southernmost areas, where the weather is marginally better.

As the searching has become a smaller operation, the organizers have felt the need to reassure the relatives of the missing that they are still committed to finding MH370. The update release on May 20 includes the following:

Our work will continue to be thorough and methodical, so sometimes weekly progress may seem slow. Please be assured that work is continuing and is aimed at finding MH370 as quickly as possible.[17]

The fear of the families remains that the commitment to find the plane has dwindled both because of increasing costs and because of the difficulties the search team has encountered.

The unspoken question has always been, what happens after this larger 46,000-square-mile area has been searched, if no aircraft is found. Even the governments were asking themselves how much longer they could continue spending the money on the search for the missing airplane when it seemed like there was nothing left to find.

The answer came in June 2015 in a depressing statement from the tripartite group. Without fuss or fanfare, they simply announced:

In the absence of credible new information that leads to the identification of a specific location of the aircraft, Governments have agreed that there will be no further expansion of the search area.[18]

These are exactly the words the families dreaded hearing. The current forty-six thousand square miles of search area contain their last vestiges of hope. If the plane is not found in this area, then the search will be over for the time being.

Until now, the question of who is paying for all this searching has not really been an issue. During phase one of the search, just after the plane went missing, international regulations say that costs are paid by the various countries in their own area. Everyone looks after their own costs. That's the way international search and rescue works.

Once the search became more focused on the southern Indian Ocean, an agreement to share costs was reached by the Malaysians, as "the state of operator and registry," and Australia, as "the probable state of occurrence," in whose flight information region it has happened. It has not been publicly stated if the Chinese government has also contributed to the ongoing costs.

The search for MH370 has been the costliest of its kind. Even allowing for the fact many of the resources deployed are defense and military assets and are already paid for, the bill for external search companies and extra costs like fuel still amounts to well over $60 million. The Australian government has been making regular provisions in its budget to cover those expenses, and they have been just about matched by the Malaysians. Such costs, albeit high, need to be put into a proper context. Boeing currently quotes the 777-200 list price around $269 million (although the 200 is not really bought anymore, airlines preferring the larger, more efficient 300 model, which costs $339 million). It may be cruel to put it in such terms, but the current search costs are less than half the price of a new aircraft.

As the costs of the search mounted, it was not surprising that government officials were asked if the plane's manufacturer, Boeing, or the engine manufacturer, Rolls-Royce, should contribute. According to the Australian deputy prime minister, Warren Truss, the answer is yes.

> They have a vested interest in understanding what happened on MH370 so they can be confident about the quality of their product or take remedial action if there was some part of the aircraft that contributed to this accident. So I think we will be looking for increasing involvement from the manufacturers and their host countries.[19]

In July 2015, I asked Rolls-Royce if they had been requested to contribute to the cost of the search, and the company told me, "We have not been asked and have not contributed." Since an engine maker has never before been asked to contribute to search costs, they don't expect to be asked.

The work to refine and narrow down the primary search zone has continued even as the deep-sea search is under way. In 2015, research was commissioned to reexamine the Inmarsat data, the performance of the Boeing 777, and meteorological factors that could determine where the plane went down. Results were independently obtained from the Australian Defence Science and Technology Group and Boeing. In the words of the ATSB report published in December 2015, "it is significant that they were in general agreement."[20] Both groups pointed to the southern part of the existing search zone as the most likely place for the plane to have crashed.

The ATSB report also put to rest some of the theories on what happened during the end-of-flight scenario. The ATSB now says that as the fuel began to run out, the right engine would have flamed out first. The left engine would have remained running for up to fifteen more minutes before it too flamed out. Then the plane would have banked and entered a slow, long left turn, which would have increased in speed as the powerless plane fell from the sky. The distance it traveled would have been no more than ten nautical miles from where the engines finally gave out, so the search zone has now been recalibrated to within twenty miles of the seventh arc.[21]

Because the authorities now believe the plane ran out of fuel, theories that one of the pilots did a controlled ditching of the aircraft into the ocean, as suggested by authors like Captain Simon Hardy, have also been discounted. The ATSB report says the Inmarsat data, specifically the last handshake at 08:19, where the plane was logging back onto the satellite system, shows "this evidence is therefore inconsistent with a controlled ditching scenario."[22] Any idea that the pilot tried to land the plane on water must now be dismissed.

As the search moves into its final phases, the authorities say they are committed to finding the plane. Whatever happens, the Malaysians say they won't give up and don't expect the Australians to quit either. But it is tough to see how they can continue searching when they don't have anything new to go on. Once the ATSB have finished this latest search, they will have exhausted the area deemed most probable by the data. To extend it farther would be pointless unless justifications for doing so arise. Of course, there is no shortage of critics who say it was a wild-goose chase from start to finish. Once again, I think this is unfair. If there is one thing that infuriates me when I am covering stories like this, it is listening to armchair quarterbacks with no experience to back up their pronouncements. The hand dealt to Houston and the searchers was far from ideal and they had to do what they could with the information they had.

The unprecedented nature of the plane's disappearance and the issues it has raised mean that even if the physical search stops, the Inmarsat handshakes and other data will continue to be analyzed for years to come, while the searchers wait for the moment when they feel confident to go back out to find the plane.

CHAPTER EIGHT

THE CAUSE: NEFARIOUS

I know what happened to that plane. Everyone here
knows what happened to it. The Americans took it.

—CABDRIVER

I t was late in the afternoon, and I was in Kuala Lumpur doing the final interviews and research for this book. More than a year had passed since MH370 had gone missing, and obviously life in the Malaysian capital had moved on. But if you scratched the surface, people would quickly start talking about the missing plane. Heading back into the city with an hour-long car ride ahead of me, I settled back in the cab, knowing I had plenty of time to listen to the latest theory. The cabdriver, knowing he had a captive audience, warmed to his task.

Theories vary, but basically the story goes something like this: the Americans had been using highly secret drone technology in Afghanistan or Iraq or Turkey or Syria (it doesn't matter which theater of action, they all get mentioned at some point). The command and control software of the drones had fallen into the hands of the Taliban or Hamas, or now ISIS terrorists, who were intent on raising money by selling it to China. To prevent the Americans from finding out and stopping the sale, it was decided to put the device onto a commercial airliner and fly it to Beijing as commercial cargo. MH370 was chosen as the random flight for this purpose. The drone technology was listed on the flight manifest as mangosteen fruit (of which there was a sizable cargo on board). But the Americans discovered what was planned and took action. Since 9/11, all Boeing aircraft have been equipped with top-secret technology that allows the US military to take control of commercial planes and fly them like drones. The planes are controlled from an AWACS aircraft flying above them, or by controllers on the ground.

This system was activated on the highest authority, which for most people usually means the president of the United States, or at the very least the CIA director. Once under US control, MH370 was flown to a hush-hush, remote US military base at Diego Garcia, an atoll in the middle of the Indian Ocean. The island is owned by the British and leased to the US military for fifty years. The two countries jointly run the strategically vital air and naval base, allowing the allies to exercise military power in the Middle East and Southeast Asia. This furtive flight to Diego Garcia explains why there are so many eyewitness accounts of a large plane with markings similar to Malaysia Airlines flying across the Maldives on the night of the disappearance. The islands are just six hundred miles from the US base. Once the plane arrived there, the technology was retrieved and either returned to Washington or destroyed.

As for the passengers and the plane . . . well, here the theories get a bit convoluted. One story states that the passengers were all killed by switching off the oxygen en route to Diego Garcia, then the plane was put back into the air and crashed into the ocean, sinking rapidly because all the doors had been removed. A more basic theory says that the plane was put into a Faraday-style hangar where no signals could be received, and the passengers are still being held hostage on the atoll (from which iPhone photos have been sent out, with metadata showing the location of Diego Garcia—clearly the Faraday isn't working too well).

There are a large number of online proponents of this theory, and if you look at the comments section of those websites championing it, there seem to be no shortage of people who believe it.[1] What surprised me during my visit to KL was the sheer number of people who believe that the US or another government was involved in hijacking MH370. Time and again I was told that one government or another was responsible for taking the plane, killing the passengers, and making off with the technology. Nor is it just the usual conspiracy theorists who believe this—lots of people who are not prone to outrageous views believe that there is much more to the story than meets the eye. If it wasn't the Americans who took the plane to Diego Garcia . . . well, there are numerous variations on this theme: some say it was Captain Zaharie Shah who flew the plane to the atoll, having practiced landing there on his home-constructed simulator (no one ever says why he flew it there, just that he did). Each theory usually adds another layer of conspiracy; for instance, the above scenario is frequently embellished with the idea that the Americans didn't steal the plane, but rather shot it down, as Captain Zaharie flew it toward Diego Garcia, and that attack is what is being covered up. Or that a large number of scientists from a secret US technology company were on board the plane and they were the real target. Yes, it is true, there were twenty employees from the US firm Freescale Semiconductor. The company makes chips for various purposes, including defense. There were numerous suggestions that somehow stealth technology was involved. This time Israel and Iran have been dragged in as possible culprits to join China and the US. In reality no one has so far managed to create a connection to any specific allegation other than the tragedy of so many employees from the same company being killed at once.

For the record, the US has repeatedly denied that the plane flew to Diego Garcia. Former White House press secretary Jay Carney said, "I'll rule that one out," when asked at the regular briefing.[2] Also, in an emailed statement to me, Boeing specifically denied that is has the capability to take control of aircraft.[3]

Having been at the heart of the coverage, I have both relished and dreaded writing this part of the book. Until now, what I have written has been based on statements and known facts. Such facts may be few and far between, and there are frequently disagreements about how to interpret them, but they do have some rational basis. Yet now I must consider the various theories and hypotheses about what happened to the plane, from the straightforward to the outlandish.

In essence, all the theories can be broken down neatly into clear categories: the Nefarious and the Mechanical. Did something go wrong with the aircraft, or did somebody intentionally do something wrong? When I first used "nefarious" on-air, some colleagues raised eyebrows, since it is not a word frequently used these days on television. Most people prefer talking about criminal activities. But in my view, nefarious better describes the entire range of activities about which we are talking. The Oxford dictionaries define "nefarious" as "(typically of an action or activity) wicked or criminal." It is the perfect word to describe the many possible deliberate human actions that could lie at the heart of the missing 777.

It is crucial to add that there is no evidence to support any of these theories. They usually originate with experts, pundits, pilots—

anyone—who has made what they believe are educated guesses. Such people deliver their theories with all but papal authority. Then there are those who have looked for evidence, and found it in some very unusual situations. But—again—anyone who says "this is what happened" is simply offering up their thoughts on the few facts that we have. There is no unequivocal view.

Pretty much from the moment the plane went missing, the main view formed around the idea that the pilots were responsible. This nefarious theory can be neatly summed up in two words—"pilot suicide." It's worth reminding ourselves about Captain Zaharie Shah and First Officer Fariq Hamid. Captain Zaharie was fifty-three years old. He joined Malaysia Airlines in 1981 and had flown a variety of aircraft before being promoted to captain on the 777 fleet in 1998. He had been in that role for fifteen years, and also served as a training and rating captain, which is one reason he had been paired with the inexperienced Fariq Hamid.

Those to whom I spoke at the airline, who had known him for years, attest to his excellent flying skills, his charm and friendliness. He was married, with three children. He had two homes, one near Kuala Lumpur Airport, the other in the city's suburbs. He was a distant relation of the Malaysia opposition leader Anwar Ibrahim. Zaharie was known to have political views and indeed was a supporter of Ibrahim and the opposition party, but no one has ever suggested he was a rabid fantasist. His chief claim to eccentricity was that he had built a flight simulator in his home that he used to practice flying—and he had posted several videos on YouTube, including one explaining how to perform maintenance on air-conditioning units, which he introduced sitting in front of the homemade simulator.[4]

Not much is known about the first officer, Fariq Hamid. He was among the newest minted first officers on the 777 fleet. Aged twenty-seven, single, and still living at home, Hamid was engaged to be married to Nadira Ramili, a pilot at another airline. Some have made much of the fact that he had a very limited social media footprint, which is seen as unusual for someone of his age. But frankly, besides anodyne allegations that he had two cars or was a bit of a loner, there is nothing about Hamid that is out of the ordinary. One scandal, though, did come out in the days immediately following the disappearance. Two Australian women said that on a flight from Phuket to Kuala Lumpur in 2011, they had been invited to fly in the cockpit with Hamid and his colleague from takeoff to landing, in what was obviously a breach of cockpit security. They described the pilots as smoking throughout the flight and the encounter as "sleazy." They released photographs of themselves with the captain and Hamid. I found the whole story to be nasty, and frankly of marginal relevance. The reality is if the women were invited to the cockpit, it was the captain's responsibility, not Hamid's, as the first officer. These women were quite happy to be on the flight deck and now were just as happy to be on television revealing what might have happened.

When it comes to the pilot suicide theory, the proponents say the captain, as the more experienced, older pilot, was more likely to have committed such a nefarious act. What evidence is put forward for the proposition? In the first few days of the investigation, a media feeding frenzy took place when it was discovered that Zaharie had built an amateur flight simulator, also known as a sim. This sim included several computer screens, cockpit control panels, and a yoke, or wheel. It is more sophisticated than a basic flight sim package you might have at home, but a far cry from the ultraexpensive sims found in airlines and training centers. After several days of delay, the Malaysian police finally dismantled this contraption and took it away for forensic examination. Widespread reports quickly leaked that Zaharie had downloaded flight plans of a route into remote parts of the Indian Ocean, where a landing attempt would be made on a small runway. There were allegations that these computer files had been deleted, so that afterward, no one would be able to work out what he had been planning. The machine and data were sent to the FBI for a more thorough analysis and to try to re-create the deleted data, neither of which the Malaysian police could do.

As this process was under way, the Malaysian police leaked on several occasions that Zaharie was now the "prime suspect" as a perpetrator of some nefarious act. They leaked more information about the captain: apparently he had no social or family engagements on his calendar in the period after the plane went missing. And just for good measure, there were rumors that he and his wife were estranged and no longer living together. One report had his wife and children moving out of the house on the day when he was to fly MH370. Everyone in the media was pretty certain Captain Zaharie had done it. The reasons could be many; his outrage over the arrest and imprisonment of the opposition leader Anwar Ibrahim for alleged homosexual offenses; a wish to expose the lack of democracy in Malaysia and how an innocent person could be arrested on trumped-up charges; and possible distress over the failure of his marriage. The only problem with all of this was that not much was true.

First, Zaharie was a supporter of Ibrahim, but so far no one has suggested that he had shown any radical tendencies or was a zealot determined to avenge what some perceived as Ibrahim's persecution by the government. Anyway, it's not clear how crashing a 777 would accomplish anything other than to embarrass Malaysia in the eyes of the world. Second, the FBI examined the sim's computer and stated that nothing had been deleted; files had simply been overwritten by later use. In the widely reported words of the FBI investigators, there was nothing suspicious about the simulator or its use.[5] In other words, there was nothing with the simulator, other than its mere presence, to suggest anything was wrong. The FBI may have changed its position a few months later, when they started suggesting that there were indeed flight paths to remote landing strips in the Indian Ocean on the sim, but so far this is just a rumor.

On the issue of the captain's marriage, I have spoken to those who say yes, there may have been marital difficulties, but as one Malaysian captain put it to me, "If your marriage breaks down, you don't then go out and murder several hundred people." Anyway, there are those who testified to the fact that the captain's marriage was just fine and that he and his wife didn't live apart; rather his wife spent weekdays at their second home while the captain stayed in town because of work.

We need more than conjecture, rumor, and gossip about the captain's personal life and habits in order to determine whether he might have committed this act. The report published on the first anniversary of the incident addresses the captain's financial, physical, and possible psychological state. Section 1.5.8, "Psychological and Social Events," states categorically:

> The Captain's ability to handle stress at work and home was good. There is no known history of apathy, anxiety, or irritability. There were no significant changes in his life style, interpersonal conflict or family stresses.[6]

If the captain's wife had recently left him, and on the day of the crucial flight no less, this statement can't be true and must be considered absurd. No one would doubt for a moment that marital separation would classify as family stress; to leave such a crucial fact out would discredit the entire report.

The report goes on to note that "no behavioral signs of social isolation, change in habits or interest, self-neglect, drug or alcohol abuse" were discovered among the flight or cabin crew.[7] This contradicts those unnamed sources who told various newspapers that the captain's world was crumbling, that he was "terribly upset," and was in the "wrong state of mind to fly."[8] If this allegation were true, one would have expected a reference in the Factual Information Report released on the anniversary: there is none. If the stories and rumors prove to be true, then the report is a heap of rubbish.

The authorities went further and reviewed closed-circuit videos of the flight crew going through airport security to see if there were any behavioral discrepancies, and were unable to see any. Everything appeared normal. Taking all of this together, even if the Malaysian Department of Transport wished to put the best possible gloss on the situation, in order to defend the country and its pilots, as many have suggested, it beggars belief that they would leave out such crucial facts as a failed marriage or a state of unreasonable upset over political events. In air accident investigations, the truth eventually wins out, even if it ends up being disputed by one side or the other.

The truth, which is inconvenient to those who want to vilify the captain, is currently that there is no evidence that he did it. I am not saying he didn't do it, but I am saying there is no evidence that he did. The homemade simulator has thrown up nothing. The family background has thrown up nothing. The financial check has thrown up nothing. There is no evidence that he was stressed, deranged, or otherwise likely to bring down the plane. And remember, this is a captain with more than fifteen years' experience in the left-hand seat. It just does not make sense that he would suddenly commit an act of pilot suicide.

Cases of pilot suicide are extremely rare, and those that have happened are well known.[9] The most recent, of course, is Germanwings

9525, on March 24, 2015. The plane was an Airbus A320, flying from Barcelona to Düsseldorf. When the captain went to the restroom, the first officer, Andreas Lubitz, locked him out of the cockpit, then set the autopilot to one hundred feet, causing the plane to descend toward the mountains. Lubitz increased the rate of descent several times while the captain tried unsuccessfully to get back into the cockpit, finally using an ax to try to break down the reinforced door. After ten minutes the plane crashed into the French Alps, killing all 150 people on board. The facts and details of this case are so horrific because in using the door-locking system to keep the captain out of the cockpit, Lubitz was using the post-9/11 security measures designed to protect pilots in order to commit an act of mass murder. The retrieval of the FDR and CVR quickly established the facts, and to date no one has seriously questioned Lubitz's intention.

Within days of the incident, it became clear that Lubitz was suffering from a variety of psychological conditions. There were medications for anxiety and depression in his apartment, along with ripped-up sick notes declaring him unfit for work on the day of the deadly flight. The further back prosecutors looked, the more mental problems they discovered: in 2008, his training was suspended for eight months because he was suffering from depression. He did eventually get his pilot's license, which contained medical restrictions requiring regular examinations. In the five years preceding the crash, Lubitz had consulted at least forty-one doctors. He complained about failing eyesight, but doctors could find no physical reason for this and some judged its cause as psychosomatic. As his condition worsened in the month before the crash, Lubitz made one visit to a general practitioner, three visits to a psychiatrist, and three visits to an ear, nose, and throat specialist.[10] Investigations into his Internet searches in the days before the crash revealed he had been researching the operation of the cockpit door-locking mechanism and suicide methods. The belief now is that fearing the loss of his eyesight, and with it his career, Lubitz decided that life was no longer worth living and crashed the plane. There is no need for me to go into the wider implications of this tragedy—which include psychological testing of pilots, and what Lufthansa knew, should have known, and could have known. Rather the point is that in the wake of the crash, the facts of Lubitz's mental condition were established quickly and the motive for his suicide/murder became obvious. The evidence was overwhelming.

The Germanwings case of pilot suicide is eerily similar to the crash in 2013 of an Embraer 190, belonging to LAM Mozambique Airlines. This time it was the captain who locked out the copilot and set the autopilot to descend, killing thirty-three people. The cockpit voice recorder leaves no doubt of what happened.[11] Here, so far, no motive has been established for why the pilot decided to crash the plane, and the final report has yet to be published.

Other major cases of pilot suicide occurred on EgyptAir 990 and Silk Air 185, both of which have given rise to conflicting explanations. In the case of EgyptAir 990, a Boeing 767 crashed off the US coast in 1999. The NTSB in Washington was delegated by the Egyptians to conduct the investigation. The Americans rapidly focused on the actions of one of the relief pilots, Gameel Al-Batouti, a fifty-nine-year old senior first officer. Al-Batouti had been with EgyptAir since 1987, and before that had been a member of the Egyptian air force and a flight instructor. He was, by any standards, extremely experienced.

According to the NTSB, shortly after the 767's departure from JFK to Cairo, Al-Batouti managed to get the other pilots, including the captain in command, out of the cockpit, whereupon he pushed the yoke forward and put the aircraft into a dive. When the captain returned and tried to recover the airplane, Al-Batouti is believed to have switched off the engines, dooming any hope of recovery. The report of the NTSB says that in the final moments of the plunge, the flight data recorder shows the left and right elevator at the tail, controlling the pitch of the nose, moving in opposite directions because the captain's controls were pulling the nose up while the first officer's were pushing it down. Throughout this, Al-Batouti is heard on the cockpit voice recorder whispering eleven times under his breathe, "I rely on god."[12] Meanwhile the captain is heard saying "pull with me." The NTSB's conclusion was clear:

> The probable cause is . . . a result of the first officer's flight control inputs. The reason for the first officer's actions was not determined.

The Egyptians strongly disagreed with this conclusion. They called the US report "limited . . . incomplete . . . inadequate . . ." and accused the NTSB of having "used selective facts and speculative conclusions to support a predetermined theory."[13] Instead they said the crash was caused by faulty mechanical parts in the tail section, which caused the plane to go into a nose dive.

The NTSB didn't attempt to pinpoint Al-Batouti's motives, but some months later one emerged. Apparently, EgyptAir's chief captain of the 767 fleet, Hatem Rushdy, was a passenger on the flight to Cairo. Rushdy had been investigating allegations against Al-Batouti of improper sexual behavior during his US layovers. It seems that women had complained of Al-Batouti's making unwelcome sexual advances. According to a whistle-blower, Al-Batouti had been told he was being taken off the lucrative and prestigious transatlantic route and was likely to face demotion. The theory is that he crashed the plane in order to seek revenge. Even though the Egyptian authorities have always denied the pilot suicide theory, most experts in the industry accept the US conclusions.

The second case where there is a disagreement about pilot suicide concerns Silk Air 185, flying from Jakarta to Singapore. Here a Boeing 737-300 crashed into the Musi River in south Sumatra, Indonesia, killing all 104 people on board. It was a violent, brutal impact that left few remains of the aircraft or of those on board. The cockpit voice recorder was unable to help in the investigation because it had stopped recording at the crucial time—allegedly, a circuit breaker had been pulled. The report by the Indonesian investigators failed to come up with a reason for the crash, saying that "the technical investigation has yielded no evidence to explain the cause of the accident."[14] The Americans strongly disagreed.

They believed that the captain got the first officer out of the cockpit, then pulled the cockpit voice recorder circuit breaker, stopping the recording. According to their investigation, the plane's trajectory and movements were entirely consistent with nose-down manual inputs. As a motive for suicide, the US focused on several previous flying incidents involving the captain where there had been loss of life: notably one in which three of his fellow officers in the Singapore Air force were killed. The Silk Air crash took place on the anniversary of that earlier crash. Also, risky trading in stock markets had left him financially strapped. Crucially, the captain had taken out a life insurance policy that became effective on the very day of the accident. When this information was put together with the descent profile of the aircraft, the US investigators were in no doubt that the captain had deliberately crashed the plane. The Indonesians have never accepted this view. Like EgyptAir 990, most people in the aviation industry prefer the American version of events to the Indonesian report, which merely says there is no evidence to support such conclusions.

The countries involved in the cases of disputed reports did not want to believe that one of their own pilots had caused a crash (in the case of Silk Air, Indonesia wanted to avoid offending its tricky neighbor Singapore). National pride and politics meant you didn't say one of your pilots killed himself and committed mass murder. No one in the aviation community, however, believed them. The beauty of the ICAO Annex 13 procedure is that all the accredited parties to the investigation are involved; they get to see the reports and test results, and they are part of the hearings. Final reports are circulated and everyone gets to comment very publicly on their content. (Of course, each party has its corner to defend, and so, frequently the NTSB or the Europeans are said to tend toward finding contributing errors on the part of pilots so they don't have to lay too much blame on the plane manufacturer, Boeing or Airbus, while quietly making recommendations for modifications.)

All of this brings us back to MH370, and the suggestion that one of the pilots was responsible for the crash. If we just take the hard facts in our possession, there is strong circumstantial evidence to suggest that yes, one or the other did commit a heinous act.

1. The ACARS was disabled at around 01:07.

2. The radio call "Good night Malaysian 370" was said at 01:19, with no indication that anything had gone wrong.

3. The transponder was switched off at 01:21.

4. All this happened at the transfer between air traffic control centers, the perfect moment to go dark.

5. The plane was deliberately turned back and flown across Malaysia and around Indonesia before heading south.

6. The final resting place is somewhere in the most remote place on earth, guaranteeing that no one will ever find out what happened.

Add in the gossip and rumor—the captain had a flight simulator and practiced this route, the captain had marital problems and was a political fanatic—and suddenly the case seems open-and-shut. When put like this, even I can buy into the theory that the pilot committed suicide and murdered everyone else along with him.

Except all the incidents of commercial pilot suicide we have discussed display a very different set of actions. In all the cases reported by ICAO, the act of the culprit is fast, immediate, dramatic. They get the other pilot out of the cockpit and then push the nose down, putting the plane into a dive. They don't plot for weeks, devising a highly complicated method of execution requiring detailed knowledge of the plane's complex technology, such as disabling the ACARS systems. If Captain Zaharie Shah or First Officer Fariq Hamid wanted to commit suicide, there were plenty of opportunities to do it over the South China Sea, or even over the remote parts of Malaysia. Also they would have known their plan would be ruined if Malaysian radar tracked the plane on its trek across the country and the air force sent up jets. They couldn't have known that incompetence by a military radar operator in Malaysia on that night meant no one reacted, or that neither Thailand nor Indonesia would show any interest in the aircraft, let alone that Singapore, with its obsession over security, would allow an unidentified plane to fly by. Because of incompetence and bad luck, no one responded, an occurrence that, according to all the pilots I have spoken to who regularly fly this airspace, could not have been taken for granted.

In the case of MH370, a suicidal pilot would likely have had to depressurize the aircraft. This is done by switching off the air control on the control panel; it's not necessary to take the aircraft up to ridiculous altitudes of forty-five thousand feet, as has been suggested. After killing all those on board by hypoxia, the aircraft is put on its final heading and then the pilot kills himself or waits seven hours for the fuel to run out. Alternately, if he doesn't kill the passengers, the pilot ends up sitting in the cockpit with hundreds of people screaming in the cabin behind. In all cases, the pilot either dies with everyone else from hypoxia or sits there awaiting the crash. This does not tally with the evidence of MH370. I just don't think it is what happened.

If pilot suicide doesn't bring us any answers, there are many other nefarious activities that could have been involved. Not least, that the plane was shot down by either the Americans or the Chinese (other nations are sometimes included, but these are the two usually mentioned) and the entire episode is being covered up. One book, released just eleven weeks after the plane went missing, suggests that it may have been shot out of the sky after accidentally getting caught up in American and Thai joint military tests.[15] Most of the shooting-down theories have a Diego Garcia component to them.

How likely is it that MH370 was shot down? While the number of cases of civil airliners being mistakenly shot down are rare, they are marginally more frequent than those involving pilot suicide. Most involve war zones where rebels shoot down a civil plane, usually by accident. The most recent, tragically, involved Malaysia Airlines again. In July 2014, another Malaysia Airlines 777, this time MH17 from Amsterdam to Kuala Lumpur, was brought down by a missile while flying over eastern Ukraine; 298 people died. This happened only 128 days after MH370 went missing. The official report and appendices run to more than five hundred pages and reveal the debris field was huge. There were six wreckage sites spread over twenty square miles of the Ukrainian countryside.[16] Horribly, the continuing war meant the human remains could not be retrieved for several days. It was a grossly inhuman end to an atrocity that should never have happened. After an exhaustive review of all possible causes (including whether MH17 was hit by a meteor), the final report of the Dutch investigators concluded "the aeroplane was struck by a 9N314M warhead as carried on a 9M38-series missile and launched by a Buk surface-to-air missile system."[17]

The prevailing view is that anti-Ukrainian separatists, believing the 777 was a Ukrainian military aircraft, fired a BUK-M1 missile supplied by the Russian army. The Russians say it was the Ukrainian air force that shot down the plane by mistake. The wreckage recovered is being reassembled in the Netherlands as the Dutch investigators determine exactly what did bring down the plane.

Before MH17, we have to go back some years for incidents in which large civil aircraft planes have been shot out of the sky: Korean Airlines 007 and Iran Air 655. With KAL 007, the Korean plane was shot down by the then Soviet Union in 1983, killing 269. The Boeing 747 was going from Anchorage, Alaska, to Seoul, South Korea. An autopilot mistake meant the plane was flying miles off its original flight plan, and was in restricted Soviet airspace around Sakhalin Island. Initially, the Soviets said they knew nothing about what had happened, then claimed the passenger jet was engaged in spying. It wasn't until ten years later, after the fall of the Soviet Union, that the new Russian government released wreckage and transcripts that showed how the Soviet air force had intentionally shot down the plane. Further tests allowed investigators to discover how the autopilot mistake that led the plane off course happened. The second case is Iran Air 655, shot down by a missile from the American warship USS *Vincennes* in 1988, killing 290. The US mistook the Airbus A300 for an F-14A fighter plane. Although the Americans admitted that they had shot down the plane, it took eight years before they apologized and paid damages.

So was MH370 shot down? I discount this as a possibly valid theory because there is simply no evidence to support it. In the cases above, we knew about the shooting down almost immediately after it occurred. As we saw with MH17, when an airliner is violently brought out of the sky, the crash leaves a massive debris field, and so far nothing of the kind has been reported. If the attack had occurred around the South China Sea, the Bay of Bengal, or the Indian Ocean, with the plane breaking up in midair, we might expect some debris to wash ashore to nearby countries, as in the case of KAL 007, when body parts and paper cups washed ashore in Japan.

Also, the KAL and Iran Air examples involved Russians or Americans who either promptly accepted responsibility or admitted that they knew about it and then tried to justify their drastic and lethal actions. In the case of MH370, no one has come forward to even whisper that they were responsible. (I know: someone will bring up TWA 800 as being accidentally shot down by the US Navy off the coast of New York. The US has absolutely denied this and the NTSB has determined it was the center fuel tank that exploded.)

Some of the victims' relatives are not so convinced and believe MH370 may have been accidentally shot down by the Malaysian air force as the plane crossed the country. The Royal Malaysian Air Force has specifically denied to CNN that they scrambled planes to intercept the 777.[18]

Still, Sarah Bajc, whose partner, Philip, was on board, isn't so sure. When I met her in Kuala Lumpur she told me the plane could have been shot down over Peninsular Malaysia.

SARAH: They could have cleaned it up. That's rain forest. A
totalitarian government.

QUEST: Somebody would have leaked it.

SARAH: Well, leaks may still happen. It takes a long time
here. I'm just saying we don't know.[19]

If MH370 was shot down, was there a motive, or was it an accident? Or was the plane hijacked? In asking such questions, we head
off into the realm of the incredible. The novelist Marc Dugain, who
used to be the CEO of now-defunct Proteus Airlines, suggested in a
December 2014 *Paris Match* article that the plane was on a suicide
mission to Diego Garcia, being flown either by the disgruntled Captain Zaharie or by hijackers, when the Americans shot it down. He
claimed that part of the empty fire extinguisher washed ashore and
was found on one of the islands before being seized by the military.

All the wilder theories choose to ignore the Inmarsat data, the
heart and soul of the entire search operation. Inmarsat and others
have shown the plane flying for seven hours after it went missing, and
its offset calculations give specific directions about which way it went.
If you accept the Inmarsat data, then you must reject all the more
extreme theories. The two are simply inconsistent.

One man who has tried to square the Inmarsat circle is Jeff Wise,
author of the book *The Plane That Wasn't There*[20] and a *New York* magazine article, "How Crazy Am I to Think I Actually Know Where That
Malaysia Airlines Plane Is?"[21] Jeff and I have come to broadcasting
blows a few times on CNN. Even though he was absolutely right during
the underwater search in saying that the pings did not come from the
black boxes, there have been other times when I felt his haste to dis-
believe what we were being told by authorities was neither helpful nor

useful to the viewer. The focus of the *New York* magazine piece is the possibility that the plane was hijacked by or at the behest of the Russians. The hijackers managed to get into the electronics and electrics bay (E&E), which is under the cabin floor. The entrance to the E&E is through a hatch under the cabin floor carpet, in front of first class, by the cockpit door. Jeff gives a long explanation of how the SATCOM equipment was tampered with in order to transmit false Inmarsat readings. The plane then flew north to Kazakhstan, where it landed at a Russian cosmodrome in which it has been kept ever since at the behest of President Putin, for some unspecified purpose, which may include having it turn up one day "packed with explosives." Jeff admits that he has no idea why Putin did this.

Jeff tells a good story, but as a theory about how the plane went missing it misses the mark. After all, I would love to know how his Russian/Ukrainian hijackers would manage to pull up the first-class carpet, lift up the hatch, and jump into the E&E bay without someone in the galley noticing and raising the alarm, especially as they were only forty-five minutes into the flight and drinks and dinner were being prepared. Even Jeff admits the level of planning and arrangements for this scheme to work (right plane, right equipment, right satellite, right destination) would be incredible. Of course, now that the flaperon has been conclusively determined to come from MH370, the Kazakhstan theory has lost the little credibility it had to begin with.

I decided not to spend too much time delving into the possibility that a passenger somehow hijacked the plane for the simple reason that there is no evidence for it. Admittedly, we haven't heard much from the Malaysian police, but what they did say is that they haven't found anyone suspicious on board while continuing to investigate those on the passenger list (having told us at one point that everyone was in the clear). We know the two stolen passports turned out to be a tragic case of youngsters trying to escape to the West. All things considered, if this had been a traditional terrorist attack, there likely would have been a claim of responsibility; but no group has come forward to take the credit for stealing a 777 with 239 passengers. And if it was something more along the lines of state-sponsored terrorism, as Jeff Wise suggests, well, we are just clutching at straws, forcing together random facts in order to weave a story. It may make a good yarn, but it doesn't stand the test of credibility.

Pulling all the strands together, the nefarious options are by far the easiest to understand and in many ways the most interesting. There is a simplicity to the notion that the pilot did it, or that someone hijacked the plane. While I don't think either happened, if I had to choose one over the other, the pilot suicide scenario is more likely. When it comes to hijacking, no one has claimed responsibility for taking the plane, there have been no demands for ransom that we know of, and there is no evidence that the plane landed anywhere.

Before I leave the nefarious options, let me clear up one of two other "theories" that have made the rounds: first, that the plane flew over the Maldives on its way to Diego Garcia. There were numerous eyewitness accounts of a large plane with red markings flying unusually low across the islands, which are only several hundred miles from the US base. The head of the country's civil aviation authority decided to go back and have another look at these stories. In the end, he concluded that what the islanders had seen was not a Boeing 777; it was a fifty-seater Bombardier Dash 8 belonging to Maldivian, a local airline. True, both airlines do have red and blue lettering on the fuselage and their planes could be confused in poor light. There is an obvious difference in size, but perhaps only veteran plane spotters can make this distinction. In any event, it seems the Maldives theory can be put to bed.

To those who still cling to the idea that the plane has somehow been stolen by terrorists or a government, landed somewhere, and is being readied for some suicide mission, I urge you to remember some basic facts of aviation. Landing a 777 is not an easy task. Like all planes of its size, it requires a runway that is a minimum of several thousand feet in order to land and stop safely, and that would increase to eight thousand feet if it was close to its maximum landing weight (which MH370 wouldn't have been). It is challenging enough to put down such a jet on ten thousand feet of smooth runway with all the navigation aids at your disposal. An attempt to land the plane on anything other than a decent runway would probably collapse the nose gear, making future takeoff impossible. And even if you did land it on a runway without damage, you have to obtain fuel and be able to get the thing back in the air. Ideas of landing on beaches or jungle runways are just not realistic, not without destroying the aircraft. Always remember: the Inmarsat data said the plane continued to fly for seven more hours; that fact is the killer to most of the conspiracy theories (unless of course you believe that the data has been fabricated, in which case you will never accept any of the rational theories).

There are many more nefarious conspiracy theories making the rounds. Some are more ludicrous than others. They are all brandished with the fervor of the true believer. Suggestions like pilot suicide are credible and must be taken seriously, and hijacking or terrorism must remain on the table as a possibility until absolutely discounted. As for the rest, the harsh reality is that when you pick up the strange, outlandish theories, like a piecrust, they fall apart.

CHAPTER NINE

THE CAUSE: MECHANICAL

We don't know what exactly happened in the cockpit so
we don't know if it was a security issue or a safety issue.

—Raymond Benjamin, secretary general, ICAO

I f I don't like the nefarious options because they don't fit the profile or there is little evidence to support any of them, then I must look at the possibility of a mechanical problem with the aircraft, or perhaps something in the cargo hold that brought down the plane. After many months of considering what, if anything, mechanical could have caused the incident, I realized the question is not as straightforward as it seems. As I have stated, planes do not simply fall out of the sky, especially not during the cruise phase of flight. Recall: most incidents happen on takeoff or landing. Cruise incidents where the plane is destroyed are few and far between. When they do happen, the reasons are usually pretty clear.

Because of the unique circumstances of MH370's disappearance, any mechanical cause requires that several conditions are met. Whatever happened had to have been large and dramatic in order to take out all the communications systems at once. If you recall, the last ACARS transmission was at 01:07. The system was programmed to send reports every thirty minutes, so the next should have been sent at 01:37; nothing was received. This means that ACARS was disabled sometime between 01:07 and 01:37. Of course, disabled does not necessarily mean switched off, just that the system was incapable of transmission. The radios continued working up to 01:19 ("Good night Malaysian 370") with no suggestion from the captain that anything was awry. The transponder was switched off at 01:21. All of this is well known. Therefore, if the plane's problem was mechanical, something took place between 01:19 and 01:21 without the crew realizing it.

As the Australian report reminds us, "In the case of MH370, there were multiple redundant communications systems fitted to the aircraft,"[1] totaling eight different modes of communication. First, whatever happened had to take out all the communications tools at once. Anything less would have either allowed the crew to make a Mayday call to air traffic control, or, more likely, triggered automatic ACARS messages to be sent from the aircraft to Malaysia's base in Kuala Lumpur, in which case we would know what had happened. If you recall the case of Air France 447, ACARS transmitted two dozen warning messages of failing equipment as the aircraft fell out of the sky. Air France engineers were aware there was a problem with the pitot tube speed sensors long before they knew where the plane had gone down.

Second, the plane's movements have been described as "deliberate." Someone was commanding the turn-back toward Malaysia, and the various twists and turns across the Strait of Malacca. There is nothing erratic about these turns. Whether this was done by hands on the wheel or by changing the heading select of the autopilot, the movements were consistent with human inputs.

Finally—and this is the tricky bit—whatever happened to MH370 could not have been so destructive that it prevented the plane from continuing to fly for a further seven hours, as we know it did from analysis of the Inmarsat handshakes.

So as we think about mechanical problems we always have to keep in mind the following principles:

1. It must be serious, major, and take out the communications at once.

2. The crew must still be able to deliberately turn the aircraft back toward Malaysia, but unable to communicate what is happening.

3. The event can't be so destructive that it prevents the plane from continuing to fly for the next seven hours.

All these conditions must be met if the mechanical problem is to be a realistic option. Once you start testing various hypotheses against these conditions, it becomes clear that the options are few and far between, which is why so many aviation experts believe a mechanical reason to be unlikely.

Attention obviously focuses on some sort of in-flight fire or explosion, but not one fierce enough to destroy the aircraft. In-flight fires are among the most serious problems any aircrew can face. There are plenty of accelerants on board an aircraft, including, of course, the fuel in the tanks, the supplementary oxygen supplies, and baggage and cargo in the hold. The reality is planes are robustly built to withstand turbulence, but they are fragile objects once flames take hold.

Full-scale, in-flight fires rarely end well. Fires generate large amounts of smoke and noxious fumes that seep into the cockpit, making it difficult for the pilots to breathe or even see out of the window. Flames damage electrical wires and control mechanisms, making it physically impossible to control the aircraft's flight and operate the engines. Some fires can destroy the fuselage and leave the plane incapable of staying in the air.

There are many examples of the seriousness and deadliness of in-flight fires: Swissair 111 was off the northeast coast of Canada flying from New York to Geneva in 1998 when a fire broke out above the cockpit among electrical wiring linked to the in-flight entertainment system. Initially, the pilots thought the funny smell had to do with air-conditioning problems. Five minutes after becoming aware of a problem, they requested an immediate landing at the nearest airport and were directed to Halifax, Nova Scotia, some sixty miles away. Even that distance was too great. As the fire spread, the electrical and aircraft systems began to fail, and flames and smoke invaded the cockpit to the point where the plane became uncontrollable. From smelling the initial odor to the plane crashing was twenty-one minutes.[2]

The time from fire to disaster was even shorter in the case of Valujet 592, a DC-9 flying from Miami to Atlanta in 1996. Shortly after takeoff, at 14:10:03, one of the pilots said, "What was that?" in response to a noise. Twenty-four seconds later, someone is heard shouting, "We're on fire, we're on fire." The plane tried to turn back to Miami but crashed into the Florida Everglades at 14:13:42. From crisis to crash took less than four minutes.[3] The fire began among old cabin oxygen cylinders that were being sent for recycling. They had been improperly stored and loaded into the aircraft hold, ignoring safety warnings about the treatment of such potentially incendiary material.

Because of these well-known cases of on-board fires, especially those starting in the cargo hold, it was important to know what exactly MH370 was carrying in its cargo belly. In the early days of the inquiry, the Malaysians flatly refused to release information about the plane's cargo, once again needlessly hiding behind the ICAO Annex 13 process by saying they could not release any details that were part of the investigation. Even the Australian authorities, who were doing the searching, complained that "they had experienced difficulty obtaining the MH370 cargo manifest which would be useful for identification against debris recovered."[4] Finally, on May 1, along with the official preliminary report, the various air waybills and cargo listings were released, and immediately attention focused on two items of great interest: MH370 was carrying 2.7 tons[5] of lithium-ion batteries for Motorola China and 5 tons[6] of mangosteen fruit. Both aroused great suspicion for very different reasons.

The issues surrounding the transport of lithium-ion batteries on planes are well known and documented. These batteries are more efficient, giving longer and stronger power; they are also highly volatile, susceptible to thermal runaway, and if damaged, they can burst into flames. When they do combust, "li-on" battery fires are exceptionally hot and very difficult to put out. Even with a halon gas suppression system, li-on batteries have been known to continue to smolder, frequently reigniting after being thought to be extinguished. Carrying them on planes improperly can be extremely hazardous and there have been many cases where fires have resulted from planes carrying these batteries as cargo or as part of their own power supply. In 2010, a UPS cargo 747 crashed en route from Dubai to Cologne, Germany. The plane had been carrying a large quantity of lithium-ion batteries, and the final report of the investigation "conclude[d] with reasonable certainty that the location of the fire was an element of the cargo that contained among other items lithium."[7] The same was true of UPS

Flight 1307 in 2006, where a fire believed to be caused by these batteries led to a successful emergency landing but the total destruction of the airframe.

The FAA in the US has been so concerned about li-on batteries that it regularly releases a list of reported incidents. There have been 152 of these since 1991.[8] As passengers carry more smartphones, tablets, e-readers, and devices that use these batteries, the number of incidents has risen. The FAA has reported an average of 8 incidents a year. Lest anyone doubt the real danger of these batteries, the entire fleet of brand-new Boeing 787 Dreamliners was grounded in January 2013, less than sixteen months after the planes' entry into service. There had been several incidents of the new planes' own lithium-ion batteries suffering thermal runaway, generating large amounts of smoke and in some cases small but fierce fires. The 787 was using a recently developed and different type of li-on battery, which is believed to have had certain design and manufacturing defects that made it susceptible to thermal runaway. The 787s were allowed back in the air only after Boeing had redesigned safety features to vent any smoke or flames.

Captain Zaharie Shah and First Officer Fariq Hamid probably didn't know they were carrying li-on batteries in the hold: the airline's cargo manifest merely describes the pallet's contents as consolidated goods.[9] The shipment's air waybill does specify li-on batteries, and contains clear warnings that a flammable hazard exists, but the cockpit crew would not have seen the waybill. Nor did the dispatchers issue a NOTOC—Notice to the Captain—which is used to warn the crew of any dangerous cargo on board, and gives them the right to reject it. The airline claims that since the batteries were packed in accordance with IATA's international regulations, a NOTOC of dangerous cargo wasn't necessary. The reality is that we have no idea if the goods were packed properly. The official Factual Report has lots of color pictures showing how they *should* have been packed, but there is no evidence they were actually packed that way.

Some commentators believe that the batteries probably started smoldering, letting off toxic fumes that caused many on board to become unconscious. This theory suggests that there may have been a fire, which led to the pilots' disabling of all the communications equipment before the pilots succumbed to the fumes and the plane continued to fly on autopilot, deep into the night.[10] The 777 pilots I have spoken to don't give this theory much credence for all sorts of technical and procedural reasons, not least of which is a variety of warnings that would have been issued by the cargo bay sensors.

Should we get all excited about the li-on batteries? Are they the key that unlocks this mystery? In my view, no. The battery issue falls apart upon closer inspection. Originally the airline said there were 2.7 tons of batteries on board. Later they revealed more details showing that, of the total consignment being sent from the Motorola factory in Penang to its manufacturing plant in Tianjin, only 221 kilograms were li-on batteries.[11] The rest of the consignment is described as chargers and radio accessories. Of course, 221 kilograms is still a quarter of a ton, and could burst into flame, but it is not quite the same thing as several tons. Now, you may wonder why the Malaysians originally said the plane was carrying two tons of the stuff, then suddenly claimed otherwise.

Whether or not the figures were fudged (which I don't think happened), it doesn't alter the situation: even if these batteries had caught fire, they certainly didn't explode and blow up the aircraft, because if this were so, the debris would be all over the South China Sea and the plane wouldn't have flown for another seven hours. Also, a li-on fire is especially fierce, and very likely to have spread to other pieces of packing and cargo. Any smoke and flames in the hold would have been picked up by the plane's sophisticated fire detection systems, alarms would have gone off in the cockpit, and automatic ACARS messages would have been sent to the ground.[12] We can reasonably assume the pilots would have declared an emergency on the radios and told the ground they were turning back to land. (Before someone suggests that the battery fire or explosion took out the radios first, a look at the loading position of the batteries shows they were stored at the rear of the aircraft and immediately in front of the wing, a long way from the radio equipment.)

So now to the mangosteens. This is a delicious fruit that is very popular in Southeast Asia and exported worldwide, bringing in high prices. Here I must confess I am bewildered. For many months, I didn't pay attention to the fruit because I was so distracted by the li-on batteries. In any case, I have never been quite certain what the issue is when it comes to the fruit. Certainly MH370 was carrying a great deal of the tasty fruit, five tons' worth. Ironically, while the much more dangerous li-on batteries didn't merit a specific mention on the manifest or Notice to Captain, the mangosteens were written up clearly and got their own Notice to Captain. The NOTOC was sent via the ACARS system just before departure because the fruit was perishable. Any serious flight delays or problems with the air and heat in the cargo hold very likely could cause them to be ruined.

The conspiracy theorists had a field day with the mangosteens. Some pointed out that the fruit was out of season, and there was none in the orchards of Johore, Malaysia, from where they were said to have come. The police, their suspicions raised, said they would interview the fruit pickers. Now we know that the mangosteens came from both Malaysia and Indonesia.

Behind all the suspicion is, of course, the suggestion that the mangosteen cargo wasn't really fruit, but a cover for something that took down the plane. Or that the alleged fruit crates contained the drones that I referred to in the last chapter. This possibility might make a good plot twist for a thriller, but there hasn't been a shred of evidence to support it. Malaysia Airlines said it frequently transported lithium-ion batteries and mangosteens together from Kuala Lumpur to Beijing, and provided documents showing both in the cargo hold thirty-two times in the first three months of 2014.[13]

I have spent a great deal of time saying what I believe didn't happen; now it is time for me to focus on what did take place, and how the plane might have fallen from the sky. What follows is a theory, a suggestion, a possibility. It must be treated with the same caution as all the others. The germ of my thinking came during my first visit to Malaysia when I went to interview the prime minister. During this trip, I took the opportunity to speak to as many pilots and aviation experts in the country as possible. There was one thread that kept recurring . . . Most could not believe that one of their colleagues, whom they knew well, could have committed pilot suicide. It was their belief that something happened in the cockpit that incapacitated the crew and kept them from getting back to the ground before they all perished. The question was, what could that have been? To answer it, I have to repeat the fundamental principles that must be met for any mechanical theory: the event or action must take out all the communications equipment, so the pilots can't declare an emergency; the plane must remain controllable and be flown deliberately; and the event or action can't be so catastrophic as to prevent the plane from flying for several hours.

Those I spoke to believe what happened took place in the electrical and electronic bay (E&E), which is beneath the passenger cabin floor, at the front of first class, as you may remember from my summary of Jeffrey Wise's theory in the last chapter. The bay goes under the cockpit all the way forward to the radar dish in the nose of the plane. The E&E bay is the electronic brain of the plane, housing the electrical, electronic, and computer systems. It also contains all the radio equipment in a single electrical rack: the transponders, the radios, the control units for the ACARS systems . . . all of it. Take out the comms rack in the E&E bay and you take out the ability of the plane to communicate, except—and this is crucial—by the satellite communications unit, which is in the roof of the plane at the back. Now, this is where things get interesting: along with the plane's computers, also located in the E&E bay is a very large oxygen cylinder that supplies the emergency masks used by the pilots. This cylinder is at the top of the bay, sitting right underneath the cockpit.[14]

The theory goes that there was a rupture or explosion in this oxygen tank that, at a stroke, destroyed or disabled all the radio communications equipment nearby, along with many of the other computer systems in the E&E bay. Such explosions of auxiliary oxygen tanks have occurred before. In 2008, Qantas Flight 30, a Boeing 747, flying from Hong Kong to Melbourne, was very badly damaged when one of the passenger oxygen tanks, stored in a rack in the cargo hold, exploded. The force blew a large thirty-square-foot hole in the jumbo's fuselage, leading to a rapid depressurization. The exploding cylinder rocketed into the cabin above, where an emergency exit was located, and did significant damage to the plane before falling back down below and being sucked out of the hole.[15] If the explosion had occurred a few feet farther back, it would have been underneath passenger seats and very likely killed someone. After months of testing, the Australian investigators could find no reason, as a result of design, maintenance, or usage, why the cylinder had exploded. The ATSB were left declaring, "It was clear that this occurrence was a very rare event."[16]

If such an explosion of the cockpit oxygen tank had occurred on MH370, the consequences would have been terrible. There would have been the immediate damage to all the communications equipment, which could also have required the pilots to cut power to much of the plane. It is likely there would be a rapid depressurization of the aircraft, and very possibly serious injury to the pilots sitting above. As this theory goes: the crew, realizing the seriousness of the situation, immediately turns the plane back toward Malaysia to make an emergency landing. The highly experienced captain knows that the quickest and most likely place to head for is not Kuala Lumpur Airport but Penang Airport, where he has been many times. The airport's runway at 10,997 feet length is one of the longest in the region and perfect for an emergency landing. If you look at the profile of the flight back across Malaysia, the variance in speed and the height alterations fit the characteristics of an aircraft in trouble. Incidentally, from what I have been told, all reports of massive changes in altitude are incorrect. According to sources in Malaysia, the country's primary radar calibration was not working well enough to give a proper reading on altitude; hence the Factual Report doesn't refer to any large altitude changes.

One captain believed the routing of the plane, and the turns it made, suggest an approach to the runway at Penang. If so, the plane never made it. If there had been an explosion, the depressurization of the aircraft left those on board hypoxic and the crew injured and disoriented. The plane then overflew Penang and headed farther out into the Strait of Malacca before a last attempt to turn back to safety failed, sending the plane south. Those on board had already succumbed to hypoxia and a ghost flight continued for the next seven hours.

I am not saying the oxygen tank scenario is the only way an incapacitation of the plane could have happened. Others have put forward suggestions that the front tire might have overheated; as it retracted into the wheel well it smoldered and caught on fire.[17] Or there may have been different causes for an electrical fire in the E&E bay, requiring the pilots to cut the electrical power by pulling circuit breakers in the cockpit and disabling the ACARS and radios along with the other equipment. There is another point in favor of the electrical/mechanical cause. As mentioned earlier, the first and last of the seven Inmarsat handshakes showed that the plane was initiating a log-on to the satellite system after some sort of power break. When the signal was restored, no aircraft identification was present and the frequency was described as "abnormal."[18]

I think it is entirely possible that there was some form of electrical problem, caused by an explosion in the E&E bay or an electrical fire that either destroyed the radio equipment or required the cutting of electrical power to large parts of the plane. The flight crew turned the aircraft back to Malaysia, setting course for an airport they knew well, before finally perishing along with everyone else on board.

Before we dismiss this possibility on the grounds of improbability, let's consider that no one would have thought some ground mechanic's failure to check that a cabin pressurization was switched on could ever cause a 737 to be lost, but that is exactly what happened with Helios in 2005. No one would have believed that an electrical fault in an in-flight entertainment system would have caused a wide-bodied MD-11 to crash, yet that is the story of Swissair 111. Or that a seven-year-old botched repair on the tail would doom a Boeing 747, which is what happened to JAL123. Or that a 777 would crash-land because a very cold crossing from Beijing led to ice buildup in the fuel lines—the facts of BA38 at Heathrow. The list goes on and on. Possible in-flight emergency situations are so numerous that speculation is foolish. Instead, I content myself with looking at the way the plane was being flown and the facts that we know. There was a clear, defined, deliberate turn-back. There was a power loss to the satellite link and no other communications. The plane flew at erratic speeds and made marginal changes in altitude. The pilots flew across the country, where they must have known their craft would be seen, especially as it crossed the military base and headed out into the Strait of Malacca.

There are holes in this theory of mine, I readily concede. Any smoldering fire would have set off the sensors in the hold. An alarm and ACARS warning signal would have likely been sent to the ground, probably before the pilots pulled the circuit breakers. If there was a fire, why didn't Zaharie or Hamid call Mayday before taking any action? And of course, if there was an explosion with so much damage, how did the plane keep flying on autopilot as is suggested it must have done? There may have been toxic fumes from the smoldering lithium batteries in the hold that got into the plane's air supply, which incapacitated everyone, as some have suggested.[19] There are plenty of holes to destroy my theory, as indeed there are with every theory that is out there. I just happen to believe some version of this mechanical scenario is the most likely, when taken with the facts that we know.

The important point is that I am not wedded to any specific theory of how this accident happened. I know from long experience of covering plane crashes that what turns out to be the final proximate cause is often something that was never even thought of early on in an investigation. For instance, with AirAsia 8501, everyone initially thought the weather played an important part in causing the crash. No one would have suspected that there was a problem with the rudder control system and the pilots disconnected a crucial computer, then lost control of the plane. Plane crashes from mechanical causes are never obvious.

Another theory for the lack of debris has been put forward by a group of mathematicians in the *Notices of the American Mathematical Society*.[20] Examining the different angles at which the plane might have entered the water, they concluded that if the plane hit nose first at a ninety-degree angle, straight in, then it would not have broken up and there wouldn't have been much debris on the surface. They even suggested that it might have gone down to the bottom virtually intact. It is an interesting theory, and while it may be true, others have said it is more likely that after the plane ran out of fuel, it glided, until one wing dipped and the plane went into the water at an angle. We don't know and won't know until the black boxes are found. One sour note to the nose-dive theory: the flaperon that was found would have to have become disconnected in the dive, otherwise the leading edge would have been crumpled upon impact. It is relatively unscathed, casting doubt on the possibility of a nose dive.

Whether you prefer the nefarious or the mechanical theories, one overriding feeling persists: someone knows more than they are letting on. It is the most common comment I have heard: someone is covering up for a mistaken shooting down of the plane, or they have facts about another country's involvement. This is not simply another conspiracy theory. I have interviewed the highly respected CEO of Emirates Airline, Sir Tim Clark, many times over the years. A man who is not afraid to say what he thinks needs to be said, Sir Tim runs the world's largest international airline,[21] containing the biggest fleet of A380 Superjumbos and 777s in the world. In a newspaper interview, Sir Tim gave voice to what others had been reluctant to say. He described himself as "totally dissatisfied" with the current situation.

> Every single element of the "facts" of this particular incident must be challenged and examined in full transparency, exhausted to the point that there is no other way that we can think of this other than a complete mystery. There is plenty of information out there which we need to be far more forthright, transparent and candid about.[22]

Sir Tim questioned everything from the role of the Malaysian military to the integrity of the Inmarsat handshakes. As he reminded us, his airline operates the largest number of 777s in the world, so he has more of a vested interest than most in knowing what happened. Sir Tim does believe someone took control of the aircraft, but does not think it was a case of pilot suicide. Fundamentally he thinks something is being hidden. "I do not believe that the information held by some is on the table," he says. The fact that someone of Sir Tim's caliber believes there is much being hidden should give us all pause. As far as I am aware, he is not prone to believing conspiracy theories. His views are worrying, and need to be taken seriously.

Since the plane went missing I have spent many hours discussing with CNN colleagues, aviation journalists, former investigators, airline CEOs, pilots, and even some of those involved in this case about what might have happened. Which theory they choose to believe largely depends on their perspective on aviation and those who fly planes. Policemen and prosecutors are far more likely to believe it to be a case of pilot suicide or hijacking. Those with a background in aviation are less likely to want to believe the pilots did it.

As for me, a journalist who has covered this story from day one and continues to follow every twist and turn: I am prepared to be wrong. I can accept that the chance of a failure of all the communications systems while the plane continued to fly a specific route is cause for suspicion. Yet I am just not prepared to say one of the pilots murdered 238 people without further evidence. For the moment, I am on the mechanical side, and I accept that when the plane is found, and the full facts are known, I may be totally and utterly wrong.

CHAPTER TEN

CNN GOES THERE— AFTER THE PLANE

I am a little jet-lagged from my trip to Malaysia.
The lengths we have to go to get CNN coverage these
days. [Laughter and applause.] I think they're
still searching for their table.

—PRESIDENT BARACK OBAMA, MAY 23, 2014[1]

The president was speaking at the White House Correspondents' dinner, the annual event that allows the commander in chief to roast the press, wreaking revenge on his media tormentors. As I listened, I thought, when the president of the United States starts making jokes about your coverage, something has happened.

Now, seven weeks after MH370 went missing, CNN's coverage of MH370 had become part of the story. As one of the correspondents leading our reporting, I was at the center of coverage that attracted widespread comment, sometimes criticism, and often bewilderment about how the world's number one news network had become "all plane, all the time." Before you read this chapter, I offer the following caveat: I am extremely proud of the work we did, which is why I dedicated this book to my CNN colleagues. I would not have included this chapter if I felt that it would destroy my credibility and ability to say something meaningful about how we covered this story, what I saw, and what I learned.

When I got the call on the night of March 7, I was fully prepared for many hours of broadcasting. Whether we love planes or are scared of flying, there is a huge interest in aviation, which means news stories about planes are always popular. This can become a morbid fascination when the stories include crashes. When we fly, we put our lives totally into the hands of another person, knowing that if something goes wrong, the outcome will probably be fatal. There is an almost unquenchable appetite for facts and details when planes crash. We want to know everything, especially what it must have been like for those on board. My job is to provide some of those facts and put them in perspective. Part of this involves reminding the viewers how safe it is to fly. In 2014, there were only 939 fatalities out of flights carrying 3.6 billion passengers.[2] Flying remains the safest form of public transport.

None of this was on my mind as I headed into CNN's New York bureau to begin what I knew would be trying hours. I spoke on-air about the few facts that were known: the airline involved, the model of the plane, the route it was taking, any previous incidents with this type of aircraft, airline, or airport, and so on. MH370 was a wide-bodied 777, carrying hundreds of people. The Boeing 777 until now had not suffered a full-scale in-flight crash, so I knew this was going to be major "breaking news" coverage across all our main networks—CNN USA, CNN International, and CNN Español.

How long our different networks would keep up the intense level of coverage would depend on a whole host of factors. CNN International, which is where I do most of my daily work, broadcasts globally so its viewers are directly affected by the events, and would expect detailed coverage. Our US domestic network always has a pressing interest in aviation stories, but the staying power of such stories largely depends on whether the plane was flying to or from the USA, the number of Americans involved, and whether or not the plane was a US-made Boeing. These factors make a story more relevant to a US audience. At least that is the way I have seen these stories go before. This was Malaysia Airlines, which no longer even flies to the United States, so I didn't imagine there would be many US citizens on board, but the aircraft was a very popular, successful, and profitable model built in Seattle, and it was the first crash of its kind. I guessed the story would lead the US networks for several days and then drift down the program schedule. The decisions of one man showed how wrong I could be.

In January 2013, fourteen months before MH370 went missing, Jeff Zucker became the new president and CEO of CNN. Jeff had been executive producer of NBC's *Today* show, president of NBC Entertainment, and head of NBC Universal until it was taken over by Comcast. Now Phil Kent, CEO of Turner Broadcasting, and his boss, Jeff Bewkes, CEO of Time Warner (the parent companies of CNN), had given Jeff the job of turning CNN around. Everyone knew his number one task was to restore the network's USA ratings, which had fallen to disturbingly low levels. Jeff established his modus operandi almost immediately. He made it clear that the policy of "the news comes first" was still CNN's mission. Even as he introduced new, expensive documentary series, he repeatedly said that covering the news was at the core of what we do at CNN. But there would be changes. No longer would we have a smorgasbord of stories, dipping in here and there. When there was a big story that resonated with viewers, CNN would dramatically ramp up coverage, or, as Jeff described it to me, "go all in on it."[3]

The first instance of this philosophy in practice occurred barely a month after Jeff's arrival, with the "poop cruise." The Carnival Cruise ship *Triumph* had suffered a fire and engine failure that left her stranded in the Gulf of Mexico. For three days, the ship drifted with very limited power and overflowing toilets, creating a disgusting environment. Sewage was leaking into the corridors and food had to be rationed. CNN deployed correspondents and crews to cover every aspect of the event; we even sent a helicopter to follow *Triumph*'s progress as she was towed into port. The viewers watched and the critics noticed.[4] It marked a deliberate shift in the way CNN would cover such big events. Jeff described the significance of this story.

> What [the prominent coverage of the story] actually proved
> was how we were going to treat stories like that, of inter-
> est . . . or important. And the reason that I think that that
> attracted so much external attention was because we had
> never done that before.[5]

The new ground rules were in place and the stage was set for the coverage of MH370.

With any plane crash story, I am usually guaranteed a front-row seat in the coverage, as is CNN aviation correspondent René Marsh. Once it was known within CNN that I had just been to Malaysia to do a story on Malaysia Airlines, and had actually flown with First Officer Fariq Hamid, I found myself at the story's center, broadcasting every hour. A plane crash with hundreds of passengers still missing was always going to attract a great deal of coverage. The fact that we had a correspondent who actually knew about the airline, its history, and its way of doing business was a huge advantage.

CNN's formidable news-gathering operation was being led by the senior director of coverage, Cynde Strande. Over many weeks, she and I would have hour-long discussions on the minutiae of ACARS, radar blips, air traffic procedures, locator beacons, and airline politics. When the plane went missing, Cynde deployed reporting teams to Kuala Lumpur and increased coverage in Beijing, MH370's destination. All of this was to be expected. But by early the next week, I could feel a difference in tone and emphasis. Sometimes when producers asked me to do live reports (or live-shots as we call them), they would buttress the request with some version of "Jeff wants us to cover this in a big way." This requirement got stronger as the story became bigger and other networks ran with it too. We were determined to own the breaking news coverage of MH370 and dedicated whatever resources were necessary to do it. Jeff described his philosophy like this: "I thought it was a very compelling story initially because I thought everybody could relate to it."[6]

Watching CNN gearing up for such massive coverage was an impressive sight, even for someone who had been at the network for thirteen years. With our marching orders clear, the deployments began. From CNN's Asia base in Hong Kong, we sent satellite equipment, engineering staff, and more correspondents to Kuala Lumpur to establish twenty-four-hour coverage. As the story became more complicated, with tentacles reaching down to Perth, western Australia; Inmarsat in London; and Jakarta, Indonesia; wherever was required, we went. We had so many people in places like KL and Perth that we sent senior field producers—known as "circus masters"—to organize the troops and resources, making sure our coverage was comprehensive and coherent. When you have so many people in the field, there is always a danger they will end up tripping over each other, that some stories will get duplicated while others are missed. As the name suggests, the circus master is in charge. Including news-gathering backup, I counted more than twenty-five people between Perth and Kuala Lumpur. Add in those in the rest of the world, and there were at least three dozen people in the field covering the story. We were spending a fortune and no one minded. The message from the top was clear: spend whatever we need to own this story.

CNN was more fortunate than other networks because we already had a team in Washington called TRACS, which specialized in transportation and aviation stories. In DC, producers Mike Ahlers and Aaron Cooper and correspondent René Marsh had excellent contacts within US government agencies to ensure we knew the latest thinking. Add the formidable reporting strength of Barbara Starr at the Pentagon; Jim Sciutto, our chief national security correspondent; Evan Perez at the Justice Department; and Pamela Brown, also in Washington, and we consistently remained ahead of the game with original reporting.

To ensure the flow of information across the network, almost as soon as the plane went missing, an internal email alias was established under the name *missingplane. CNNers anywhere in the world could report developments quickly to anyone network-wide who had an interest in the story (the alias still exists, for any new details). Emails were flying around CNN with subjects like "Urgent—Search Area Expanded"; "Malaysia Airlines—life rafts spotted?"; and "Malaysia Latest—Iranian man purchased tickets for stolen passport holders." When you looked at our shows, the difference in emphasis could be seen immediately. With previous crashes, our US network might have done five, ten, or fifteen minutes per hour; now they were devoting most of their airtime to MH370.

We threw everything at it, and then tried to throw more. One morning I had come off-air with *New Day* and was called to speak to one of the senior executives on the fifth floor. The exec wanted to know where we could get a cockpit to show concretely what we were broadcasting about. I said we couldn't hire the sort of simulator used by the airlines to train pilots. I had discovered that when a plane crash occurs, there was an unspoken agreement among simulator owners not to let the media rent the devices in order to re-create the incident. The news exec looked at me sympathetically, as it was obvious I had no idea what we were talking about. "No," the exec continued, "we don't want to rent a simulator: we want to charter a real 777 and send you up in it, to get the pilots to show us what it's like in the cockpit and what might have happened." I was dumbfounded. A real Boeing 777. Jeff had decided at the morning meeting that this would be another way to distinguish our coverage and wanted to explore the options. I warned that we were talking serious money here, tens of thousands of dollars, possibly more. No one was fazed. If we could charter a 777 and show what we needed to show, it would be money well spent. I put out feelers to the aviation world and the unanimous verdict came back: "No Way!" Word of our project had gone around the world. Some weeks later I got an email from CNN's commercial head of Asia in Hong Kong. He had been asked by a major Asian carrier if it was true CNN wanted to charter a 777. They wouldn't rent to us either.

If we couldn't get a real 777 and no airline or training facility would let us use a professional simulator, we went for the next best thing: a fully functional but fixed simulator that we discovered outside Toronto. Unlike professional machines, which mimic the pilot inputs by moving the whole simulator up and down on hydraulic legs, this one remained stationary, but it had an authentic, full-working cockpit, and for television purposes, it was perfect. We immediately block-booked (to ensure no one else got into the act) the machine for our coverage. Our correspondent Martin Savidge spent more than ten days sitting in this sim with the instructor pilot Mitchell Casado. From nose dives into the water to fuel exhaustion and engine flame-outs, Martin and Mitchell demonstrated scenarios of what the pilots might have done and how it would have looked and felt in the cockpit. Even though this was derided by some in the press, it proved to be extremely useful for viewers. There is nothing better than being able to say, "This is a theory; now we'll show you why it may or may not work." Or "Now see what happens if you do this, or that." Despite the criticism, I know for a fact that what we were doing on TV was being done by many airlines and pilots in the privacy of their own 777 simulators, to see what might have happened. In the end I was quite envious of Martin's getting to spend so much time in a sim, practicing flying techniques between live-shots. He jokingly told me he had been in the device so long he was now well on his way to instrument rating. (In a strange postscript, the pilot Mitchell Casado was fired from his job shortly afterward; his boss said he had been improperly dressed during his TV hits and it had been embarrassing.)

Everyone at CNN was involved. Tom Forman made excellent use of the new virtual reality studio in Washington, each day coming up with different graphics to show what was happening. Stephanie Elam in Santa Barbara demonstrated how the underwater locator beacons worked. Michael Holmes visited the ATSB laboratories in Canberra to see how they would decode the black boxes if they were ever found. Kyung Lah and Will Ripley spent hours on air search and rescue planes to dramatize the difficulty of this mission. Correspondents were everywhere: Atika Shubert, Nic Robertson, Kate Bouldan, Sara Sidner, Paula Hancocks, and Paula Newton shuttled between Malaysia and Australia as the story moved, while Andrew Stevens, Jim Clancy, and David McKenzie kept broadcasting in Kuala Lumpur and Beijing, hour after hour. I have no doubt forgotten someone in this role call of our coverage, and for this I am sorry.

The results of all this coverage quickly showed up in the network's ratings: viewers turned to CNN in large numbers. If I compare prime-time ratings on Wednesday, March 12, to Wednesday, March 5, before the plane went missing, the number of viewers aged twenty-five to fifty-four (the age group known as "the demo") was 125 percent higher because of our MH370 coverage. This was significant because it meant we were increasing our viewership with this strategically important group. Some shows had spectacular success. In the first week of MH370 coverage, Anderson Cooper's *AC360°* beat Fox News's Bill O'Reilly three days in a row.[7] Overall, in the first ten days of coverage, CNN's viewership was up 68 percent in total viewers and 79 percent in the demo. As the twists and turns continued, the numbers remained high. It was clear viewers wanted more and more details of the missing plane and were tuning to us several times a day to find out the latest. Even weeks later, when the numbers started to drift back, they settled at higher levels than before.

This increased coverage, especially given my special knowledge of Malaysia Airlines, meant I was working round the clock. Not that I minded: everyone was. MH370 was the aviation story of a lifetime and I would have been unhappy not to be part of it. The challenge for those of us who understood aviation stories was to make sure my colleagues had the necessary information and analysis to know where the story was headed so we didn't take too many wrong turns. Usually with a plane crash, there are only a couple of us doing the coverage, so it's pretty easy to help editors and producers differentiate between what is reasonable to broadcast and what is out of the ballpark. But with this story, all bets were off. Every show on every network was covering MH370 from wall to wall, and it soon became clear that the best I could hope to do was to make sure the network knew what we were thinking and to be available to give guidance on the intricacies. Emails would go back and forth, checking, double-checking. The special editorial morning call dedicated to MH370 could take up to an hour as we parsed the latest briefing from the Malaysian government or tried to understand the minutiae of operating ACARS and satellites. Huge amounts of time were spent defining a definitive timeline of events then debating the minutiae of avionics transponders and flight recorders.

CNN was now in full war mode, dispatching large numbers of troops to cover the story. As we began focusing on the shortcomings of officialdom, we started to feel the wrath of the Malaysian government, which now believed we were being unfairly critical of their operation. Hishammuddin Hussein, who was doing the briefings, had regularly been pulled apart by our experts and pundits. Now he started fighting back. For example, when we reported that sources had told us the Malaysian air force had scrambled jets on the night of the seventh as the plane flew across the country, Hishammuddin finally snapped and tweeted that the story was a "false allegation" and a "total fabrication," telling reporters that "CNN is losing all credibility."[8] A year later, he still bristles when he talks about CNN:

> I was told that somebody decided this was a story you were going to cover wall to wall, room to room and just descended on Malaysia. And it happened to be me, sitting right in front of the camera. It's not fair. You have to be put in my

position to be able to know what it's like having 6 reporters from CNN alone every day at 5:30—bashing back—not wanting to know what my answers are going to be. They had a script. They don't care what I say. They just want a response to something that has already been scripted.[9]

The suggestion that my colleagues had scripts is of course not true. I reported these criticisms to Jeff Zucker, the CEO of CNN Worldwide, my ultimate boss, and he denied them outright.

If they didn't have any new information, nobody was forcing them to do a press conference. Nobody said, "Mr. Defense Minister, you must do a daily press briefing at 5:30." I think the way that the government handled the story left a lot to be desired and that became part of the story.[10]

For the transport minister, Hishammuddin, resentment against the media, and perhaps CNN, runs deep. As he saw it, he had been trying as hard as possible to be as transparent as possible, yet the media, especially my network, were saying his briefings were a complete shambles. He was trying to show the world that his country was doing a good job, while networks like CNN were reporting the opposite.

It's not the right thing to do. You guys are so powerful, you can bring governments down, you can bring countries down.[11]

It wasn't only the Malaysians who were taking note. It is a measure of how CNN is viewed that almost immediately the TV critics and others were commenting on our wall-to-wall coverage. It was just a matter of time before Jon Stewart's *Daily Show* laid into us, deriding our use of graphics and the extent of our coverage.[12] Others chimed in: the former CNN talk-show host Larry King described our coverage as "absurd" and said he was glad he was no longer at the network.[13] Everyone online, it seemed, had an opinion. Erik Wemple, in the *Washington Post*, deplored what he saw, describing it as "very unsatisfying coverage."[14] BuzzFeed's Dorsey Shaw analyzed the amount of time we spent covering the story. He discovered that on Wednesday, March 12, from 4 to 10 p.m., we devoted 256 out of 271 minutes to MH370. He called this level of coverage "insane."[15] March 12 was also the day when all our prime-time shows doubled the number of their viewers and Anderson Cooper beat O'Reilly. Whatever the critics may have thought, the viewers apparently were watching in record numbers.

There was another development that had a dramatic effect on our coverage. CNN, like all networks, employs analysts who bring their expertise to a broadcast when it is necessary. These experts often cover political, defense, military, and security matters. They are not staff journalists or correspondents involved in the hour-by-hour coverage, but they are expected to give instant analysis in their special area of knowledge. Before MH370, we didn't really retain aviation analysts; instead, we would just call up a range of experts we had regularly interviewed in the past and put them on the air. With the demands of MH370, this was not sufficient. We had to sign up several analysts to share the load of broadcasting, and pretty soon had an entire cadre of CNN aviation analysts broadcasting on the network. Some I had worked with before and interviewed many times. Mary Schiavo was a former inspector general at the Department of Transportation and always gave superb analysis. There were newcomers to the world of twenty-four-hour television news like David Soucie, a former federal aviation investigator, who has written his own book on MH370[16]; and Les Abend, a 777 captain who, when not flying, swapped his left-hand cockpit seat for the studio. Both David and Les realized that they knew little about the workings of twenty-four-hour news broadcasting and the responsibilities that go with it. Being consummate professionals in their own fields, they set about filling the gaps in their knowledge. It was a privilege to work with them and others such as Peter Goelz, in Washington, who had been the managing director of the NTSB, and Tom Fuentes, former assistant director of the FBI.

Our "resident analysts" would be supplemented by ad hoc aviation experts. Lots of them. Often it seemed the more the merrier. As the resident aviation correspondent, I was very much aware of this change. In the past there might be a reporter at the scene, followed by a live-shot with myself. Now I often found myself in the studio with two, three, sometimes four experts in different disciplines chewing over the latest developments. It was a very different experience for me, and an engaging and constructive way of covering a story.

Experts on air-crash investigations, underwater searches, ocean topography, pilot training, audio analysis, psychology, and so on were brought in. The level of the experts in the green room where we wait before going on-air was world class. Their presence created an extraordinary hotbed of discussion and debate as we challenged each other's views on the latest developments. Mary Schiavo described those green-room interactions as "very productive."[17] She said:

> That team in the green room was as good as any investigative team with which I have ever had the honor of working,

and the years of experience and cumulative degrees and training was unlike any other and may never be replicated or surpassed.[18]

One former colleague whom it was wonderful to have back on board as an aviation analyst was Miles O'Brien. He and I had worked together for years when he was CNN's aviation and space correspondent, before he left in 2008. Miles is blunt, often undiplomatic in his views, but his analysis is always worth listening to. We frequently disagree. I think he doesn't appreciate the difficulties of actually running an investigation or airline; he thinks I am too much on the side of the authorities or airline. This is just fine. Miles is the best in the business and I know our disagreements are only professional.

For me, dealing with so many pilots or pundits took a bit of settling into. I was used to being the aviation correspondent, and pretty much had the field to myself. Now there were experts everywhere. With so many world-class experts on tap whichever way the story went, we were always prepared to give specialist analysis on what a piece of breaking news meant. From a purely practical point of view, it was necessary to have so many guests because there was so much airtime to fill and one or two people couldn't do it all.

These guests were not CNN journalists or correspondents, they were analysts and contributors. As outsiders, they were not familiar with the CNN bible on standards and practices and our policy guidelines. Normally this doesn't matter. Analysts are usually on-air for a maximum of five minutes. But this was different. The sheer amount of MH370 coverage in the weeks of March and April meant some of them would be on for twenty, thirty, forty minutes at a time or more. So there were a few times when I would firmly indicate to a producer that a particular issue or question should first be addressed to me or another staff correspondent in order to put it into the perspective of the network coverage before opening it to the analysts for discussion.

There were two occasions when I lost my temper with our outside contributors. The first was during a *New Day* telecast, after the Malaysians announced the Inmarsat data and we were now coming to grips with the meaning of this stunning new development. Jeff Wise kept insisting on-air that he was very suspicious of it all, and wouldn't believe anything until he had seen the Inmarsat data. He had a point and I didn't quarrel with his right to make it. But he was the only analyst on the segment acting as a de facto correspondent. I thought the CNN morning viewer wasn't helped in understanding this development in a short three-minute segment if we spent the time trashing what we were reporting. It leaves the viewer wondering, What was all that about? Jeff and I had words in the green room as I pointed out the risk of leaving the viewer more confused than at the start. I think Jeff frequently tried to go further in his analysis than the facts, and found the constraints of twenty-four-hour news coverage difficult. You can hear his frustration as he described his view on CNN's use of analysts:

> I soon realized the germ of every TV-news segment is: "Officials say X." The validity of the story derives from the authority of the source. The expert, such as myself, is on hand to add dimension or clarity. Truth flowed one way: from the official source, through the anchor, past the expert, and onward into the great sea of viewerdom.[19]

The second incident almost had me leaping out of my seat. I was broadcasting on a Don Lemon CNN Special Report at 10 p.m. One of the large group of panelists was the US aviation lawyer Arthur Rosenberg. In response to a viewer's question about the safety of flying to Mexico, he made this extraordinary statement:

> My personal feeling is I would rather fly an American flag carrier knowing that the quality assurance of the pilot and the equipment are ruled by the FAA.[20]

I sat there fuming, incredulous, as I heard what I believed to be dangerous nonsense. I had to interrupt Arthur, saying "forgive me" before laying into him.

> I can't let you get away with that one. There are many international carriers, I can reel them off from Singapore Airlines, Cathay Pacific, Qantas, British Airways, Lufthansa. I can go on forever, so I cannot allow the suggestion that somehow a US carrier is that much safer than one of the other major global carriers.[21]

I simply could not let Arthur's comments go unanswered. Arthur may believe it to be correct, but to my knowledge his view is not generally held by the aviation community. This show was being simulcast on CNN International and his comments could damage our credibility. Don, and indeed the other panelists, watched with some amusement as Arthur and I battled it out, finally agreeing to disagree.

Arthur and I would joust frequently on Erin Burnett's show, *Out-Front*. He gives as good as he gets, and is always gracious afterward. At that stage in the MH370 story, I had not made up my mind about the cause of the plane's disappearance, nefarious or mechanical. Arthur was firmly in the nefarious camp and made no bones about it. Night after night he and I argued, with Erin joining in. My point always remained the same: we simply didn't know and it wasn't fair to impugn the pilot.

All the CNN shows, in their own ways, took different tacks. Some wanted short, sharp, up-to-date reports, while others wanted to delve into the details. *The Situation Room* with Wolf Blitzer is a good example. The show had assembled its own team of experts, including Peter Goelz, the former head of the NTSB, and Tom Fuentes, the former assistant director of the FBI. *SitRoom* decided to make huge amounts of time available so the team and Wolf gave us the space to really come to grips with what had happened and its implications. It was a pleasure to be a part of, and the viewer was better informed as a result.

There was so much coverage and so many unknown experts on our air that eventually it became a legitimate concern. Our core group knew the ropes of twenty-four-hour news and were good at negotiating the line between analyzing a development in context and going off into rampant speculation. But others did not, and sometimes the numbers of people taking part were multiplying. While this was a very small part of the total coverage, I was worried that this risked diluting the quality of the output. I wrote to Rick Davis, the head of standards, expressing this concern. My view was simple: just because you can fly a small plane, or are an instructor or investigator, does not mean you can weave your way through the thicket of live-broadcasting on one of the most complex aviation stories ever. This was not an occasion for every pundit pilot to opine, "Well, I think this or that." Our viewers turned to us for careful, considered, expert assessments and our regular team of aviation analysts were superb at providing this.

Far and away the biggest criticism we received came as a result of the "black hole" incident on March 19, 2014. I was with Don Lemon on the CNN Special Report "The Mystery of Flight 370," answering viewer emails and tweets. It was the end of the hour-long show. I knew we were heading into dicey territory because I had already handled a viewer's question about what role, if any, psychics could play in finding MH370. The exchange went like this:

> QUEST: Jeff Wise, this is—it may seem an odd question, but I know these people have been used in murder investigations on many, many occasions. "Investigators sometimes use psychics. Why hasn't anyone considered the services of a credible psychic specializing in missing persons?" I mean, it sounds incredible, but they have been used before.
>
> WISE: I think it's difficult to find a credible psychic.[22]

I thought the psychic question was strange, but I could justify it. A viewer genuinely asked it, probably knowing that some police forces have consulted with psychics in their investigations. Then we went even further: a questioner asked whether MH370 could have disappeared into a black hole. It is worth reprinting the exact transcript:

> LEMON: Whether it was hijacking or terrorism or mechanical failure or pilot error, but what if it was something fully that we don't really understand? A lot of people have been asking about that, about black holes and on and on and on and all of these conspiracy theories. Let's look at this. Noha said, "What else can you think? Black hole? Bermuda triangle?" And then Deji says, "Just like the movie 'Lost.'" And of course, it's also—they're also referencing "The Twilight Zone," which has a very similar plot. That's what people are

saying. I know it's preposterous, but is it preposterous, do you think, Mary?

SCHIAVO: Well, it is. A small black hole would suck in our entire universe. So we know it's not that. The Bermuda triangle is often weather, and "Lost" is a TV show.

Even before we came off-air, I knew the "black hole" was going to become a talking point. Sure enough, the critics had a field day. The *Huffington Post* said, "When you've dragged out the story so much that you're onto the purely fictional causes for what appears to be a monumental tragedy, it might be time to just stop and think for a second."[23] The *National Review* called it "nonsense."[24] Time and again I have questioned myself about whether we should have asked that question and I always come down on the side of yes. It is a fact of twenty-four-hour coverage that you do have the time and the luxury to delve into areas that other shows can't. I asked Jeff Zucker about the question and criticisms. "I think this has been blown out of proportion," he told me. "If you go back and look at the tape, Don was just reacting to questions that were submitted from viewers. No one remembers that it was a viewer question or that Don dismissed it."[25]

As the weeks went by, CNN stayed with the story pretty much nonstop. We followed it through the air searches for wreckage, the towed pinger locator listening for the black boxes, the Bluefin underwater search. The critics said it was never ending and feelings were starting to grow that it was now too much. The pilot Les Abend said, "As the fourth week approached, the back stage rumblings of overkill made its way into my head."[26] Some senior producers were also uneasy. The word I always got back was the viewers still had this amazing appetite for the story and we were fully invested in covering it and would continue. But there were grumblings within the newsrooms.

Senior editors would roll their eyes as another hour of "The Mystery of MH370" programming got under way. I am told that those at the top were aware of their views.

If there was one person who is credited with driving this level of coverage for so long, it is my boss, Jeff Zucker. I asked Jeff directly whether we continued the depth of coverage for too long:

> No. It's a tremendous mystery. I get on a plane all the time. I want to know what happened. There's a lot of layers to this story and as every day went by and it wasn't solved, it became an even greater mystery and so that is what I think made it a great story.

To those critics who say CNN's coverage of MH370 came at the expense of other important stories, such as the war and crisis in Ukraine, Jeff robustly answered:

> We didn't ignore the other major news story of the time that was going on, which was Ukraine. We gave more attention to Ukraine than anyone else. We had 4 correspondents on the ground in Ukraine. Had we not been covering the plane, I don't think we would have given any more coverage to Ukraine. So I have no regrets about that.[27]

On this issue of whether we had done too much coverage, I got a different and important perspective from Mary Schiavo, the former inspector general of the US Transportation Department who now represents families in air accident claims; Mary didn't flinch from saying we were right in doing what we had done:

These families who have lost loved ones scour the news for information. They wanted every piece of information we could deliver. No family member has ever told me we did too much or were too sensational.[28]

The network remains committed to the story and stands ready to ramp up coverage the moment there are further developments. When the flaperon was found on the African side of the Indian Ocean, we immediately dispatched correspondents and crews to Reunion Island. Such was our speed that we got there a few days ahead of Malaysia Airlines and most of the French authorities from Paris. Again, I was struck that the viewers' appetite to know about MH370 developments had not gone away.

MH370 and the flaperon dominated the airwaves again, but this time for a much shorter period. Donald Trump was standing for the republican presidential nomination, Hillary Clinton's email scandal was heating up again, the Iran nuclear deal was on the agenda, so the will to stay with the story at heightened levels was more muted.

As the deep underwater search drags on, and with fresh suggestions that the search teams are looking in the wrong place, I continue to be amazed at how nothing about this story is easy, or goes according to plan. For instance, with the flaperon, what should have been an easy task, identifying whether the piece was from MH370—yes or no—dragged on for weeks.

Before I leave CNN's coverage of MH370, you may recall that in chapter one I recounted how I had flown and filmed with Fariq Hamid, the first officer on MH370, two weeks before the incident. We were filming *Business Traveller* in Malaysia. Although nothing more than a sad coincidence, the conspiracy theorists were quick to suggest otherwise. Every day I received tweets such as "@CNN stop using @richardquest as an expert on flight 370. He is complicit." "@richardquest Y were u flying w 370s copilot Fariq Hamid just weeks before? Vry strange coincidence u r now heading the media hunt! Surreal?" One article even asked, "Can you see why this particular so called 'coincidence' may need some further investigating?"[29] It was bizarre and I am not entirely certain what these people thought had happened. Do they believe I knew MH370 was going to disappear? Or, perhaps, that I had a hand in it? Or, as some darkly suggested, the whole thing was a media hoax. To this day, I still get tweets and emails from people wanting to know "what I was really up to."

The critics may have gotten a kick out of poking fun at our coverage, but I am convinced that CNN and those of us involved will have the last word. The facts of this missing plane are unique and worthy of breaking the broadcasting mold. There have been some incredible moments during the broadcasting, moments I had never experienced before and am unlikely to experience again. Frequently we would be on-air, usually late at night, on *Anderson Cooper 360°* or a Don Lemon CNN Special Report. We'd be wrapping up the events of the day when announcements would be made from Kuala Lumpur or Perth, where it was already the middle of the next day. David Gallo, David Soucie, Les Abend, and I would then have to make sense of these developments, on live television. It is a testament to the willingness of executive producer Charlie Moore and the producers at *AC360°* to do things differently, and throw the running order out the window and stay with our ruminations live on-air. We would be reading the documents, commenting back and forth among ourselves as we tried to make sense of it all before attempting an analysis. These moments were the antithesis of the era of prepackaged, formulaic news coverage. It was why twenty-four-hour news had been invented. Here the viewer was being invited to see firsthand the process by which raw news is analyzed and brought into perspective. What I will always remember are the debates and discussions about what should be reported, and how we pushed the coverage into new areas of knowledge, ensuring that nothing was missed. I may never see such size and scale on a single story again in my career. That is, until they find the plane, when you can be assured of one thing: CNN will be there.

FINALLY . . . SOMETHING

If it's a plane crash, then people have died.
You have to respect them for that.

—JOHNNY BEGUE

Sixteen months after MH370 went missing, I was on assignment in Florida for CNN *Business Traveller* when I got the email. My producer Saskya Vandoorne wrote, "Twitter is abuzz with MH370 . . . probably a false lead but a wing has washed up near the Reunion Island." She enclosed a picture of the object found in the western Indian Ocean. I was about ten miles from Legoland, where I was filming the next part of our show on theme parks. As I looked at the photo it was obvious that this was something significant. It was a part of a large aircraft wing, probably one of the flaps. As I said right at the start of this book: you know when something big happens in the world of CNN, your BlackBerry goes into overdrive. Saskya may have gotten to me first, but there were plenty behind her. Suddenly everyone was emailing: What is it? Is it part of MH370? Could this be the breakthrough they have been seeking? Have they found it? I knew there and then that Legoland would have to wait. I called Meara Erdozain, the vice president of programming. All she wanted to know was where I was and how quickly I could get back to a major CNN broadcasting center. It was going to take too long to fly to New York, so she instructed me to head immediately to the Orlando Airport, where there are hourly flights to Atlanta, the headquarters of CNN.

On the way to headquarters, I had an hour or two to think about what had been found. Certainly it looked like a part of an aircraft wing. But I had been wrong many times on this story: I was wrong about the debris in the South China Sea, wrong about the debris in the southern Indian Ocean, wrong about the pings heard underwater. I didn't want to be wrong again. This wasn't a matter of pride; rather, I had learned from experience that this story was throwing up challenges to aviation journalism in a different way from anything I had seen before. The usual rules simply didn't apply. Yet all my instincts said that obviously this was part of the missing plane. The question was, what could I say that would get this point across while at the same time pointing out that there was always room for doubt?

Within hours, larger, better photos of the missing plane part had been published and we were comparing it to online schematics of the Boeing 777 wing. The pictures suggested that the piece was part of the control surfaces of the wing. Rather than the flaps, it appeared to be one of the plane's two flaperons. A flaperon is a hybrid piece of equipment that combines the functions of the flaps and the ailerons, hence the name flaperon. The ailerons control the left and right banking of the aircraft by going up and down into the airflow, helping raise or lower the wing to make turns. The flaps extend on takeoff and landing and increase the wings' size, giving the plane greater lift at slower speeds. The flaperons are part of a plane's steering mechanism, and allow the pilot to bank the plane. At slower speeds they also extend marginally out of the wing in order to give greater stability and lift. As a passenger, you can see the flaperon in action if you sit behind the wing. It is on the trailing edge and is located nearer the fuselage. You will see it bouncing up and down on takeoff and landing as it stabilizes the aircraft, unlike the flaps, which extend in several sections then retract into the wing. The flaperon remains active throughout the flight (although at higher speeds it is far less noticeable).

The piece had been found by a local beachcomber, Johnny Begue. He had been at the beach looking for stones to crush spices with when he saw it.[1]

> I realized it was part of a plane by the roundness. I called my friend who helped me lift it up the beach. We thought about the families, families we don't know. And then we thought we shouldn't sit on it because if there was a crash something like that there are dead families so we should respect them, so we said we'll put the flowers there to make it pretty.

Begue stopped his friends from cleaning the barnacles off the flaperon, a move that in hindsight would be a help to the investigators as they tried to work out the provenance of the piece. The flowers would not stay there long because the police on Reunion soon arrived and the piece was on its way to the authorities for further study. After some initial confusion over a number reportedly printed on the piece, it was confirmed as 657BB. It was described in the Boeing 777 maintenance manual as "flaperon Leading Edge Panel."[2] Another piece of debris was also recovered on the beach: the remnants of some sort of suitcase or backpack.

The suitcase was much less likely to yield information than

the mechanical part, and so the latter is where most of the attention was focused. While we waited for the aviation investigators to make a final determination on the source of the flaperon, I was being asked one vital question, hour after hour: Was it possible for a piece of debris from MH370 to have traveled 2,500 miles from the most likely crash site? It became obvious that the answer was, unequivocally, yes. If you look at a map, you'll see that Reunion is on the opposite side of the Indian Ocean from Australia. It is a straight shot across the water from the most likely search zone to the coast of East Africa, where the island is located. Experts were put on-air reminding us that they had long predicted that the currents of the southern Indian Ocean Gyre, swirling around, creating a great sea garbage tank, would eventually cause the debris to drift across to the other side. CNN weather staff created graphics showing how it had taken only eight months for debris from the Japan tsunami to make its way across the Pacific Ocean, washing up on the shores of western Canada and the United States. It all came back to me. In March 2014, the experts were telling us that eventually, something would be washed up on the western side of the Indian Ocean. It was all backed up by solid scientific evidence from the University of Western Australia, which showed us its drift-modeling forecast, which indicated that after eighteen months, wreckage would land in that region. According to Professor Charitha Pattiaratchi:

> It is entirely consistent with what we know about the ocean currents from our computer modelling. The debris coming in there can only have originated to the east of the region where they found it. The current goes anticlockwise. It goes north from the crash site and then goes west.[3]

The ATSB in Australia also released a drift-modeling video, which proved exactly this point. If we were surprised by this development, our expert oceanographers were not.

Needless to say, at CNN we moved our coverage into top gear. My colleagues in the studio were brushing up on their history, remembering what had happened all those months ago. I was in a fortunate position, as I had just finished the first draft of this book, so all the facts were fresh in my mind. Correspondents were being dispatched to Reunion Island, to Kuala Lumpur, and to Paris. In an amazingly short period of time, we had all areas and aspects covered. The message from CNN was clear: we owned the story the last time round, and if this was the moment when a critical clue in the mystery had appeared, we were not about to cede the ground.

As the news of the find flashed around the world, it was particularly noted in Paris, where a new bureaucratic wrinkle was about to be added to the proceedings. Reunion has been under the control of France since the seventeenth century. It is now classed as an overseas territory and considered an administrative region, or prefecture, of France. Even though the French had played only a limited, advisory role in the MH370 investigation so far, the fact that the flaperon had washed up on French soil meant the French authorities took responsibility for handling the debris, which had to be transported to France for specialized examination. Thus, late on Friday, July 31, the flaperon was crated and boarded onto an Air France 777 flight bound for Paris. As I watched the video of the plane taking off I thought of the strange juxtaposition of one 777 carrying in its belly a vital part of another 777, taking it on a journey to release any secrets it had carried for the past sixteen months.

As the piece was making its way to France, Boeing sources made it clear that yes, their experts recognized this as a flaperon from a 777 but they couldn't say whether it was from 9M-MRO without further tests. This was backed up by comments from the Australian deputy prime minister, Warren Truss, who said the flaperon was a "major lead" and was "not inconsistent with a Boeing 777."

It was a very strange situation: everyone agreed that this was a 777 flaperon, but no one would say it's *the* flaperon. Yet what else could it be? There were no other missing 777s in that part of the world. Though no 777 had reported losing a flaperon in flight—it's the sort of thing a pilot would notice pretty quickly—everyone stopped short of weighing in definitively on the piece of debris. The French transferred the flaperon from Paris to Balma near Toulouse, and the headquarters of the Direction Générale de l'Armement (DGA). The DGA is part of the Ministry of Defense and is a specialist laboratory and testing center for the military and civilian aerospace industry. In many ways it was the perfect place to send the flaperon, as the DGA did much of the work on the wreckage of Air France 447, which had been in the water for years. This gave them expertise in analyzing pieces exactly like this one.

In an odd turn of events, it wasn't the aviation investigators at the Bureau d'Enquêtes et d'Analyses (BEA) who were in charge. Instead, the judicial authorities in France were now calling the shots because four of the passengers on board MH370 were French citizens. With a hijacking or other criminal act looming as a possibility, under French law the judicial authorities were given primacy to inquire into what had happened. The inspection of the flaperon was to be conducted under the control and presence of three French judges carrying out their legal mandate. Inevitably a bureaucratic circus ensued. In Paris, meetings had been held between the French and Malaysian governments to determine how to handle this development. In Toulouse, there were representatives from the BEA, NTSB, the Malaysian DCA, Malaysia Airlines, the Australian ATSB, the Chinese, Boeing—it seemed everyone had to be there to make sure proper protocol was followed during the inspection of the flaperon. Its analysis didn't begin until four days after the piece arrived in France. It left me and my colleagues wondering what on earth was going on and taking so long.

Finally, on Wednesday, August 5, 2015, it was time to reveal what they had found. An announcement was expected at 8 p.m. Paris time, from a French prosecutor, and then a statement from the Malaysian prime minister, Najib Razak. That was the plan, yet the Malaysians weren't going for it. Ten minutes before the French were to present their findings, the prime minister spoke. From everything I have heard, the Malaysians were determined that because this was their plane and their investigation, it was their right to speak first. Here is the crucial part of Razak's statement:

> An international team of experts have conclusively con-
> firmed that the aircraft debris found on Reunion Island is
> indeed from MH370. We now have physical evidence that,
> as I announced on 24th March last year, flight MH370
> tragically ended in the southern Indian Ocean.

It was lost on no one that Razak used the word "conclusively." I was broadcasting live at the time he said this, and it was obvious to me that he was leaving no room for doubt about where the plane had gone down, or so we thought.

Within minutes of the prime minister's statement, the deputy prosecutor in France, Serge Mackowiak, held his news conference. We waited for a similar announcement of "conclusiveness." It never came. Instead, Mackowiak said, "In view of the experts' report we can say today there exists very strong presumption that the flaperon found on the beach of Reunion comes from the Boeing 777 of Malaysian Airlines flight MH370."

The difference in language was obvious. What was a cut-and-dried conclusion for the Malaysians was a matter of "strong presumption" for the French. The anchor Brooke Baldwin and I parried this back and forth trying to make sense: Was it merely a semantic issue or were there real, substantive differences in meaning between what the two officials were saying? We had no idea. The prosecutor said that Malaysia Airlines representatives had seen specific similarities that linked the flaperon to the plane. But he didn't say what they were. No one mentioned the presence of a serial number, which would seem to be the only conclusive proof of its origins.

This was a shambles. The first time potentially hard evidence of the plane is found and the authorities managed to make a complete mess of it by differing in their wording. It beggars belief that something like this was able to happen.

The families, scattered around the world, had been given an early warning of a few moments about the announcement. Some received it by text message, others by email, while luckier ones got a phone call from Malaysian embassy officials. They were given the prime minister's version of the announcement: This flaperon was part of the plane. The plane went down in the southern Indian Ocean. Yet all of a sudden we in the media were questioning this conclusion. Not surprisingly, the families of the Chinese victims were having nothing of it. Soon they were out on the streets, protesting in front of the Malaysian embassy in Beijing.

In the following days we learned more of the Malaysians' decision to use the word "conclusively." The transport minister said Malaysia Airlines had recognized one of their maintenance seals on the part, along with the type and color of paint. No doubt these are the "elements" referred to in the French deputy prosecutor's statement.

To the uncertainty over the flaperon, now there was about to be added confusion over other debris that was found on the island. The new transport minister, Liow Tiong Lai, declared that Malaysian searchers on Reunion had found parts of a window, seat cushions, and other debris. He told my colleague Andrew Stevens:

> These debris are all aircraft materials, window pane materials, cushion materials, so once we had collected we immediately handed it over to the military police. We cannot be certain it is from MH370, but it is definitely aircraft materials.[4]

There was only one problem: no one else claimed to know anything about this other debris, let alone said they had custody of it. It was another example of a stunning lack of communication between all the parties, which further frustrated and enraged the families. At the time of writing this book, many of these issues remain unsettled.

Now that the French authorities had said with "certainty" that the flaperon was from MH370, one key question had been definitively answered: the plane had indeed gone down somewhere in the southern Indian Ocean. Many of the more fanciful theories about the disappearance, including the ones about landing on Diego Garcia or in the Maldives, could now be put to rest. (The conspiracy theorists will never let up, and will claim the flaperon was planted by the Chinese, Americans, or someone else who shot down the plane.)

An in-depth examination of the part will probably reveal how and when it separated from the aircraft, and whether this occurred in flight or as the plane hit the water. Microscopic examination of the tears, rips, and scratches will provide answers. A scientific analysis of the barnacles and sea life growing on the flaperon should tell how long it had been in the water. Possibly the kind of marine life the investigators find will reveal where the piece first rested.

What the flaperon will not reveal is the exact location where the plane went down. This was confirmed by the ATSB in its report published in December 2015: "While this debris find is consistent with the current search area it does not provide sufficient information to refine it."[5] It seems the flaperon won't reveal the secret of where the plane is.

Nor will the flaperon reveal what happened at 1:19 after "Good night Malaysian Three Seven Zero." Unless there was an explosion (almost certainly there wasn't) and residue is found (highly unlikely after all this time), the only information that the piece can possibly yield will be how it separated from the aircraft.

All of this, of course, is enormously disappointing to the victims' families, who have ached for any factual information about the plane's whereabouts. As I write this chapter, with so much still unresolved, I am left to reflect on how the flaperon incident only served to heap more confusion and misery on those who were most vulnerable. I was astonished that there wasn't a better plan in place for informing the families of important developments. Any liaison arrangements with the families from last year did not appear to have been maintained or kept up to date. The Malaysians and French did not coordinate properly on announcements, so that each country delivered a differing message. Even though something like this was entirely predictable, it was still a disgrace. Everyone involved should have done better.

CHAPTER TWELVE

THOSE LEFT BEHIND

I would like to know what happened.

—Sarah Bajc

If there is widespread agreement about one part of the MH370 story, it is the appalling way the families have been treated and, in many cases, left to languish in their grief and misery. No account of the vanishing of MH370 can be complete without a look at their ordeal. I have witnessed many scenes of airline accident grief, but in thirty years I have never seen relatives accorded such callous treatment.

As I described in chapter 5, the relatives of those on board had been placed in several hotels in Kuala Lumpur and at the Metropark Lido Hotel in Beijing. Unfortunately, in the case of the Lido, the provision of support, care, and comfort was far from the reality. The families were besieged by reporters and photographers every time they attempted to go from one place to another, especially to the grand ballroom, where the briefings took place. It was just about impossible to create anything like an environment of support in such chaotic circumstances. The video from Beijing told a truly horrific story of what the families were going through. The relatives were angry at the lack of information they were being given and were taking it out on the low-level officials sent to speak to them.

To understand what the families were going through staying at the Lido, I asked CNN's Beijing correspondent, David McKenzie, who spent weeks covering this side of the story, to describe the day-to-day ritual. "It was awful," he recalls. "The family members were stuck in this hotel. They got into this terrible rhythm of going together to breakfast and going to meetings, trying to get some sense from the Malaysian and Chinese authorities . . . they were living in this vortex, kind of grief. There were lawyers trying to talk to the family members; there were government officials; there were journalists."[1]

In those first weeks, the worst moment by far was the arrival of the text from Malaysia Airlines announcing the death of all on board. As we saw, the text's arrival started rumors, panic, and waves of anguish among the relatives, many of whom didn't understand the English text and were hearing the translation at second or third hand.

Over the weeks, as I watched the treatment of the relatives both in Kuala Lumpur and Beijing, I remembered my own experiences with Pan Am 103, twenty-five years earlier. It was December 1988. I was a young BBC Radio reporter based in New York. We were having our office Christmas lunch at the Russian Tea Room when our beepers all went off simultaneously. The message: call London immediately. Using the restaurant pay phone, I called the news desk and was told a Pan Am plane had crashed over Scotland. My instructions were to get to Kennedy Airport as quickly as possible to witness the arrival of relatives who were meeting a flight that would never reach its destination.

It was raining hard and it took seemingly forever to get a cab. When I finally got to JFK, there was little if no attempt to identify or stop the reporters from roaming the Pan Am terminal, looking for anyone we could interview. I saw one mother, who I later learned was Janine Boulanger, looking up at the flight information screen, which read "Pan Am 103—See Agent." Her husband joined her and whispered in her ear. Janine went rigid, like a plank, and fell to the floor, where she writhed in agony, screaming, "My baby, my baby!" It was the closest I had ever come to witnessing a heart break. Without thinking, I turned on my tape recorder to get a recording for the morning news. In doing so, I still think I acted professionally, but once I realized what was taking place, I should have switched it off and turned away. Unfortunately, I did neither. I remain ashamed of this moment even after all these years.[2] Later, another relative spat as she passed by the reporters, saying, "He's dead, he's dead, what more do you want."

These thoughts came back to me as I watched the footage coming in from Beijing: people being removed by stretcher, others screaming at the cameras as they were carried from the room. I remember thinking, Why on earth were the authorities allowing the ranks of the media to get so close to the room where these poor people were being told this horrible information? Once it was clear what was happening, why didn't they find another way to get them out of the ballroom, or attempt to protect their privacy as they left? Of course, one has to question the media themselves, who decided to record and show these pictures, my own network included.

Each of the 239 people on board MH370 left behind a grieving family. One person who has been more vocal than most in criticizing the authorities and giving voice to the relatives' complaints is Sarah Bajc. Sarah's partner, Philip Wood, worked for IBM in Beijing, where she was a teacher at an international school. Philip was fifty years old when he disappeared with MH370. Returning from a visit to his family in Texas, he was heading to Beijing to the home he shared with Sarah and her three children from a previous marriage. The family was preparing for a move to Kuala Lumpur, where both Philip and Sarah would be working.

Sarah remembers every detail of that Saturday morning. She was particularly anxious for Philip to be home as the movers were coming later that morning to begin the move to Malaysia. She had sent a car to meet Philip at the airport. The flight was due to land around 6 a.m., and when he hadn't arrived by eight, she tried to find out what happened. Initially, she saw an announcement on the Malaysia Airlines website that the flight had been delayed, yet she knew it had taken off on time from Kuala Lumpur the previous evening. Growing more concerned, she continued searching online and found reports that the plane was missing. As she was listed as Philip's next of kin, she finally received the call from Malaysia Airlines six hours later saying the plane was missing and they had little more information about its whereabouts.

Sarah has been one of the leaders of the campaign questioning the official version of events. Along with other family members, she has been involved in the hiring of a private investigator to look into what happened. Before I met Sarah in "real life," I interviewed her several times on live television. Although she wasn't the only relative we spoke to, in many ways she became the voice and the face of the English-speaking families.

When I went to Kuala Lumpur I knew I had to meet Sarah. Seeing her on television, I had often wondered what was driving her actions. I could understand her anger at losing her partner, but I couldn't understand why she (or many of the other relatives and friends) didn't accept what seemed obvious to everyone else: that even though the circumstances were extremely unusual, MH370 had probably crashed and her partner had perished along with the others.

Sarah has been exceptionally critical of the way MH370 has been handled by the Malaysian government. She doesn't know what happened to the plane, but she is pretty sure the families are not being told the truth. We met in an Irish pub in Kuala Lumpur at the end of a school day. "We don't have the facts because they haven't really released a lot of facts," she told me. In the weeks and months that followed the official announcement, the families struggled to obtain information from the airline and the government. "We don't know why it went off course, we don't know where it went because Malaysia has not been transparent. They say one thing and then they say something else and then they contradict themselves yet again."[3]

In addition to the horror of losing their loved ones, Sarah and the others have had to deal with some preposterous stories that only exacerbated their pain. In Sarah's case, there were reports that Philip had sent a text to a freelance journalist, attaching a black digital photograph embedded with Exif data that located him on Diego Garcia, home of the enormous US military base. The text supposedly said:

> I have been held hostage by unknown military personnel after my flight was hijacked (blindfolded). I work for IBM and I have managed to hide my cellphone in my ass during the hijack. I have been separated from the rest of the passengers and I am in a cell. My name is Philip Wood. I think I have been drugged as well and cannot think clearly.[4]

It is amazing that anyone took such an obvious hoax seriously. Nevertheless, there are pages and pages of online discussions about it. Distressingly for Sarah, as the story went viral around the world, she was called on to respond to it. Today, she just sighs about the experience: "When I read that I dismissed it on 3 primary counts. Firstly, I would have been in his last call so it would have been me on autodial. Second, this wasn't the way he would have spoken. If he could have had the opportunity to have a phone, I am sure he would have contacted me or his father. So I discounted it."[5]

Like all who have studied MH370, Sarah knows just about every fact of the case and she goes back and forth on the different theories. I would like to know what she currently believes, since she doesn't think that either of the pilots committed suicide and she is pretty sure the Diego Garcia stories are untrue. But she remains open to the possibility that the Malaysian air force accidentally shot the plane down. "There is a lot of evidence to support that there has been an intentional cover-up of that," she says. "People make mistakes, accidents happen. I could reconcile with human failure or a systems failure or an equipment failure. Those are part of life. But the fact that somebody's intentionally hiding the ability to reconcile that for me is very, very angering. It's angering."[6]

The theory of a possible cover-up is at the heart of what she and many relatives believe is going on. Whether the issue is what happened to the plane or how Malaysia handled the search and investigation doesn't matter to Sarah. She is convinced someone knows something and is not letting on. The fact that the private investigator hired by the relatives is making little progress because regular sources refuse to speak to him only reinforces this view. Apparently, a colleague of the detective said she's never seen anything like it. Sarah says, "It's their opinion that there is an act of cover-up within the government and more than one." I ask whether this cover-up is a result of incompetence or a deliberate act. "We don't know that, but it's still unacceptable. I believe they destroyed evidence. So if you're talking about ever finding the truth on this, the likelihood is getting smaller and smaller."

Sarah has given more than 250 interviews and spent at least 1,200 hours searching for, cajoling, and demanding answers from anyone who might be able to help. Such endeavors have taken a heavy emotional toll, on Sarah as well as other angry, frustrated relatives. The lack of progress in their quest leaves them without closure. Sarah has had no choice but to go ahead with the move from Beijing to Kuala Lumpur. Since she and Philip weren't married, it appears she's not in line for any financial compensation. With three children in college she had to be smart because, as she said, "What else was I going to do?"

Whenever I interviewed Sarah on CNN or read articles about her, I was always a bit wary of her refusal to believe the official version of the crash. Repeatedly, she would say that there was no physical evidence that the plane had gone down in the ocean, and talked in terms of Philip's coming back. After more than a year-long disappearance, now she seems more accepting. "Not that I don't want Philip to come back, but the reality is he's probably not coming back," she says.[7]

Having lived, breathed, and slept this crisis since the day the plane went missing, Sarah, like the other relatives, is angry, frustrated, and bewildered, but mostly these days she is exhausted. "I think we are all tanked out. I mean not only has it been an emotionally exhausting time, it's been physically exhausting. How many times can you be punched and still get back up? I think we're all at that point where we're just wiped out," she says.[8]

After speaking with Sarah for more than an hour, and hearing the views of someone who has been battling with the authorities to get answers, I began to have a different feeling about this story. I have met relatives of plane crash victims many times. Usually I meet them during brief interviews in which they remember the person they loved and lost. Meeting with Sarah was more of a forensic dissection of what happened and speculation about possible reasons for a cover-up. While MH370 has been a big part of my life for the past two years, I have always been looking at it from a professional journalist's perspective. That's my job. With Sarah, I was talking to someone whose interpretation of the past year was very different from mine, because she had been living it 24/7, hearing every theory, every nuance. For her, it wasn't a job; it was her life.

Then Sarah asked me a question. "So you're willing to donate any of your proceeds to the investigation?"

I didn't have to think for longer than a couple of seconds. "Yes," I replied.

She was surprised. "Really? Every person who's published a book, I've contacted and said, 'Are you willing to donate a portion of your profits?' They all said no. I don't even care about the money. It's just the point."

In the interest of transparency, you should know that I have made a small donation from my advance for this book to the private investigator who is looking into what happened on behalf of the families.

Before Sarah and I parted ways, I had only one question left. "Do you think we'll ever find out?"

"I don't know," she admitted, "but I can't hinge my sanity on that."

CHAPTER THIRTEEN

THOSE IN CHARGE

There are pundits who continually spout their claims
about what happened and there are people like me who
make informed assessments.

—David Soucie[1]

I have spent most of this book immersed in the facts of the MH370 mystery, and have done so in the hope of bettering the reader's understanding. I know from years of covering crashes that being an aviation correspondent frequently means focusing on the literal details about the plane and about what investigators are discovering. But a plane crash is fundamentally about the human tragedy that arises in its wake: those people who were on board and those left behind grieving. MH370 was carrying 239 souls from fifteen countries. I have learned that everyone who comes into contact with plane crashes is affected in ways rarely seen in other stories.

Two people at the very center of the MH370 crises were Hishammuddin, the acting Malaysian transport minister, and Ahmad Jauhari Yahya (AJ), the CEO of Malaysia Airlines. Both men agreed to meet me in Kuala Lumpur. Until now, neither had spoken much about his view on what was happening during the crisis and how it was handled.

THE MINISTER

I think the first realization is "This cannot be happening."
And then "Where is it?" It is unprecedented.
—HISHAMMUDDIN HUSSEIN

Throughout this book one name has continually popped up in press conferences, in the giving of statements, and in the making of announcements: Hishammuddin Hussein, who in March 2014 was Malaysia's defense minister and acting transport minister. In those roles he became the voice and the face of the Malaysian government's response to MH370. He was the minister responsible for holding the daily press briefings, standing front and center before the world's media. Hish, as he is known to friends and colleagues, was inextricably linked to every aspect of Malaysia's handling of MH370.

In doing this job he bore the brunt of the criticism that was constantly being leveled against Malaysia. He was vilified, criticized, mocked, and ridiculed by the families who called him clueless, hapless, incompetent. To the world's press, as Malaysia's representative, he seemed to embody everything that was going wrong in the search and the investigation. In those first few months, I sat through hours and hours of Hishammuddin's briefings, and during my visit to Kuala Lumpur in April 2014, I saw him in action. I realized quickly that Hishammuddin's fundamental problem was that he rarely had any facts to tell us. Those he did have kept changing and he himself kept changing what he was telling us. Time and again, we heard him backtrack on facts he had given only a few days previously. For instance: the "all right, good night," the final words spoken in the cockpit, became "Good night Malaysian 370"; and the five passengers who checked in but didn't board the plane eventually became four who never checked in.

So who is this man who became the object of the world's scorn? Any idea that this well-spoken, urbane minister is just another garden-variety Malaysian politician is misleading. In Malaysia, he comes from a leading political family and is a political animal through and through. His father, Hussein Onn, was Malaysia's third prime minister. His uncle was the country's second prime minister. He is a first cousin to the country's current prime minister, Najib Razak. With a law degree from Britain, Hishammuddin is a lawyer by training and a politician by profession. But none of his previous ministerial posts prepared him for the prime minister's request that he take the lead in the case of MH370.

When I went to Malaysia in 2015, I wanted to hear his side of the story, and hear him explain why he made the decisions he did. After several days of negotiations with his advisers, I was finally granted an hour with him at his office in the Ministry of Defense, outside Kuala Lumpur. The minister's office is huge, with a large desk, comfortable sofas, and a conference room to the side with a big table. On the walls and stacked around the room are various interesting pieces of the art he collects. I made it clear that I would treat our meeting like any other journalistic interview. I asked the questions I wanted to ask; it would be up to him to choose to answer, evade, or just demur.

I had sat through hours of this man's press conferences; I had heard him called just about every insult imaginable; I had wondered myself if he was incompetent, a fool, a fabricator, or somebody who had been dealt an impossible hand of cards and had played them as best he could. Now I got to ask him, directly, crucial questions, such as why he did not release sooner the information that the plane had turned back or announced that it had kept flying for seven hours. "Would it have made any difference?" he replied. I believe it would have made a big difference to the perception of truthfulness, I told him. "I am not dealing with perceptions," he retorted. "What if what I said was wrong? I just add more conspiracy . . . more doubt. Because the public are not going to give us the benefit of the doubt." This was his reason for sometimes saying so little.

In truth, Hishammuddin could never have satisfied the demands of the international press. From the very start of the crisis, he had been on the defensive, telling the world two days after the plane vanished, "we have nothing to hide."[2] There were hundreds of journalists every day clamoring for information about a search that Hishammuddin now agrees was full of confusion. "How can it not be confusion?" he admits. "If you're going through something that's so unprecedented and in real time." Admitting now to confusion is a very different response from that which we were hearing at the time. During those first hectic days after the plane vanished, he had responded to accusations of confusion saying "it is only confusion if you want it to be seen as confusion."[3]

When Hishammuddin described himself as "this poor acting minister of transport of Malaysia" and said that "Malaysia is poor . . . we don't have the assets," he was not seeking our sympathy; rather, he was hoping for understanding. He was right when he said he was facing a state of affairs that was on a larger scale than anything he, or indeed anyone in the government, had faced before. He knew that many of the passengers' families believed the government was hiding something and would never accept what he said. "I don't blame them! Until we get to the truth of it. Until we get to the black boxes," he acknowledged. "That is part and parcel of being government nowadays. You have to take the good and the bad; and the bad is that people are not going to believe you until you show the facts into their face. Unfortunately for 370 we don't have all the facts."[4]

I tried to get a statement from him telling us that more information would be released about what happened on the night with the radar operator, and I failed. I tried to get the minister to admit where things could have been done better, and all he said was "obviously we had to manage it better" and "there will be a full report later."[5]

As if to prove again that truth is stranger, and more ironic, than fiction, in July 2014 Hishammuddin's stepgrandmother, Puan Sri Siti Amirah Kusuma, was a passenger on MH17, and was killed when the plane was blown out of the sky over Ukraine. The Dutch report into the crash said the plane was brought down by a BUK missile. It's believed anti-Ukrainian separatist rebels fired it at the 777, mistaking it for a military transport plane. The Russians suggest it was the Ukrainian air force that shot down the plane by mistake.

Even allowing for the horrendous delay in retrieving the bodies from the sunflower fields of Ukraine, her remains were among the last to be recovered and identified. For a man who has been unable to give closure to the families of MH370, Hishammuddin now had to face the uncertainty over who killed his own relative. He told me, "I went through it with my grandmother. Until you found her you still feel like she might not be on the plane. The plane might not have left. She might have survived, parachuted out or something. But we only found her knee. Just her knee. What we buried. And that was enough for me to have closure."

A visiting high-ranking military officer from an allied nation was awaiting his turn with the minister, but before I was ushered out of the door, I wanted to know if Hishammuddin felt that history would be kinder to him, and to his handling of the aftermath of the disappearance, than his contemporaries were. He thought long before he answered. "I think that in the circumstances we did the best we could. And for what it's worth people are going to judge us for that." Then he continued, giving us an insight into some of the local, primarily Malaysian issues that weighed on his mind at the time: "[The citizens] have not gone to the streets and brought us down because of my handling of MH370. And that was one of my priorities."[6]

I think, though, there was something else at play here. All the major political decision makers in Malaysia realized that the world's attention was on them. They wanted to ensure that the country was seen to be handling this crisis in a professional, first-world way. They were so intent on following the rules, doing everything by the book, that they lost sight of what was happening. Far from being widely praised for their work, they ended up being roundly criticized.

With this in mind, it becomes clear that there is an astonishing gap in the minister's perception of what happened and the rest of the world's. He thinks he did his country proud in his appearances before the press. "In that 45 minutes that I was on TV at 5:30 every day, I didn't embarrass Malaysia," Hishammuddin told me. "If you can get away with the present media today, with not embarrassing your nation, no matter what mistakes we make along the way, that's the best you can get out of it."

A few weeks after MH370, he gave us a glimpse of how he viewed the world. "I think history will judge us well."[7]

THE CEO

The reality just sets in. It's not about losing an aircraft.
You're losing lives.
—AHMAD JAUHARI YAHYA, CEO

Nothing prepares an airline CEO for "the call," telling him one of his company's planes is missing, probably crashed. He knows this is one of the risks of the business he runs, and he is trained to handle the situation, yet still he isn't prepared for "the call."

My first meeting with AJ, the CEO of Malaysia Airlines, was during my trip to Malaysia to film *Business Traveller* in 2014, when I flew in the cockpit with Fariq Hamid. After the flight, I had dinner with AJ in the first-class lounge. He wanted me to try the new menu and services Malaysia Airlines was offering their most preferred passengers. The chef had arranged for me to try just about everything on the menu. The food was excellent.

A newcomer to aviation, AJ had been CEO for only two and a half years. I wanted to get his perspective on the handling of a major accident, which is the toughest part of being an airline CEO. How would he handle the intensity of the public's interest? Did he believe he should be out front speaking to the press and meeting the families, or leading from behind the scenes? As the evening came to an end, I asked him, "How do you prepare for the phone call in the middle of the night?"

AJ told me he had read and memorized the airline emergency manual; he had rehearsed where he would go and what he would be expected to do. Hearing his answer, I knew he didn't have the slightest idea of what it would truly be like after a major accident.

One year later, after he had endured the disappearance of MH370, I asked him the question again. AJ recalled the first few hours of the crisis.

> When 370 went missing I had a call from my commercial director at about 6 in the morning, to say this is not a drill. We lost a 777 flight to Beijing. We're still trying to find out where it is right now. We have no idea where it is. We lost a 777. I went to the office straightaway. We had already set up

a response. We tried to call the aircraft and they didn't respond. We tried to call via SATCOM, not the normal radio. They didn't respond. Nothing. Nothing. We just lost the aircraft.[8]

AJ agrees, that no amount of training gets you ready for this moment. "Nothing. You can do all the drills in the world, but having something that actually happened, nothing will prepare you for this. Until the reality hits you, nothing prepares you for that."[9]

Not surprisingly, no airline CEO likes talking about this part of the job. Tony Fernandes, the CEO of AirAsia, Malaysia Airlines' rival, received his first phone call in December 2014 when one of his A320s crashed into the Java Sea on a flight from Indonesia to Singapore. Fernandes agreed with AJ. "There is no amount of rehearsal, or practice or reading that can prep you for this moment. It is the single worst feeling I think I have ever had in my life. That moment, that phone call will haunt me forever."[10]

CEOs like AJ at Malaysia, Tony Fernandes at AirAsia, and Carsten Spohr, who dealt with the Germanwings crash, say the way an airline disaster unfolds is different from anything for which they had been prepared. The speed of events, the constant and endless demands for information, seeing the television news repeatedly showing video of hysterical, distraught relatives, the overwhelming media attention. Ultimately, as CEOs, they had to deal with the fact hundreds of people had been killed in one of their planes.

What often distinguishes the reaction to such an event is the character of the CEO and whether he is one of those leaders who has always been seen and perceived as being out in front. AJ is a businessman, with a reputation for strength and determination. He has run some very large utility companies. He performs Ironman challenges.

He is no pushover. But he is not your typical airline CEO. He doesn't fit the usual profile of airline chiefs. Having met most of the world's top airline CEOs, I have found them to be generally larger-than-life personalities. Aviation is a complex, frequently controversial industry with earnings in the billions. The CEO of an airline must be knowledgeable about a wide range of subjects, not only in his own company and in the industry it is part of; he must also have a wide geopolitical perspective. The airline CEO must be ready, willing, and able to answer questions about the safety of flying over war zones, about the political ramifications of building new runways, and he must deal with allegations of illegal government subsidies, environmental concerns about carbon trading, and disputes over increasing air taxes. At the same time he must handle strategic discussions on mergers and acquisitions, and of course, remember to run his airline profitably . . . Even the weather can end up a matter of concern for a CEO as he deals with the fallout (literally) from volcanic eruptions leading to interruptions in flying! In short: any subject that might end up on the front pages of a newspaper can and does affect the running and profitability of an airline.

Today's airline CEO needs to be a swashbuckling innovator, a diplomat, a brutal corporate fighter, and a politician. He needs a much greater view of the world than, say, a chief executive of a utility company. The airline CEO frequently is a figure known to the public: think Richard Anderson at Delta; Willie Walsh at IAG; Michael O'Leary at Ryanair; Alan Joyce at Qantas; Akbar al-Bakker at Qatar. When you run an airline you don't have to be a "real character," but most CEOs are, and it helps.

AJ was definitely not cast in that mold. He is a quiet, unassuming man who had spent his career running engineering and utility companies such as Malakoff. While the latter were large and complicated corporations that required a CEO with a vast amount of knowledge in all areas of operation, they did not put their CEO as much in the public eye. The airline world was entirely new to AJ. Now, in a trial by fire, he was to discover that running an airline is like running no other company. His position was made worse because Malaysia Airlines is a flag carrier, and thus viewed by its leaders as a symbol of national pride.

In truth, very few CEOs from other industries make a successful transition to running airlines. Carolyn McCall, who left the Guardian Media Group to become CEO of EasyJet, is the most notable exception. McCall built huge loyalty with staff, shifted the branding of the airline, and led it to greater profitability and shareholder value. But she is the exception!

AJ, like Minister Hishammuddin, now acknowledges that the Malaysian response to MH370 was far from satisfactory. "There was obviously serious confusion in the early days when we were not aware of what actually transpired," he admits.[11] "We didn't have the plane and we don't know where it is." As a result of this, all the preparations they had rehearsed no longer made any sense. AJ remembers them plowing on regardless: "There was . . . the knee-jerk, off the cuff response in the beginning. It wasn't a measured response. They put out a typical response." I was surprised that for the first time, I was hearing someone who was at the center of the crisis speak with candor. Were they out of their depth? His answer was honest. "Yes. Where it wasn't typical, they put out a typical response for an untypical situation. That's where we had that breakdown. We had an untypical situation here and trying to come up with a typical response doesn't work."

It is no wonder that the whole thing fell apart. Things went from bad to worse. The politicians interfered. The families' tempers flared. Boxed between political masters and the strict rules of secrecy, AJ found himself seen but rarely heard.

While AJ and the staff were still reeling from the loss of MH370 and its 239 passengers, 121 days later he got "the call" again, this time about MH17.

> The second time I couldn't believe it. They said, "We lost an aircraft, MH17." I said, "This is just not true. Can you please call and confirm that. Please be more certain whether we actually lost the aircraft or just lost communication with the aircraft?" And then after half an hour, they came back and said, "They sighted the wreckage."[12]

Malaysia Airlines had now suffered 537 passengers and crew being killed and two 777 planes lost in the space of a little more than three months. AJ recalls:

> My mind went blank. Literally blank for a few minutes. You have to recompose yourself. And say, "Okay. Let's get on with it. Let's deal with it." Because that's the reality. You can't run away from reality. You just have to deal with it.[13]

AJ found himself in an impossible situation. All the planning in the world could not have prepared him or the airline for the vanishing of MH370. They couldn't arrange for the families to visit a crash site. They couldn't give them the closure they sought and needed. AJ and his airline had nothing to offer, not even the promise that information would be forthcoming, still less the return of their loved ones. They were doomed.

AJ retired from Malaysia Airlines in June 2015. He was replaced by Christoph Mueller, a lifelong airline man who has held senior posts with Lufthansa, Sabena, Brussels, TUI, and was CEO of Aer Lingus, where he engineered the turnaround of the Irish flag carrier. Mueller's biography on the Malaysia Airlines' website describes one of his strengths as "structural repositioning of companies in difficulty."[14] He quickly put these talents to work at Malaysia by shrinking the airline to cut its costs. He laid off 30 percent of the staff, closed numerous loss-making routes, and sold off planes, including two of the company's flagship A380 Superjumbos. He has yet to decide if the name and brand of Malaysia Airlines are beyond repair.

CHAPTER FOURTEEN

NEVER AGAIN

*A large commercial airliner going missing without a
trace for so long is unprecedented in modern aviation.
It must not happen again.*

—TONY TYLER, DIRECTOR GENERAL, IATA[1]

Aftter an accident, finding the plane is essential. Of course, the
recovery of bodies must be a top priority of the airline. But to
discover what happened, and how to prevent its happening
again, it is also necessary to retrieve, and to analyze the contents of,
the black-box recorders. MH370 rightly created huge concern among
both travelers and the aviation industry. Time and again on various
shows, as I explained the difficulty of the search, anchors would look
incredulous and ask the same question: "If we can find the location of
our lost iPhones easily online, how come a modern jetliner could just
disappear without a trace?" It was no use explaining that an iPhone
will only be found if it is switched on, logged onto a nearby cell tower,
registered with Apple, etc. The point the anchors were making was
obvious: every day people are using ordinary technology to find something as small and commonplace as a cell phone. Yet in the case of

MH370, tens of millions of dollars were being spent during months of searching the deep ocean in appalling conditions, and no one could find something as large as a 777, which costs $250 million! Months after it disappeared, we had no certainty where the plane had flown, or where on the ocean bed it lay.

To track a plane with certainty, air traffic control must know where it is at all times, even when the plane's communications equipment has been switched off, disabled, or has failed. The goal must be to receive as much information as possible from the aircraft while it is still flying. Looking at MH370, I can trace all the problems back to what happened on the night when the 777 had been able to evade the most sophisticated air traffic technology. The plane's transponders had been switched off, the ACARS system was disabled, and there were no radio signals. The plane had "gone silent." It was able to continue flying without anyone noticing partly because of terrible human errors made by air traffic controllers and radar operators. But, even discounting these initial mistakes, it was the long, seven-hour flight over the southern Indian Ocean that turned an incident in Southeast Asia into the world's biggest aviation mystery. It is only stating the obvious to say that surely the technology should be put in place so that no plane can fly for so long, anywhere in the world, without air traffic control knowing its whereabouts. The public has rightly said it's a disgrace, and the industry has to make sure it can never happen again.

What is galling about MH370 is that this was not the first occasion when a major jetliner went missing and it took several years to find it. The industry had had to cope with some of the very same issues five years before, in June of 2009, when Air France 447 went missing over the South Atlantic. By now you will recall that this was the A330 that had a problem with speed indicator pitot tubes. The pilots flew the aircraft into a stall and it crashed.

No radar was tracking Air France 447 when the crash happened, and no air traffic control center was following it in real time. Most fliers are amazed to learn that planes are not always tracked by radar when they are in the air, crossing the globe. Air traffic control radar constantly monitors the airspace over landmasses like Europe or the United States, where the sheer number of planes in the sky demands full coverage. Any plane that deviates from its flight plan is quickly noticed. With Germanwings 8501, only three minutes and fifty-three seconds passed after Andreas Lubitz initiated the unauthorized descent over the French Alps before the air traffic controllers were calling him on the radio demanding an explanation (and some would say even this was too slow). During the next ten minutes, until the plane hit the mountains, fourteen additional radio calls from four different sources attempted to contact the pilots. Suffice it to say, over most stretches of populated land, air traffic control responses are typically swift.

There are, however, large parts of the globe where no radar exists, including the airspace over the world's oceans. Radar coverage requires ground-based facilities. At sea, both the distances and the costs involved mean it is neither practical nor reasonable to build floating sites for oceanic radar.

Of course, the absence of radar doesn't mean that planes aren't being supervised as they cross the oceans. Consider the thousands of aircraft that cross the Atlantic each day between North America and Europe. As the plane travels over water, traditional radar coverage ends about 250 miles after they leave behind the Canadian or Irish coast. Radar doesn't return until they are within similar range of land on the other side. Instead there is a complicated system of "tracks" where planes fly specific east- and westbound airways, which change daily with the changes in the jet stream. The pilots are given definite times when they must join the track to begin their oceanic crossing.

The planes are spaced out, roughly ten minutes apart, and this long chain of aircraft moves through the sky. Throughout the journey they communicate their position regularly, using high-frequency radios or, more usually today, satellite-based systems. A similar track method called PACOTS is used across the North Pacific between the US and Asia. If tracks aren't being used, then planes are directed to waypoints along standard airways. Again, the aircraft regularly reports its position so air traffic control can safely space out the planes.

Air France 447 was out of Brazil's radar coverage and had just passed over waypoint ORARO, heading for waypoint TASIL. Fortunately, the plane's ACARS system was programmed to send its location automatically every ten minutes. Five minutes had elapsed between the last transmission and the crash into the water. After calculating the maximum distance AF447 could have traveled in those five minutes, the investigators came up with a search area of forty nautical miles, covering seventeen thousand square kilometers. It took several days before the first floating debris was spotted. Finding the aircraft on the ocean bed involved three full-scale search operations over two years. In the end, AF447 was found just 6.5 miles from the last known position of the flight and searchers were able to retrieve the black box.

As a result of AF447, experts set up two groups, the Flight Data Recovery Working Group and the Triggered Transmission of Flight Data Working Group, to see how searches could be improved in the future. The conclusion after Air France 447 was that planes should transmit their location more frequently and the battery life on the locator beacons should be extended to ninety days from the current thirty days.

Now for an awful truth in aviation: unless there is a major emergency, nothing happens fast. In fact, everything happens very slowly. All the recommendations from AF447 ended up being bogged down with ICAO, the UN agency responsible for aviation. There were plenty of working groups, air navigation meetings, briefing papers written, but nothing much was done. Even the deadline for extending the battery life on the locator beacons to ninety days would not be implemented until 2018. Almost no progress was made on improving location information. As a result, five years after AF447, as MH370 developed into a worse situation and the underwater locator beacons ran out of battery power after thirty days, it was as if the Air France disaster had never happened, and nothing had been learned.

The solution in all aviation matters is to set up a working group or a task force to look at a problem and report back. This time the airlines realized that this was an emergency, and the traveling public was getting worried. The industry body, IATA, was given the job of sorting out the post-MH370 mess and making suggestions. IATA, unlike ICAO, represents airlines, not governments. One likes to think airlines have a great vested interest in not losing any of their valuable passengers and expensive planes. Indeed, IATA recognized that there were legitimate questions about why this problem hadn't been sorted out after the Air France crash. The frequently-asked-questions section on its website asks, "Didn't the industry face the same issues after AF447 and do nothing?" and "Why was this not done before?"[2] Both are good questions, which I have asked many times on my programs, yet I have never received a satisfactory answer.

There was one big difference this time, though: the public had become engaged in the debate. Partly as a result of massive coverage from networks like CNN, passengers were now asking how this had happened and why something hadn't been done to prevent it. The industry could no longer ignore the questions. By February 2015, a final agreement was reached that a system must be put in place whereby planes could report their position at least every fifteen minutes. The tracking rule would be performance based, which means the airlines themselves could decide which technology they would use, provided it met the fifteen-minute rule. Luckily for you and me, airlines felt the urgency of this change more than ICAO, and most major carriers moved fast to ensure their planes report positions at least every fifteen minutes, usually even more frequently.

One change could be made relatively quickly, and at not too great an expense. On MH370, the transponder was switched off at 01:21, and thereafter the plane flew silent and was unidentifiable. The transponder switch is conveniently located on the pedestal between the pilots, and with a simple turn, it is easily switched off. It has been suggested that airlines make it impossible for anyone in the cockpit to switch off this electronic signal, which gives the plane's call sign, altitude, speed, and other basic information.

Many who are involved in this debate have asked why the pilots would want to switch off the transponder during flight anyway. Since it is an important part of safe air navigation, surely it should always be switched on. In answer to this, some argue that after aircraft touchdown, having multiple planes transmitting details in such close proximity can be a hindrance to controllers. Thus pilots switch the transponder off when taxiing or when parked at the gate. Today, when more advanced ground controls systems are readily available, this is less of a problem. Another argument against preventing pilots from switching off the transponder is that in case of a fire or electrical emergency, pilots must be able to switch off any of the aircraft systems in order to shed electrical load. Ask most pilots and they will tell you that their job requires them to have maximum flexibility to handle any untoward situation. If switching off the transponder is an option, they want to keep it. The weak point here is that today's modern jetliners require so much automation and computer-controlled flying that pilots are discouraged from disengaging too many systems because of unforeseen knock-on effects elsewhere on the aircraft. Also there is a whole host of systems deep in the electronics that the pilots don't really have access to. All in all this is a battle the pilots will probably lose. It seems likely that some sort of restriction on a pilot's ability to switch off the transponder will be introduced.

Another issue in the debate is whether the data captured on black boxes should be streamed from the aircraft to air traffic control in real time so that frantic searches for the devices before the battery runs out becomes a thing of the past. The usual objection to this involves satellite bandwidth and cost. If all planes were constantly streaming, a huge amount of data would be generated, and satellite capabilities would need to be increased. That involves more expense, which eventually leads to higher ticket prices. Airlines have rightly said that streaming every bit of data is probably impractical and a waste of time. The data being streamed would need to be more targeted and forensic.

One possible way around this is to configure the system so it only transmits essential data when the plane behaves unexpectedly—for instance, when it suddenly changes altitude or deviates from its flight path. The machine can be set up to recognize out-of-the-ordinary occurrences, and if they happen, to automatically do a satellite data dump of what is in the black box memory, including the plane's current longitude and latitude coordinates for rescue. It would also send anything that would help an investigation, such as the speed, altitude, cabin pressure, position of the control surfaces, engine performance, and so on. All of this is possible and likely to happen in the next few years.

There is one other option that is regularly batted around as a possible solution to the black-box problem: install deployable black boxes that would be ejected from the aircraft in an emergency. These are already in use on military aircraft, and Airbus and Boeing are looking into whether they can be adapted for civilian jets. This is unlikely to happen in the short term. Constructing machinery to eject black boxes would require a redesign of the fuselage, as well as many of the electrical and mechanical systems. It is a complicated solution, when there are already easier, cheaper options on the table.

What has come out of the whole messy process is the clarion call that "something must be done," and there now appears to be a real willingness to get on with it. Regular reporting of aircraft positions; triggered transmissions of data before crashes; deployable black boxes; longer-life batteries on emergency locator beacons—these are all perfectly acceptable solutions to a serious problem that the industry now faces. It just needs them to get on with it and decide what to do.

One condemnation leveled against airlines is that they fight the changes because it is expensive to introduce many of the measures being proposed. An airline with hundreds of planes may incur large capital costs in the tens of millions of dollars installing extra equipment. This would entail the cost of purchasing satellite services to receive and process all the extra data from companies like Immarsat and Iridium. I don't buy this argument. Of course, there needs to be a cost-benefit analysis of whether it is worth spending this much money (safety has unlimited potential and demands). I can't see any CEO saying, "Hmm, let me weigh this up. Do I spend the extra couple of million? Nah, let's just take the risk and maybe lose a plane." However much people may want to portray them as moneygrubbers, I don't know of any global airline CEO who would ignore a safety risk for a few million dollars.

There is a safety solution that has often been suggested but remains hotly contested: putting video cameras in the cockpit. The video would be recorded on the black boxes and, like data, could be transmitted by satellite in the event of an emergency. This subject has been under discussion for years. It was first seriously raised by the NTSB in the United States in 2000, and is regularly included on the list of "most wanted safety improvements."[3] The NTSB believes:

> Automatic information recording devices, such as image recording systems, would provide critical information to investigators about the actions inside the cockpit immediately before and during an accident.[4]

Pilots and their unions disagree. Their usual argument has been that there are already many recording measures in place telling investigators what happens in the cockpit. To add cameras would be effectively spying on the pilots. They worry that the video might be used by airlines to check up on pilots to make sure they are following the rules. It could be used against them in internal disciplinary hearings. Also, in the event of accidents, they worry that the video would be leaked to the media during an investigation and would inevitably end up on television. Today there is little sympathy for these anticamera "spying" arguments. A huge number of workers, from shop assistants to factory workers to transport staff, have closed-circuit TV cameras watching over them at work: the cameras are always watching and recording. It is hard to see why it's okay for a checkout person in a grocery store to have their privacy infringed but it's not for the pilot of a 777. Provided the recordings are similar to the cockpit voice recorders, and over-record every couple of hours, or erase at the end of the normal flight, I don't think this argument stands up. The question of potential leakage of the recordings during an investigation is also weak. There have been almost no leaks of actual cockpit recordings. Often the transcripts of conversations are leaked, but the actual audio is never officially released and, from what I can see, has rarely been leaked.

The more serious argument against cameras in the cockpit is that they won't make much difference. The existing recorders already provide a huge amount of information. Adding grainy and shaky video is not likely to make much difference. If you already know what the pilots did, does it matter if you see them doing it? The authorities clearly think it does, and they site the controversial crashes I have written about in this book, including EgyptAir 990, ValuJet 592, Swissair 111, and SilkAir. To this list, I might now add Germanwings 8501. Cockpit cameras would give the final confirmation that Lubitz intended to crash the plane (not, frankly, that there is any doubt about it, considering the actions he took in the final ten minutes and his known state of mind). In the cold light of day, pilots probably know that cameras in the cockpit are likely inevitable; it's just a question of when.

Accident investigations are long, time-consuming affairs. It is not unusual for at least a year to pass after a serious crash before the publication of the final report, sometimes even longer. These reports are incredibly detailed, running usually to hundreds of pages with appendices. They will outline any tests performed on aircraft parts to see if they failed. There may be elaborate reconstructions of the aircraft based on the wreckage. Nothing is left unlooked at, unsaid, unconsidered. The air accident report under ICAO Annex 13 is usually unbiased in its conclusions, the gold standard of reports. It is used by the industry as the way to make sure a particular accident doesn't happen again, somewhere else. During the investigative process, everyone involved is obliged to maintain the dreaded Annex 13 code of silence. It is a draconian rule. Parties who are on the periphery fear being excluded from the proceedings if they are seen to have released any information to the media. Once Annex 13 goes into effect, a wall of silence descends upon an inquiry and every question is met with "Annex 13. Can't say a word." In the case of MH370, the Annex 13 net captured Malaysia Airlines,

Boeing, Rolls-Royce, and the French electronic-systems company Thales Group, Inmarsat. Most of these companies' spokespeople have never said a word publicly about what happened, how the companies handled the situation. I can understand why a certain air of decorum and discretion must be maintained: air accidents are incredibly complicated, and it would be easy to take particular details out of context. That should not, though, mean no one can speak about an accident while an investigation is under way. If the aim of such an investigation is the prevention of a future occurrence, its findings won't be tainted by anyone else speaking about it. This won't change the conclusions. It won't prejudice any outcome. The investigators, working away, won't be influenced by extraneous events. MH370 is the most extreme example of an accident investigation in which no one is speaking on the record, and everyone is blaming Annex 13 for the fact they can't or won't speak. There surely must be an easier way to make information available than through the statements of a single organization, which may be predisposed to keep silent!

I can't leave this subject without also talking about the industry in which I myself am involved. The media latches on to plane crashes for all the reasons I stated earlier. They tap into our most basic fears and vulnerabilities. We all fly. We are all concerned. We all want to know what happened. Unfortunately, this is taken by some as an excuse to throw all journalistic norms out of the window. Some journalists believe, somehow, that they are going to discover what happened and solve the mystery as if it's the "Air-Crash Investigation" show. Bingo, this was the cause, and this is how it happened. All solved before the top of the hour!

I have never seen my role in such unprofessional terms. All I am on the air to do is to try to give the viewer an understanding of the range of issues that are on the table. It may be explaining the more risky phases of flight, and why what happened in any given case is particularly unusual. Journalists draw on previous accidents that contain similarities and explain what was learned from them. If there is one thing I have learned in all my years of experience, it is that the final cause of an accident frequently turns out to be totally different from what was initially hypothesized. For instance, at the beginning of the investigation of Qantas 32, the A380 whose engine blew up, no one could have known the cause would turn out to be the manufacture of a defective oil stub pipe. Or that the Concorde's crash in Paris was the result of the plane running over a metal strip that fell off the previous departing aircraft. Or that the crash of the Helios flight was a result of the air pressurization system not being switched on, a mechanic's mistake. Maybe, in covering MH370, we all went too far in trying to solve the mystery.

The European Union working paper summed up the situation as follows:

> AF447 and MH370 cannot be considered as isolated cases. There is a growing number of long-range aircraft that fly over oceans to connect distant continents. It is important to improve the ability to quickly locate (missing) aircraft for saving potential survivors and preventing effectively future accidents.[5]

This goes to the heart of the matter. The newer, longer-range aircraft such as the Boeing 787 and 777, and Airbus A350 and A380, now can connect almost any two points on the earth with flying times scheduled as taking more than fifteen hours. Qantas 8 from Dallas to Sydney flies the length of the Pacific; Delta 201 from Johannesburg to Atlanta rarely sees land, most of the journey passing over the South and North Atlantic oceans; Etihad and Emirates go from the Persian

Gulf to Los Angeles via the polar route, spending hours in the air over the Arctic Ocean.

Changes in the aviation industry are always slow. Both the planes and the industry are so complicated that any new equipment or procedures must be thoroughly tested. There is no point in solving one problem if you merely end up creating another, and without the kind of thoroughness practiced by the aviation industry, such blunders would often occur. But this should not be an excuse for doing little or taking too long in the investigation of an accident. For the second time in a decade, the devastating tragedy of a lost plane has occurred. The industry must actually do something about it and make the changes necessary before it happens again.

CHAPTER FIFTEEN

WILL THEY FIND
THE PLANE?

We owe it to the grieving families, we owe it to everyone
who travels by air, to get to the bottom of this mystery.

—TONY ABBOTT, AUSTRALIAN PRIME MINISTER[1]

I t was Chris Cuomo, the anchor of *New Day*, who first asked me, shortly after MH370's disappearance, "Richard, will they find the plane?" I answered without a moment's hesitation, "Of course they will." He followed up with another question: "And if they don't?" I didn't flinch. "They must find it."

In the following days, then weeks, months, and now years, Chris and all my other anchor colleagues have asked me the same question again and again. My answer has always been the same. "Yes, they will find it. They must." As the time has gone by, sometimes I think I detect a certain wry smile on my colleagues' faces as the words I uttered with such certitude come back to haunt me. So far I have been proved wrong, and with the exception of the single flaperon, nothing of the plane has been found. Some are now saying that the plane may never be found, that the task is too great. Assuming the Inmarsat data is correct, and the plane is lying along the seventh arc, the water is too deep, the ocean canyons too wide, the area too large. The search teams could be trolling right over the wreckage and never notice it.

Many people have asked me how I can write a book about MH370 when authorities haven't found the plane and the ending to this story remains unknown. My answer has always been that the need for a book like this does not hinge on finding the plane. The vanishing of MH370 has raised too many other issues for this to be the case. Of course we want to know what happened during those moments, on the morning of March 8, 2014, at 1:19, just after Captain Zaharie said, "Good night Malaysian 370." But if we never discover the facts, there are plenty of other issues occasioned by the plane's disappearance and it is these that must be resolved. There is the failure of air traffic control on that night, the confusion and political interference in the search operation, and the new methods of tracking planes and retrieving vital black-box data that are now being considered.

I have sat through more hours of news conferences, interviews, and debates about MH370 than most people. I have read the reports. I have seen the documents. I have spoken to those who were involved in making decisions about how to find the plane. In the face of the increasing difficulties, I still believe they will find it. I say this not out of some simplistic view that missing planes are always found, but because the plane must be found; the vanishing of such a large aircraft is simply not acceptable. There are more than 1,200 of the 777 family of planes flying around the world today. As Sir Tim Clark, the CEO of Emirates, put it, "MH370 remains one of the great aviation mysteries. I have the concern that we will treat it as such and move on. We mustn't allow this to happen. We must know what caused that airplane to disappear."[2]

After the search teams have finished covering the 46,000 square miles (120,000 square kilometers) currently designated as the most probable place where the plane went down, if nothing has been found there, the whole matter becomes much more problematic. The Malaysians and the Australians have said they will stop searching at this point, because in the absence of any new evidence of where to look, increasing the zone would cease to be feasible. They can't search the entire length of the seventh arc.

If the searching stops, a major rethink will have to take place. First, of course, the authorities will need to be absolutely certain that the search was thorough and that nothing was missed. In the case of AF447, some of the earlier searches missed the plane, even when it was right beneath them. So there will need to be absolute confidence that the two-year search did not miss the plane. After that, of course, there will probably be a full-scale review of the evidence, the science upon which it was based, and the decisions taken. The search must somehow continue. That is what I really mean when I say, "They will find the plane, they must." There can be no temptation to consign this to the history books as an aviation mystery that was too difficult to solve. If the searchers find nothing in their search, then they need to go back to square one. This will involve questioning everything that they have believed to be true and seeing if it remains valid. The inquiry should open its doors and its minds to other experts who may have a different perspective. There has been much criticism of the tight-fisted way information has been held, and there are independent experts who might have had something to contribute who have been shut out of the investigation. I am not recommending that the investigators invite every crackpot and crank into the room to have a go at the evidence. However, if they have failed to find anything, there can no longer be any justification for exclusive access to an investigative elite. The investigators have told us all along they are confident in the science and the analysis. If nothing is found, their arguments weaken and they must let others in.

All of this is in the future. At the time of this writing, there is still more ocean to be searched. So far they have spent less than the list price of a single brand-new 777-300 searching for MH370. In the big scheme of aviation, I think the lives of 239 people, the confidence in 1,200 flying aircraft, and the reputation of the industry demand that yes, they find it. They must.

NOTES

INTRODUCTION
1. Tony Abbott press conference, April 3, 2014.
2. Tony Tyler speech, IATA Annual Meeting, Doha, June 2, 2014.

CHAPTER 1: FIRST HOURS
1. Email in file.
2. McCarthy, email in file.

CHAPTER 2: KUL TO PEK
1. MH17 Passenger Information, Dutch Safety Board, 2015, page 9.
2. www.news.com.au/world/malaysia-airlines-plane-missing-desperate-search-for
   -wreckage-and-clues-two-days-after-it-vanished/story-fndir2ev-1226849847203.
3. www.themalaymailonline.com/malaysia/article/igp-says-missing-5-never-checked
   -into-mh370.
4. Hishammuddin Hussein press briefing, March 12, 2014.
5. Various CNN reports and emails.
6. Aloyah Biinti Mamat DG Malaysia Immigration, March 11, 2014.
7. Ibid.
8. Rahman press conference; from email in file, March 10, 2014.
9. Rahman interview @ 01:29.
10. Ibid.

11. in.reuters.com/article/malaysia-airlines-interpol-idINL5N0MP4WU20140328.
12. Interpol press statement, March 28, 2014.
13. Ibid.
14. Factual Information: Safety Investigation for MH370 by the Malaysian ICAO Annex 13 Safety Investigation Team for MH370, page 21.
15. www.themalaysianinsider.com/malaysia/article/okay-roger.-good-day-the-last-words-from-mh370.
16. Najib Razak statement, March 15.
17. Factual Information: Safety Investigation for MH370 by the Malaysian ICAO Annex 13 Safety Investigation Team for MH370, appendix.
18. Ibid.
19. PM interview; transcript in file.
20. All facts from the AAIASB Report into Helio crash, November 2006.
21. www.reuters.com/article/2014/04/11/us-malaysia-airplane-investigation-idUSBREA3A0NS20140411.
22. Third Meeting of Asia Pacific Search and Rescue, APSAR/TF/3-WPO6, page 3.
23. Factual Information: Safety Investigation for MH370 by the Malaysian ICAO Annex 13 Safety Investigation Team for MH370.
24. Ibid, page 6, 2.27.
25. Factual Information: Safety Investigation for MH370 by the Malaysian ICAO Annex 13 Safety Investigation Team for MH370.
26. ICAO Brief on the SAR Response to MH370.
27. ICAO Brief on the SAR Response to MH370, page 7.

CHAPTER 3: CHAOS AND CONFUSION

1. Factual Information: Safety Investigation for MH370 by the Malaysian ICAO Annex 13 Safety Investigation Team for MH370, appendix, 1.18F, page 12.
2. www.boeing.com/resources/boeingdotcom/company/about_bca/pdf/statsum.pdf.
3. Crash of Malaysia Airlines Flight MH17, Dutch Safety Board, Main Conclusions, 10.1 (1)(b), page 253.
4. Cooper email, in file.
5. Rahman press conference, March 10, 2014.
6. APSAR, Malaysian presentation, page 4.
7. Rahman press conference, March 10, 2014, in file.
8. Hishammuddin Hussein press conference, March 10, 2014.
9. Ibid.
10. Ibid.
11. ICAO Search and Rescue Brief.
12. Press conference, March 14, 2014.
13. Newspaper reports, March 12, 2014.
14. CNN internal email, March 13, 2014.

15. DG press conference, March 17.
16. Press briefing, March 22.
17. ICAO, Annex 13, Chapter 5.12(e).
18. Press briefing, Hishammuddin Hussein, March 24.
19. Press briefing, Hishammuddin Hussein, April 1.
20. *Wall Street Journal.*
21. Press statement, March 13.
22. Ahmad Jauhari Yahya, press conference, March 13.
23. *Wall Street Journal* tweet.
24. Malaysian press statement, March 14.
25. PM press statement, March 15.
26. Ibid.
27. Ibid.
28. Ibid.
29. Ibid.
30. Ibid.
31. Xinhua, March 15.

CHAPTER 4: HANDSHAKES AND CORRIDORS

1. Malaysia prime minister statement, March 15.
2. Press briefing, March 16.
3. Ibid.
4. Ibid.
5. Factual Information: Safety Investigation for MH370 by the Malaysian ICAO Annex 13 Safety Investigation Team for MH370, page 43.
6. ATSB, "Defining the Underwater Search," page 18.
7. The satellite is also moving in its orbit by several thousand kilometers, and while that is crucial in the final calculation, we don't need to concern ourselves about it to understand the principle.
8. ATSB Report, page 19.
9. Press briefing, March 17.
10. AMSA press release, March 18.
11. Press briefing, March 26.
12. Mark Dickinson, CNN interview.
13. Ibid.
14. ATSCB Report, page 31, using MH021.
15. Ibid, page 32.
16. Factual Information: Safety Investigation for MH370 by the Malaysian ICAO Annex 13 Safety Investigation Team for MH370, page 5.
17. ATSB, MH370—Definition of Underwater Search Areas, June 26, 2014.
18. Hishammuddin Hussein, press briefing statement, March 13.
19. *New York Times*, March 26, 2015.

20. Brice Robin, press conference, March 26.
21. Ibid.
22. wsj.com, March 20.
23. PM Razak, CNN interview.
24. PM Razak statement, March 25, 2014.

CHAPTER 5: THAT TEXT

1. Razak interview, 17:31:01.
2. Razak interview, 17:31:47 et seq.
3. Rahman announcement, January 29.
4. Compensation for accidents is governed by the Montreal Convention, 1999.
5. Various reports.
6. flightlaws.blogspot.co.uk for a full discussion of the difference in definition.
7. David McKenzie, CNN email.
8. David McKenzie, email in file.

CHAPTER 6: RACE TO THE PINGS

1. JCC press conference, April 1, 2014.
2. Angus Houston, JACC press conference, April 14.
3. ATSB, MH370—Definition of Underwater Search Areas, June 26, 2014, and update October 8, 2014.
4. Factual Information: Safety Investigation for MH370 by the Malaysian ICAO Annex 13 Safety Investigation Team for MH370, page 54, item 5.
5. ATSB, Flight Path Analysis Update, "End of Flight Scenarios," page 12.
6. ATSB, MH370—Definition of Underwater Search Areas, June 2014, page 35.
7. Ripley Report on CNN, from transcript.
8. www.cnn.com/2014/04/05/world/malaysia-airlines-plane-questions/.
9. Angus Houston, JCC press conference, April 6, 2014.
10. ATSB, MH370—Definition of Underwater Search Areas, June 2014, page 13.
11. Angus Houston, JCC press conference, April 7, 2014.
12. Ibid.
13. Angus Houston, JCC press conference, April 9, 2014.
14. ABC Australia tweet and *Sky News* tweets from Shanghai, April 10.
15. It should be noted that the Air France battery was tested two years later. No transmissions were ever received in the ocean.
16. Press conference, Perth, broadcast *CNN Tonight*, April 7.
17. *CNN Tonight*, April 7, 2014.
18. ATSB, MH370—Definition of Underwater Search Areas, June 2014, page 13.
19. Factual Information: Safety Investigation for MH370 by the Malaysian ICAO Annex 13 Safety Investigation Team for MH370, section 1.11.3.1.
20. A. J. Yahya press conference, April 5, 2014, quoted by CNN, etc.
21. Angus Houston, JCC press conference, April 14, 2014.

CHAPTER 7: SEARCHING DEEP

1. Hishammuddin Hussein interview, transcript in file.
2. www.bluefinrobotics.com/products/bluefin-21/.
3. Angus Houston, JACC press conference, April 14, 2014.
4. Tony Abbott, JACC press conference, April 28, 2014.
5. JACC, Update, May 29, 2014.
6. Tony Abbott, JACC press conference, April 28, 2014.
7. Ibid.
8. Warren Truss, JACC press conference, May 5, 2014.
9. Mapping the Deep Ocean, Geoscience Australia, February 2015.
10. *Malaysian Insider*, July 6, 2014.
11. Paul Kennedy from Frugo, in Geoscience Australia video.
12. JACC, Operational Update, March 5, 2015.
13. JACC, Operational Update, May 13, 2015.
14. *Guardian*, May 28, 2015.
15. Ibid.
16. JACC, Tripartite Joint Communiqué, April 16, 2015.
17. JACC, Update, May 20.
18. JACC, Operational Update, June 3, 2015.
19. Warren Truss, JACC press conference, May 5, 2014.
20. ATSB, MH370—Definition of Underwater Search Areas, December 2015, page 3.
21. Ibid, page 14.
22. Ibid, page 16.

CHAPTER 8: THE CAUSE: NEFARIOUS

1. One of the most cogent is drgauravpradhan.blogspot.com. Others are more out-landish: https://www.youtube.com/watch?v=x2RMqViKohg.
2. White House briefing, March 18, 2014.
3. Boeing statement, email in file.
4. https://www.youtube.com/watch?v=Qykj3FeG-p4.
5. abcnews.go.com/blogs/headlines/2014/04/no-clues-to-missing-malaysia-airlines-plane-in-captains-flight-simulator/.
6. Malaysian ICAO, Annex 14, Safety Investigation Team, page 20.
7. Ibid, page 21.
8. *New Zealand Herald*, March 24, 2014.
9. There are six such cases noted by the BEA in its Preliminary Report into German-wings 9525, page 27.
10. Marseille prosecutor Brice Robin, reported CNN.com, June 12, 2015.
11. www.telegraph.co.uk/news/worldnews/africaandindianocean/mozambique/10533239/Mozambique-Airlines-captain-intentionally-crashed-plane.html.
12. NTSB Report into EgyptAir 990, 2002, page 11.
13. Ibid, Egyptian Response Attachment B, page 118.

14. NTSC Final Report into Silk Air 185, 3.2 Final Remarks, page 47.
15. Nigel Cawthorne, *Flight MH370*, John Blake Publishing.
16. Crash of Malaysia Airlines Flight MH17, Dutch Safety Board, 2015, section 2.12.2, page 53.
17. Ibid, page 137.
18. Air Force statement, April 10, 2014.
19. Bajc interview @ 03:16.
20. Jeff Wise, *The Plane That Wasn't There*, Yellow Cabin Press.
21. *New York*, February 23, 2015.

CHAPTER 9: THE CAUSE: MECHANICAL

1. ATSB, MH370—Definition of Underwater Search Areas, June 26, 2014, page 34.
2. In-flight Fire Leading to Collision with Water, A98H003, Transport Safety Board of Canada, page 4.
3. NTSB, ValuJet Accident Report 1997, page 3.
4. Brief on the SAR Response—ICAO, page 5.
5. Short tons for US (2.4 long tons for UK, 2.45 tons for metric).
6. Short tons for US (4.5 long tons for UK, 4.56 metric tons).
7. Uncontained Cargo Fire Leading to Loss of Control In-flight and Uncontrolled Descent into Terrain, GCAA, page 168.
8. Batteries and battery-powered devices, www.faa.gov/about/office_org/headquarters _offices/ash/ash_programs/hazmat/aircarrier_info/media/battery_incident_chart.pdf.
9. Factual Information: Safety Investigation for MH370 by the Malaysian ICAO Annex 13 Safety Investigation Team for MH370.
10. www.mh370site.com/narrative.html.
11. Factual Information: Safety Investigation for MH370 by the Malaysian ICAO Annex 13 Safety Investigation Team for MH370, page 103.
12. Boeing Fire System, Aero, Q2 2011.
13. Factual Information: Safety Investigation for MH370 by the Malaysian ICAO Annex 13 Safety Investigation Team for MH370, appendices, 1.18J Cargo List, page 28.
14. This is the best video of what the 777 E&E bay looks like; https://www.youtube .com/watch?v=2S-Cggs1jOo.
15. ATSB, Oxygen Cylinder Failure, AO-2008-53, Final Report.
16. Ibid, Executive Summary.
17. "MH370, A Startling Simple Theory," republished Wired.com, March 18, 2014.
18. Factual Information: Safety Investigation for MH370 by the Malaysian ICAO Annex 13 Safety Investigation Team for MH370, page 53.
19. Bruce Robertson article.
20. Goon Chen et al, "Malaysia Airlines Flight MH370: Water Entry of an Airliner," *Notices of the American Mathematical Society* 62:4.
21. As measured by ASKs—he has so many A380s.

22. www.spiegel.de/international/business/mh370-emirates-head-has-doubts-about -investigation-a-996212.html reprinted full transcript www.smh.com.au/world/full -transcript-emirates-chief-sir-tim-clark-on-mh17-and-mh370-20141121-11rc70.html.

CHAPTER 10: CNN GOES THERE—AFTER THE PLANE

1. White House Correspondents' Dinner, edition.cnn.com/2014/05/03/politics/wash ington-correspondents-dinner/.
2. IATA Safety Report 2014. NB: I have added in the deaths from MH17, as I consider them to be aviation fatalities for these purposes, even though IATA does not include them because it was not an accident.
3. Jeff Zucker, Quest interview @ 07:46.
4. www.buzzfeed.com/dorsey/cnns-24-hours-of-poop-ship#.snz6ZDLMj.
5. Jeff Zucker, Quest interview @ 08:24.
6. Ibid @ 00:12.
7. www.nytimes.com/2014/03/18/business/media/cnns-ratings-surge-with -coverage-of-the-mystery-of-the-missing-airliner.html?_r=0.
8. www.fz.com/content/hishammuddin-cnn-report-rmaf-scrambling-jets-total-fabrication.
9. Hishammuddin Hussein interview @ 14:57.
10. Zucker interview with Quest @ 04:31.
11. Hishammuddin Hussein interview with Quest @ 16:36.
12. *The Daily Show*, March 25, 2014, www.youtube.com/watch?v=krFN7jHKNNo.
13. www.mirror.co.uk/news/world-news/mh370-larry-king-slams-cnn-3510827.
14. www.washingtonpost.com/blogs/erik-wemple/wp/2014/03/12/cnns-chris-cuomo -explains-coverage-of-missing-airliner/.
15. www.buzzfeed.com/dorsey/cnn-spent-an-insane-amount-of-time-covering-missing -flight-3#.syPEb29Xr.
16. David Soucie, *Malaysia Airlines Flight 370: Why It Disappeared—and Why It's Only a Matter of Time Before This Happens Again*, Skyhorse Publishing, 2015.
17. Mary Schiavo, email to Quest, May 9, in file.
18. Ibid.
19. Jeff Wise, "How Crazy Am I to Think I Actually Know Where That Malaysia Airlines Plane Is?" Jeff Wise, *New York*, February 2015.
20. CNN Special Report, Malaysia MH370, downloaded.
21. Ibid.
22. CNN Special Report, March 19, 2015.
23. www.huffingtonpost.co.uk/2014/03/21/cnn-mh370-black-hole_n_5005557.html.
24. www.nationalreview.com/media-blog/373768/cnns-don-lemon-asks-if-black-hole -was-involved-mh370s-disappearance-greg-pollowitz.
25. Jeff Zucker, Quest interview @ 05:21.
26. Les Abend, email to Quest, in file.
27. Jeff Zucker, Quest interview @ 02:29.
28. Mary Schiavo, email to Quest, in file.

29. www.thegovernmentrag.com/CNN_anchor_files_with_with_missing_pilot%20 prior_to.html#.VbJZa5UtC1s.

CHAPTER 11: FINALLY . . . SOMETHING

1. www.telegraph.co.uk/news/worldnews/mh370/11788056/Beach-cleaner-who -found-MH370-wreckage-becomes-a-star-in-Reunion.html.
2. Brian Walker, email in file.
3. www.telegraph.co.uk/news/worldnews/australiaandthepacific/australia/11772451/ MH370-debris-discovery-consistent-with-ocean-currents-from-search-area.html.
4. www.cnn.com/videos/world/2015/08/07/lai-interview-stevens-malaysia-parts -wash-up.cnn.
5. ATSB, MH370—Definition of Underwater Search Areas, December 2015, page 22.

CHAPTER 12: THOSE LEFT BEHIND

1. David McKenzie CNN interview.
2. See also BBC Reporter Tom Brook article "Shooting Pain," which looks at the ethics of what we all did that night at Kennedy.
3. Sarah Bajc interview @ 01:27.
4. jimstonefreelance.com/phillipwood.html.
5. Sarah Bajc interview @ 25:24.
6. Sarah Bajc interview @ 02:49.
7. Sarah Bajc interview @ 27:48.
8. Sarah Bajc interview @ 13:42.

CHAPTER 13: THOSE IN CHARGE

1. David Soucie, *Malaysia Airlines Flight 370: Why It Disappeared—and Why It's Only a Matter of Time Before This Happens Again*, Skyhorse Publishing, 2015.
2. Hishammuddin, briefing, March 10, 2014.
3. Hishammuddin, briefing, March 12, 2014.
4. Hishammuddin interview @ 18:36.
5. Hishammuddin interview @ 12:00.
6. Hishammuddin interview @ 24:00.
7. Hishammuddin, briefing, March 26, 2014.
8. AJ interview @ 01:01 & 02:13.
9. AJ interview @ 04:30.
10. Tony Fernandes, CNN interview, at Davos.
11. AJ interview @ 08:16 & 08:59.
12. AJ interview @ 05:51.
13. AJ interview @ 06:30.
14. www.malaysiaairlines.com/uk/en/corporate-info/leadership/board-of-directors .html.

CHAPTER 14: NEVER AGAIN

1. IATA press release, June 2, 2014.
2. Aircraft Tracking Task Force FAQ, IATA, June 2014.
3. app.ntsb.gov/news/events/2007/most_wanted_progress/presentations/aviation _recorders.htm.
4. Ibid.
5. Aircraft Tracking—Different Issues at Stake. ICAO Working Paper, European Union Global tracking 2014-WP/5, page 4.

CHAPTER 15: WILL THEY FIND THE PLANE?

1. Tony Abbott, press conference, March 31, 2014, page 4.
2. Sir Tim Clark, *Der Spiegel* interview.